My Life on a Napkin

My Life on a Napkin

Pillow Mints, Playground Dreams,
and Coaching the Runnin' Utes

RICK MAJERUS

with Gene Wojciechowski

New York

ISBN: 0-7868-6527-X

Designed by C. Linda Dingler

First Edition

10 9 8 7 6 5 4 3 2 1

To a loving father and mother, who have meant the world to me.
To sisters Tracy and Jodi, who have been kind, considerate, and caring. To
nieces Kelly and Tory, who I hold dear and special.
I've always felt that players win games, and to all those players who
have enabled me to appear in the lefthand column with such frequency,
this book is also dedicated with gratitude and gratefulness, more than they
might ever imagine. And also to all my assistants, who were there
for the team and me—late at night, early in the morning, in restaurants,
film rooms, locker rooms, and gyms all across America—and who were,
rather than keepers of the flame, keepers of the napkins: this
book is dedicated to them as well.
—R.M.

To Mom, Gina, Janine, and Joe
—G.W.

Acknowledgments

This book was a happy accident, the result of Rick Majerus's patience and trust, of the cooperation of more than thirty of his friends, family, assistant coaches, and players, both past and present, who happily agreed to be interviewed for the project. Their names and memories are sprinkled throughout these pages and I thank them for their time (sometimes hours) and honest remembrances. It is easy to see why Rick regards them with such respect, admiration, and love.

The idea itself was pitched on a shuttle boat as the little vessel puttered down the canals of the Riverwalk area in San Antonio. It was the night after Rick's Utah team had lost the 1998 NCAA national championship game to Kentucky. Luckily he didn't have too much on his mind: only the ache of a Final Four defeat, a health scare earlier in the week, two job offers and another one on the way, recruiting demands, close to five hundred phone messages, a schedule from hell, not a single day off in fourteen months, a handful of difficult upcoming roster decisions, his star freshman contemplating a Mormon mission, and now a book proposition.

He was polite about it, but his heart and his mind were elsewhere. Instead, he changed the subject to his friends who shared the little pontoon boat. He had stayed an extra day, just so he could celebrate boyhood friend Mike Schneider's fiftieth birthday. He bought dinner, and then took everyone to a piano bar for a birthday sing-a-long. That is essential Rick.

There are those who reduce Rick to two sides: the hyperintense basketball coach and the walking dinner menu. He is addicted to both ball and food, but to consider him two-dimensional is to make a serious error in judgment. He is the most multidimensional person I have ever met, a man with soft and hard edges, with flaws, but most of all, with a compassion, humility, literacy, humor, and intelligence that is as true as Greenwich Time.

My guess is that he didn't really want to do this book. He certainly didn't need the money. Nor will he benefit from some of his honesty in the book. But Rick thinks first of his players, and if in some way his players are acknowledged and recognized, then he is the first to offer a testimonial.

This isn't meant as an appreciation, but as an acknowledgment of his efforts. I have been the beneficiary of many of his kindnesses, as well as the witness of countless others. I remember the late-night dinner at a lone steakhouse outside of Hyrum, Utah, which under normal circumstances is a two-hour drive from Salt Lake City—seventy-five minutes on Air Majerus. Rick and several lawyer friends/local club coaches were fresh from a prep game when he noticed a high school reporter from a Logan newspaper eating dinner by himself. Rick quietly excused himself, walked to the reporter's table, and asked if he'd like to join our group. Rick treated him as if he were Bob Woodward himself, and when the meal was finished, he picked up the tab.

And speaking of food, it was during that same night at Mountain Crest High School, where concession stands were nonexistent, that Rick motioned for a petite blonde cheerleader to report to his bleacher seat.

"Me?" she asked.

"Look," he said, "I don't want a date, I just want you to come over here."

The cheerleader looked around and warily approached.

"Those your cookies?" he said, pointing to an already opened, two-pound bag of treats.

"Uh-huh," she said.

"I'll give you ten dollars for them, okay?"

"Uh-huh."

Rick reached into his pocket, handed her a wad of bills, and then dug in.

And I will never forget standing in an Alamodome tunnel as Rick and his team ran joyously off the court after stunning North Carolina in the Final Four semifinals. I was there for *ESPN The Magazine*, but that mattered little to Rick. He had noticed a familiar face and in his moment of celebration he stopped, looked at me with the purest smile I have ever seen, and said, "Give me a hug, you Polack!"

So I hugged. I figured I could live with one professional indiscretion.

I have seen Rick despair over the death of a friend's daughter, and exult more over a player's grade-point average than his scoring average. I have been told countless times (never by him) of his charity work, and of his special relationships with Markie Huntsman, the mentally handicapped son of billionaire industrialist, philanthropist, and Utah supporter Jon Huntsman; and with Patrick Dwyre, the developmentally disabled son of *Los Angeles Times* sports editor Bill Dwyre, a longtime Majerus friend. I know of the marathon he ran in five hours fifty-five minutes—last in the field of 837—to help raise about $39,000 for a cardiac center in Indiana. ("Me running a marathon is like Orson Welles doing the pole vault," he once said.) I'm aware of at least two sizable checks he wrote to the Huntsman Cancer Center. I have seen his Final Four Reebok sweater auctioned for $8,500 to benefit a local Salt Lake City Catholic school.

It was Dwyre, my former boss, who first suggested I do a story on Rick. That was eight years ago. I have watched him from afar and, for several amazing months in 1997 and 1998, I watched him and his Utah team from very near. I thank Rick, his assistants, staff, and players for treating me with courtesy and warmth.

Thanks also to Utah basketball secretary Kelly Miller, who answered every request as if she had nothing better to do; to Utah Media Relations Director Bruce Woodbury, who went beyond the call of duty; to head trainer Gerald Fisher and basketball managers Brian Bolinder and Ryan Hackett, for kind acts not forgotten; to Marquette University Sports Information Director Kathleen Hohl, Ball State University Sports Information Director Joe Hernandez, Milwaukee Bucks Director of Public Relations Bill King II, and USA Basketball Assistant Executive Director Craig Miller; to Rick Reilly, who should think about a career in writing; to Arthur Kaminsky, Janet Pawson, and Alan Sanders; to David Falk and his staff; to C. Uddls; to editor Leslie Wells, who never nudges too hard; to John Papanek and John Skipper of *ESPN The Magazine*; to Tom Schmit; to John Cherwa; to Mark Christiansen, for research services rendered; to Doug Trautman, the Rick of the sneaker industry, and a friend; to Betsy Hunt, who still owes me a dance at the school sock hop; to T. L. Mann, loyal critic; to Lara, who played softly; to Taylor, who dialed less frequently; to Cheryl, who never complained, not once; and to Rick Majerus, more than just another pretty sweater.

—G.W.

Foreword

I still get messages. I got them during my rookie year with the New Jersey Nets, and I'm pretty sure I'll get them during the rest of my career. Coach Majerus said he'd give advice whether I wanted it or not, and he wasn't kidding. He never kids when it comes to basketball.

I'd come back from a game and the red message light would be blinking on the phone. And it would be Coach, telling me what facet of my game I needed to work on. One time I went 2 of 4 from the foul line and sure enough, there was a message waiting for me: work on my free-throw shooting.

But I don't mind. It's good for me. It keeps me focused. It keeps me going.

I listened to Coach's voice for four years and here I am in the NBA, and I still have to listen to it. I'd laugh a little when I heard the messages, but you know what? He was right. Every time he was right.

I miss Coach. I loved my college years. They were probably the best years of my life. He was so demanding and it was tough sometimes, but I miss him.

He obviously impacted my life, both on the court and off. But you don't really understand his influence and impact until after you've left the program. During your time there it's obvious he cares about you. He always makes it clear he's there to help you in any situation: basketball situations, academic situations, personal situations. If he can possibly help you, he will.

But when you're a player, it's sometimes hard to see that compassion. You know it's there, but you're so busy learning the game, going to school, trying to understand the things he's teaching you, that you don't appreciate his efforts until you're gone.

There have been a few players who have left Utah because they thought Coach was too hard on them, too demanding. I've always said that Coach was harder on me than any player he's ever had. But I was able to take it.

Players need to keep in perspective the reasons why he's so demanding. It isn't to be mean, and it isn't personal. He's demanding because he sees potential in every player and he wants you to fulfill it. It doesn't matter if you're a walk-on or a starter; he wants you to be the best player you can be. He wants you to be the best *person* you can be. And players don't realize it while they're playing for him, but in many aspects he's a father figure. He was for me.

Coach doesn't necessarily want to be your friend when you're a player. I used to think that was very strange, especially when we would take road trips and he wouldn't fly on the same plane with us. But I finally realized why he did that. He wanted to keep himself distanced from the team because he thought we'd be more comfortable that way. He understood that we needed time to ourselves. And maybe he needed time to himself.

In retrospect, it was a smart idea on his part. We saw enough of him on the court, and he saw enough of us. That distance he established helped keep it a healthy relationship. It was like decompression time for both the team and him.

I know Coach has a great relationship with the media. He's very funny. He's very likeable. He's that kind of guy. But it's hard for the media to understand sometimes how a guy who is so likeable and so funny can also be so demanding of his players. I think he's probably one of the most demanding coaches in America, if not *the* most demanding. Otherwise, how can you get yourself to a championship game with a team that nobody picked to be there? How can you have such a successful program over the years with the talent that Utah has had—one McDonald's All-America in his ten years at Utah?

Utah has had a couple of players each year with the potential to play professionally, but after you get past those two or three guys, you're left with a lot of role players. But those role players—and this is what Coach stresses every day—know how to play defense, play hard, set screens, and do their jobs. He turns potential into something you see on the court. And he does it with every kind of player: stars or role players. That's his talent.

When I was a freshman, I didn't understand why he was so hard on me. I'd come back from practice and say to myself, God, what a jerk!

Then one day we sat down and talked. He said, "I hope you realize why I'm so tough on you, why I'm always on you. I see potential in you and I want you to be the best player you can be." And most important, he knew what it took to make me the best player I could be.

In my case, I needed to be pushed by a coach. I had never been pushed in high school. Coach Majerus isn't used to having guys on his team who are extremely talented or very athletic. Most of the guys who have come through that program are role players. So when he gets someone with talent, he really wants to push that player. He wants to make sure that when they leave the program they can say, "I worked as hard as I could. I couldn't have gotten any better."

If a recruit called me up and asked about playing for Coach, I'd tell them, "It's going to be a great experience. You're going to get to play against top-notch competition. You're going to get a great education. Coach Majerus is very hard on people when it comes to academics. He doesn't put up with people who get bad grades. You're going to get an education, whether you want to or not. And you're going to be able to play in one of the best programs in America. It's going to be very demanding, and there are going to be days when you won't want to go to practice. But you're going to enjoy your teammates and when you're done playing there for four years, you're going to have a lot of respect for Coach Majerus. You're going to really appreciate what he did for you."

It wasn't until the end of my sophomore year and the beginning of my junior year that I really felt I could make a career out of playing basketball. Coach isn't one to pass out a lot of compliments, but he did mention that maybe, just maybe, I had a chance to play in the NBA. He also made sure to tell me how much work I had left to do. And he always dropped Don Nelson's name. He'd say, "I'm just telling you the truth, Keith. I was on the phone with Nellie last night, and he says you're nowhere near the NBA right now."

As long as you're playing hard, he's going be fairly happy. I don't know how he figures it out, but he has some sort of sixth sense that tells him when you're at 99 percent, one notch below what you should be. And he'll get on you for it. It's unbelievable how much he knows about basketball.

Probably the strangest Majerus experience I ever had was during my sophomore year. We were playing in the Maui Invitational and eventually lost to Maryland, 90–78. I fouled out in about twenty-two minutes, played terrible defense, but I also scored 28 points. I was named to the all-tournament team, but Coach never mentioned that.

Even though we were eliminated from the tournament, Coach Majerus kept us in Hawaii for five more days. We were supposed to go see the sights, but first we had to practice. Our first practice after the tournament might have been the hardest workout of my career. It was about four hours long, from 10 A.M. to 2 P.M.

After the practice we went back to the hotel, changed clothes, and then went on a snorkeling trip that Coach had arranged for everybody on the team. My ears were still ringing from all the abuse I took during practice. He was on my butt like you would not believe. It was probably the toughest four hours of my life.

So we went snorkeling and somehow, during the course of everybody swimming around, Coach Majerus and I ended up next to each other in the water. Now remember, he had been on me for just about every second of that practice. But now we're standing there and all of a sudden he's talking to me like we're friends. I didn't know what to do. It was like nothing had ever happened. But that's how he is. He can be ripping you in practice, but the moment practice ends he treats you like a real person. That whole situation sums up my relationship with him. He was tough on me on the court—I mean, really getting into me—but when practice ended, the yelling stopped and he was there for me.

Coach was the first basketball teacher I had. I didn't know anything about playing defense. In high school we ran a 2–3 zone all the time. At Utah, almost everything was man-to-man. But one thing Coach could never say is that I didn't play hard. I would always try, but I didn't always have the technique down. But my last two years he didn't get on me as much about my defense. By then I had sort of figured it out.

Playing man-to-man in college definitely helped me out in the NBA. Everything we did at Utah, with the exception of the illegal defense rules, is similar to what you see in the NBA.

My first year was 1993–94 and we went 14–14. It was terrible. I was a starter as a freshman, but we had three other starters who didn't finish the season. We struggled. We didn't have any talent whatsoever.

It wasn't a lot of fun for us or for Coach. He didn't handle the losing very well. I don't think he had ever lost that many games in a season. It got to a point where he knew all we could do is go out and play hard. He knew we weren't good enough to win a lot of games. He coached hard, but it was pretty obvious that we needed more talent on the team. He told us he was going to get us some help, and he did.

The next year we went 28–6 and reached the second round of the NCAA tournament. Even though we lost, I definitely knew we had a chance to be a really good team the following season.

As usual, there were rumors about Coach leaving Utah. He would discuss the rumors with the team and with me. He'd tell us not to worry about the rumors, but we knew he owed it to himself to look at the opportunities out there. You have to listen, right? If nothing else, it helped him when it came time to negotiate something with Utah.

We made it to the Sweet Sixteen my junior year, and the Elite Eight my senior year. But we kept running into Kentucky, the Big Blue Nasty. I don't know what it was about those guys. I think we were jinxed. We played a lot of teams who played that style. But Kentucky was a little different. They played the run-and-jump style, but at the same time they were very disciplined. They were smart, and they had a lot of depth.

Even though I never made it to a Final Four, I wouldn't trade my four years' worth of Utah experiences for anything. I could have come out early, but what I really wanted to do was stay in college. It wasn't like I was going to get any worse as a player. The way I looked at it, I was only going to get better under Coach Majerus.

What I didn't know until much later is that Coach was really nervous about my decision. I guess he was worried I might get hurt, or the team wouldn't be very good.

It would have been great to have played in a Final Four, but I know I tried my best during my four years at Utah, so I can't be upset. At the end of each of those four years, we knew we had given it our best and we couldn't have done anything more. That's the best kind of satisfaction you can have. With the team we had my senior year, we couldn't have done any better.

My life has completely changed since I left Utah. It seems like it was five years ago that I played there, not almost two. But I've always said playing for Coach Majerus and with those guys was the best four years in my life. I can't speak for the future, but the memories of the university, of Coach Majerus, of the players and the assistants will always hold a special place in my heart.

—Keith Van Horn
November 1998

Preface

I still keep a basketball in the backseat of my Explorer. Habit, I guess.

I'm the kid who stood on the fringes of the playground courts waiting to get picked . . . and waiting . . . and waiting some more, until there was no one left but me. I'm the teenager who got cut from the high school team. I'm the guy who walked home heartbroken after being ignored in the CYO (Catholic Youth Organization) open-gym night games. I'm the college sophomore who got dumped from the team. I'm the fifty-year-old University of Utah coach who would think about chucking it all if I could be the last guy on the Jazz bench. Just let me wear a uniform and be part of the team.

The thing with me is, I never belonged to something. I always wanted to be a player, but I was done in by forces beyond my control: genetics and coaches who didn't understand that I would have done anything to play the game.

If I died tomorrow and could come back as anybody, I'd come back as Bobby Jones, the ultimate team guy. He played for Dean Smith at North Carolina and was later an All-NBA Defensive Team first-team pick for eight consecutive seasons—nine, if you count his second-team selection in 1985.

He was a complementary player on a Sixers team that eventually won an NBA title. He was unselfish. He set screens. He passed the ball. He rebounded. He blocked out. He scored just enough. He made his team better.

I can identify with those ideals. I like the idea that I can defend my man and maybe help somebody else out and disrupt what the other team is trying to do. I play those games in my own mind.

As a coach, I am driven by what I couldn't accomplish as a player. I seek my acceptance that way. Vicariously, I get to play now.

I'm not exactly sure how I got to this point. There was no grand plan. As a kid in Milwaukee I didn't go to sleep at night hoping that one day I'd be a Runnin' Ute. But here I am, tucked inside the cheek and gum of the Wasatch Mountains, in the heart of Mormon country, far removed from the recruiting pools of Los Angeles, even farther removed from the likes of New York, Chicago, and Detroit.

Yet, during one amazing, magical month in 1998, we did the unthinkable. We came within five minutes of a national championship, which isn't as much consolation as you might think, but it's closer than any other Utah team had come since 1944. We did it by upsetting two No. 1 seeds, including Jones's alma mater. In fact, we did it by being Bobby Jones. We did it by being a team.

There was a story in the *New York Times* in which the writer asked, "Does Rick Majerus look like a coach?" I didn't take it personally. I am what I am. I look like the guy who never got to play. I look like the guy who did whatever he had to do to squirm into the coaching profession. I don't wear a suit and tie to work. I recruited Keith Van Horn wearing shorts, a T-shirt, and sandals.

Lute Olson *looks* like a coach. John Thompson *looks* like a coach. Pat Riley *looks* like a coach. I'm just the guy in the XXXL Reebok sweater who likes Italian food.

In a lot of ways, I'm just like you. I've got to watch my diet. I try to find two socks that match. I go to the dry cleaners. I worry about my mom. In some ways I think I represent everyman as a coach. I think people kind of relate to me. I also think there's a catharsis there because they see themselves, they see me, and they think, "This guy doesn't look like a coach."

The big craze a few years ago among coaches and business people was to read Sun Tzu's *The Art of War*. I never did read that stupid book. I tried. I read the first couple of pages, but I quit when I got to the part, "It is better the arrows are going away from you, than at you." Or something silly like that.

I'd rather read one of Del Harris's basketball books.

About fifteen years ago, I went to Summerfest in Milwaukee and Bonnie Raitt was on the side stage, and the Temptations were on the main stage. Now Bonnie Raitt is on the main stage and the Temptations are on the side stage. I'm sort of the Bonnie Raitt of coaches. I started off to the side, and worked my way toward the front.

I understand the deal here. I think I'm a good coach. You have to think you're a good coach or you won't succeed. You have to have an ego. But I understand that players, not coaches, win games. I really believe that.

Maybe that's why the 1997–98 season was so special. There was no starter who came to Utah as anything other than a project, a role player, or a question mark.

Our center, Mike Doleac, didn't even know what a scholarship was when I offered one to him. Our point guard, Andre Miller, was a Prop. 48 kid whose college entrance scores were so low that almost nobody recruited him. Our other guard, Drew Hansen, was so physically unimpressive that my own staff questioned my decision to sign him. Our one forward, Hanno Mottola, was only months removed from eating deer meat in his native Helsinki. Our other forward, Al Jensen, was only months removed from a Mormon mission and looked like the Michelin Man.

That was my starting five that ruined every NCAA tournament pool in the country. They won the WAC (Western Athletic Conference). They beat the defending national champions and tournament favorite, Arizona. They beat the Microsoft of college basketball, North Carolina. They did everything but beat Kentucky in the championship game. They finished the season 30–4, and I'll probably never forget a second of any of those games.

A lot of the guys on my teams—at Marquette, at Ball State, at Utah—were like them. They were guys I could relate to. They weren't stars. They were kids who loved playing the game, just like me. They were the kind of kids who probably carried a basketball in the backseat of their car. Kids like Larry Cain, Shawn Parrish, Rick Hall, Keith Chapman, Jimmy Soto, Mark Rydalch, M'Kay McGrath.

There was a guy on our 1991 WAC championship team named Ralph McKinney. He was a walk-on guard who attended school on the GI Bill. He lettered that year, and at the end of the season we had a ring presentation. During the ceremony he leaned toward me and said, "Coach, I'll never forget this." And then he asked me to autograph a photo.

I still smile when I think about that. You don't get those kind of thrills as an accountant.

This is really the players' story more than mine. Players win games. Players help move coaches from the side stage to the front.

So I drive around with a basketball, but I'm fifty and I know there aren't many games left I can play at my age. I have a set of golf clubs, but I don't play much. I played nine holes in Hawaii during the off-season, but I'm not any good. I started beating the hell out of a tree after a bad shot, and this guy comes up to me and says, "I don't mind you doing that to the club, but that tree didn't do anything to you." And he was right.

With or without golf, I'm not giving up on basketball. I'm intrigued by a masters basketball tournament held every summer. A guy asked me to play last year, but I wasn't in shape. Maybe that will be a goal for me next summer. Bobby Jones reincarnated.

Basketball didn't pick me, but I picked it. I couldn't have chosen a better soulmate.

—R.M.

My Life on a Napkin

1

The Basketball Jones Begins

I f you were a kid when I was a kid in Milwaukee, you played three sports: football, baseball, and basketball. The sweat sports.

No one in my old Milwaukee neighborhood had golf clubs. No one had tennis rackets. None of the kids I grew up with had any of that stuff. In fact, none of the dads of the kids had any of that stuff. We were low to middle income, that's why. We weren't poverty cases, but there were no dads who wore tennis sweaters tied jauntily around their necks or who had to worry about who to invite for the member-guest tournament at the country club. It wasn't a neighborhood high in MacGregor 7-irons and Stan Smith rackets. It was more the one-car, one-phone, one-TV-to-a-family type of neighborhood.

I was born in Sheboygan, which is about fifty miles north of Milwaukee. My family lived in Sheboygan Falls until I was seven, and then moved to Milwaukee. The name Majerus is Luxembourger and Finnish. If you go to Luxembourg, you'll see thousands of Majeruses in the phone book. We're like the Smiths or Joneses of Luxembourg.

The first place we lived was 45th Street, right off North Avenue. They called them flats. Then we moved to 57th Street. That was a flat. Someone lived downstairs, someone lived upstairs. We were the family that always lived upstairs—the A-address. There aren't a lot of A addresses out on the country club golf courses. There was my dad, Raymond, my mom, Alyce, myself, and my two younger sisters, Jodi and Tracy. My mom always said, "If we could just get downstairs." That was her goal, the downstairs flat. Later we moved to 53rd Street.

Says Mike Schneider, boyhood friend, West Point graduate, army colonel: *"Even though I had four brothers, Rick was like my brother. We shared so many things. His home was always open to the neighborhood kids. His mom and dad were like surrogate parents for us. The refrigerator was always open. They always had sodas. We always slept over at his place.*

"Even then, Rick was bigger than most of us. His dad was a big man. Rick obviously had the hereditary traits of his dad: full head of blond hair. A lot of people called Rick 'Whitey.' Big barrel chest. Big full torso. A big boy, but remarkably skilled as an athlete.

"We spent most of third and fourth grades playing baseball every day at Washington Park. Basketball creeped in the fifth grade. And since athletics were the center of our universe, we spent many a night walking home from the playgrounds sharing our hopes and dreams. We had big dreams. We were going to play for a major college, things like that. The reality was, we were short white guys who could shoot a little bit, but not necessarily jump."

Rich Panella, boyhood friend, women's basketball and softball head coach, assistant athletic director at Cardinal Stritch University in Milwaukee: *"I think the first time I met him was at the Pig and Whistle, which was a custard and hamburger place near my high school. He was about fifteen and he was there for three reasons: the food, basketball, and a lot of girls from my high school hung out there.*

"Back then you went from neighborhood to neighborhood to play basketball. My neighborhood was the Italian part of town. He was wearing a T-shirt turned inside out, shorts, tennis shoes, and he had a basketball under one arm and a custard cone in the other hand. It's not much different from now, is it?"

So we played those three sports, but slowly basketball became my game of choice. I was a pitcher in baseball. A right-hander with a decent fastball and absolutely no curve. But baseball moved too slow for me.

Football had a certain appeal, but I didn't like my high school coach. I always wanted to play fullback, but they put me on the offensive line. Then there was basketball. I think I was hooked the second I snapped off my first chest pass, or ran a little pick and roll.

We lived in the city, right in Milwaukee, in the Red Line District. It was not ghetto by any stretch of the imagination, but it was an urban environment. You could go to any playground and play ball. That's another thing. In basketball you can go practice by yourself. That's hard to do in baseball or football.

Those were the days that if the Braves won twelve straight, then George Webb, a hamburger place in Milwaukee, promised everyone a free burger. So they'd win ten straight and as a kid you're thinking the Blessed Virgin is appearing if only they can win their twelfth straight, all so you can get yourself a free hamburger.

We'd go to County Stadium as kids and watch games. We'd go by ourselves. In those days, we would walk the freeway as it was being built. We'd watch from the cliff above the right-field bleachers. We'd never go to Packers games, though. That was too hard. And I wasn't a big Packers fan. But with the Braves, you had a chance to sneak in. Sometimes there would be a guy who didn't need his tickets, and he would just give them to us.

But basketball was the game I loved most. You could hide in basketball. You could be a role player in basketball. Even as a kid, I had a great knack for putting together teams. The secret was that I could always put together a team that I could play on. I could put the pieces together.

We started playing ball in fifth grade. It was a fifth-grade church team—St. Catherine's. Then I played all through grade school. In high school I kept getting cut, so I played CYO ball. I never missed an open gym night. If the gym was open, I wanted to play. I liked playing with all the best players. I was one of those wannabe inner-city guys. We'd take the bus down, or if we had a car, we'd take cars down to a place called Franklin Square in Milwaukee. I'd get some guys and we'd go play. Sometimes we played for money, but mostly for sodas and for fun.

I've loved basketball my whole life. Ever since I was in fifth grade, I've known I loved basketball. Back then there wasn't much on TV, so I remember watching or listening to the Loyola Ramblers under George Ireland. They had a Wisconsin guy from St. Catherine's. Chuck Wood was his name. I'd listen to those games. I watched the Cincinnati teams. I remember the Michigan teams with Cazzie Russell. But I always gravitated toward the role players. Those were the guys I identified with. At Michigan it was Bob Cantrell and Larry Tregoning. I remember watching the Bulls with Jerry Sloan and Norm Van Lier, and being spellbound by how much Sloan played defense. They used to talk about Sloan's backhand in the passing lane. I was a big Sloan fan. He played with such passion, especially on defense. When I was guarding someone in a CYO game, I'd always keep my backhand up, just like I was Jerry Sloan on defense and I was trying to cause a deflection. We were only seven, eight years apart, so when I was sixteen, he was with the Chicago Bulls. I used to say, "Jeez, maybe I could play defense like that."

The same thing held true in baseball. I always identified with the no-name player. With the White Sox it was Woody Woodward. I really liked that guy. His uniform was always dirty.

Says Alyce Majerus: *"He was also a big Hank Aaron fan. Hank Aaron was his idol. When he was in Catholic grade school, they had this charity thing for infants in Catholic missions in Africa. You'd save your nickels and dimes until you had two dollars. Then you could name one of the babies. Rick named his baby, Hank Aaron Majerus.*

"He even wanted his confirmation name to be Henry."

When I was a kid, I didn't have a lot of basketball posters on the wall, but I did have a special lamp that I used as a hoop. I had a rolled-up sock and I'd play these imaginary games shooting the sock through the top of the lampshade. I used to pretend I was a player. Like I said, I used to look up to that great Michigan team. A lot of kids wanted to be Cazzie Russell, but I wanted to be the no-name guys.

I played all the time. I loved playing during the summer. I never wanted to go home. I always wanted to stay out and hang out at night. And I loved the playgrounds. We'd play at Wright Street and then go to the Beer Depot and sit on the back porch and drink Diet Cokes and eat stuff. It was heaven.

Sometimes we'd go down to Franklin Square. That was the hotbed of inner-city basketball in Milwaukee, where the black players hung out. I'd put together a team and we'd go down there and play. We judged ourselves against those kids.

We played all year. Snow? If we couldn't find an open gym, there were times when we'd shovel off a part of the playground so we could shoot baskets. It didn't matter if we were wearing boots and gloves. We wanted to shoot.

My dad was a union rep, a union organizer, like the guy in that Sally Field movie *Norma Rae*. He did it primarily in the Milwaukee area, but he traveled throughout the state and then to Minnesota later on. He kept moving up through the ranks, at one point becoming one of the key regional reps.

My mom, like many moms of that era, didn't work, though she was very much a partner in my dad's union endeavors. She didn't care about the limelight. She was more concerned about standing by her man. Tammy Wynette could have been singing that song about her.

Neither my father nor mother graduated from high school, yet they accomplished so much and cared about the well-being of so many people. My mom reared a family and worked a few months each year at a wholesale outlet called Union Toy. It was a place where union workers could buy toys below retail cost.

During election years, my father would go to factory plants and stand outside the gates to talk to workers before or after their shifts. He did that with Jimmy Carter and Walter Mondale when they ran in 1976. Politicians like Henry Reuss and William Proxmire sought his support and influence.

My father also was involved in social issues. He marched with Father James Groppi, a Milwaukee priest who was very active and supportive of civil rights. There were lots of marches back then. My dad and mom were tear-gassed on one march.

Groppi was a very prominent local figure. So was Jesse Jackson, who would come up from Chicago on occasion to help the cause. We'd march across the 16th Street Viaduct. There were no black people south of what they called the Industrial Valley. There were none on the south side.

Back in the late '60s, you didn't have to be a genius to know what was going on in this country. When I marched, I was very aware of the issues. My family always marched for causes it believed in.

Says Mike Schneider: *"Ray was a hero in so many ways. He marched for civil rights at Selma. He was on the right side of that march. When the riots hit Milwaukee, my dad was a policeman, and Ray was a union leader who was trying to help keep order. Ray was in the thick of it.*

"He was also very active in the local Democratic party. I was a teenager at the time, and Ray wanted to be a Wisconsin delegate for the Democratic National Convention. So he dragged me and a couple of guys to a smoke-filled tavern and said, 'When my name comes up, raise your hands.'"

My first strike march came when I was seven. I was on the picket line in Kohler, Wisconsin, during the famous Kohler factory strike. That's when I yelled my first, "Scab!" I didn't even know what *scab* meant. I always thought it was a swear word. I never knew its real meaning until I was almost a teenager. Cars would come by and someone would throw a brick, or spit on the car. So the next time another car came by, I'd yell, "Scab!" and try to spit. You know, when you're seven years old, it's great fun to be able to spit at cars and not get yelled at by adults. After all, they're doing the same thing.

I wasn't a regular on the picket line. It wasn't like, "Seven-year-old Majerus Child Leads Strike." I was there with my parents. Jodi, who's thirteen months younger than me, would come, too. My mom would put us on leashes of sorts, so we wouldn't get away. When the men had union meetings, the women would take their places on the picket lines. In fact, we weren't really brought up on nursery rhymes. We were brought up on union songs, like "Solidarity."

Those were contentious times. I think my uncles dynamited an ore shipment meant for the Kohler factory.

I still think the union is the best thing for the workers of this country. I'm a big union guy to this day. Now, if management does a good job and the working conditions and pay scale are equitable, then I don't think you need a union. But it doesn't always work out that way.

At the height of his responsibilities, my dad was UAW secretary-treasurer, which is the union's No. 2 international office. The night of the 1976 presidential elections, my dad was down at the campaign headquarters of Sen. Gaylord Nelson. My dad had two states—Wisconsin and Minnesota. Back in those days, labor voted as a bloc. Labor also had money. They took the union dues and backed candidates who supported labor.

Somebody called the house that night—I can't remember the name of the guy—and said Jimmy Carter wanted to talk to my dad. I thought it was one of my friends playing a practical joke. We were the kings of telephone pranks in those days. We weren't real sophisticated: we'd call girls and pretend we were standing them up for prom. Stupid stuff. We were notorious for that. So when this guy dropped Carter's name, I thought for sure this was some type of ruse.

It wasn't. Carter got on the line.

"I just wanted to thank your dad," he said in that lilting Southern accent of his. "I carried Wisconsin, and your father was a big help to me there, and in Illinois as well."

I'm like a lot of sons: I think my dad was a great man. He had principles and he wasn't afraid to stand by those beliefs. He lost the presidency of the whole UAW on a black-white issue: he was going to name a black man as his No. 2 guy on the ticket.

At the time, my dad was secretary-treasurer. But the whole idea of a black man so high in the labor hierarchy didn't sit well with some of the twenty-six members of the powerful executive board. My dad was ahead early in the four-man race, but then some of his friends turned against him. Enough executive board members crossed over on one of the later secret ballots, and that was that. My dad lost the twenty-seventh Constitutional Convention election to UAW vice-president Owen Bieber.

I met Jimmy Hoffa once when I was with my father. They weren't what you would call friends. The UAW was different from the Teamsters. The UAW has always been characterized by three things: a social consciousness, a reputation (for the most part) of being nondiscriminatory, and being a very clean union. The books are open.

My dad was a kingmaker. Besides his position in the union, he later was named chairman of the Democratic Party committee that chose the site of the 1984 Democratic National Convention. He had power, but he used it judiciously. He was a very humble, hard-working, blue-collar kind of guy. I knew he was in a position of authority, but to what extent, I wasn't entirely sure. Then one day I was reading my eighth-grade civics book, and there was my dad's picture. My dad was in a textbook. I thought that was so cool. You have to remember, my mom and dad didn't even have high school degrees. They were self-made people. All my friends would look at it and say, "Hey, there's Rick's dad."

Says Alyce Majerus: *"He really was a wonderful, wonderful father. He had the patience of a saint. Nothing upset him. He was such a family man. He would tell his people, 'Any time, day or night—and I don't care what kind of meeting I'm in—if Alyce or any of the three kids call, I want you to interrupt me.'*

"When Rick had a paper route, he'd get up at 4:00 A.M. and help deliver the Sunday papers."

Says Don Donoher, former Dayton coach: *"As much as Rick learned from Al McGuire, a lot of his overall philosophy was probably drawn from his dad. Raymond Majerus must have been a wonderful man. No doubt he had a tremendous work ethic, and I would imagine he was really a tough guy. I'm sure Rick learned about loyalty and compassion from him, as well as toughness and standing up for yourself.*

"I was at Utah for the last game of the 1998 regular season. New Mexico vs. Utah. Winner wins the WAC title. A few nights earlier, a storm had dumped about two feet of snow on the city. So there's snow everywhere, huge piles in the Huntsman Center parking lot.

"But Rick isn't worried. He's got his own itinerary for himself on game night, so we don't drive over there until about an hour before tip-off. The

team has already had its meeting, done some shooting, but he's not there. That's his routine.

"But this time he pulls into the lot and somebody has parked in his spot—the spot that costs him $2,000 a year. This has never happened to Rick before. Usually there's a security guard stationed near his side of the lot, but this time there's some poor kid covered with blankets, freezing to death. The kid apparently didn't know about Rick's spot.

"Rick gets out and wants to know if the kid can get the other car towed. Then he finds another spot, pulls in, grabs his stuff, and storms toward the Huntsman. I was a few steps ahead of him, so I didn't notice him peeling back to the car in his space.

"Rick got down on all fours and let the air out of the guy's tires. This is the Utah coach . . . forty-five minutes before tip-off . . . as Utah fans are walking by. I couldn't believe what I was seeing. When he's done, he walks up to me with a satisfied look on his face.

" 'Did you let air out of all four?' I say.

" 'No, just two,' he says.

" 'Why two?'

" 'Because he only had one spare.'

"That must have been a lesson he learned from Raymond Majerus: you cross the line, you pay. It was forty-five minutes before his team played for the WAC championship, but Rick wanted that guy to know the line had been crossed."

There wasn't much question where I was going to high school: Marquette University High, a private, all-boys, Catholic school whose mission statement paid special attention to competence, compassion, and conscience. It was Jesuit-run and part of a Jesuit network of forty-five high schools and twenty-four universities and colleges. Sports were an integral part of the school. So were education, uniforms, and discipline.

Says Alyce Majerus: *"When Rick was a freshman at Marquette High, he came home one day from school with all of his books. We were eating dinner, and then I had to go to a teacher-parent conference. I said, 'Rick, don't you want any dinner?' He said no, that he was going up to his room to study. This was a little unusual for Rick, not wanting anything to eat for dinner.*

"So his father and I went to his homeroom at the school. Rick had wonderful grades, but the priest at the homeroom said, 'Did Rick tell you what happened today?'

"That's when the priest told us how Rick had pushed another boy's books off a window ledge, and how Rick had been sent down to see Father Boyle, the school disciplinarian. Father Boyle walked the halls of Marquette High in his cassock and carried a sawed-off golf club.

"Father Boyle told Rick: 'We're going to have to do something about this, aren't we? You can have five hits or memorize twenty pages of the Bible.'

"Rick thought about it for a minute or so. 'Father,' he said, 'I'll take the hits. But would you please do them fast?'

"That was the reason Rick couldn't sit at the dinner table that night. Of course, today they'd call that child abuse."

There were few things I wanted more than to make the varsity basketball team. I tried out, but I got cut.

About ten years later, when I was an assistant on McGuire's staff at Marquette, I got a call from the high school coach, John Glaser. He had been a great star at Marquette, a real man's man. He had since quit coaching and was selling stocks at the time.

When he called and asked if I'd go to lunch with him, I thought for sure he was going to hit me up for some stock buys. I thought that's why he wanted to meet with me.

We went to Karl Ratzsch's, a famous German restaurant in downtown Milwaukee, and he starts asking me about the team, the players, the season. We're talking about ball and then, near the end of lunch, he starts hemming and hawing. I'm thinking, Oh, great, here comes the stock pitch now. And at the time I didn't have much money, and I didn't know much about stocks, so I was determined to tell him that I couldn't do anything stock-wise.

Instead, he shocked the hell out of me. He looked me in the eye—and you could tell he was really struggling with what he wanted to say—and he said, "I want to tell you something. I really felt bad that I cut you. If I had known it meant this much to you, I would have never cut you."

Can you believe that? I'll never forget him saying that as long as I live. Of course, as I have a tendency to do, I jumped right in and said, "No, no, that's all right, don't worry about it. I wasn't that good. But that was really nice of you to say that. I really appreciate this more than you might imagine."

But quite honestly, it had bothered me to get cut. I wanted to play so badly. I still do. But for him to have those feelings and then, years later, be kind enough to say those things to me . . . that meant the world to me. It really did.

We're not that close. I'll see him once in a while when I go back to Milwaukee. But I'll never forget that gesture. It was one of the nicest things someone could ever do.

Since I couldn't play high school basketball, I played CYO ball or on open gym nights or in any pickup game I could find. I still put together teams. I was the guy who set picks, rebounded, made the extra pass.

Says Mike Schneider: *"It'd take you a week to run around one of his picks. You might as well run into a redwood. On the playgrounds, the baskets and backboards were attached to those metal poles. It was almost hilarious to watch somebody try to rebound against Rick, slam against the pole, and then melt into the asphalt."*

2

Letter Sweaters and All Things McGuire

One afternoon in the fall of 1968, Al McGuire broke my heart. It was my sophomore year. I was a six-foot walk-on guard at Marquette. After practice he called me over, grabbed me by the back of my neck, and said, "You're one of the crappiest players I've ever had on one of my teams and you should think about quitting."

To this day, I thought he was going to offer me a scholarship.

All I had ever wanted was to be a part of something, to be part of a team like the one at Marquette. I would have run through two walls to play on that team, to play for McGuire. I didn't care if I was a walk-on. There was a certain honor in that.

And yet, I owe McGuire so much. Without him, I don't know if I would have ever reached this level of success. I would hope that I would mean one-tenth to my team as much as Al meant to our team. He was like those stories you'd read in *Reader's Digest*. He was my most unforgettable character.

I was in high school when McGuire took the Marquette job. Marquette had dropped football a couple of years earlier, and I remember one of my teachers saying the school was putting all of its athletic eggs in one basket.

It was obvious the guy had personality and charisma. And despite not playing on the high school team, it was obvious to me that I wanted to be part of the McGuire program. So shortly after enrolling at Marquette, I tried out for the freshman team. Hank Raymonds, Al's No. 1 assistant, was the coach.

When Raymonds picked me as a walk-on, it was one of the happiest days in my life. It didn't matter if I was the tenth man on a ten-man freshman squad used exclusively as practice fodder for the varsity. What did matter is that I was on a team, an honest-to-God team. I loved it so much. The practices. The competition. The drills. The strategy. The beauty of the pick-and-roll play.

I was spellbound by McGuire. He had that Brooklyn accent and a Brooklyn mentality. I've never forgotten some of his sayings.

➤ "The most expensive thing is cheap labor."
➤ "It's only important to win in war and surgery."
➤ "Behind every bum on every street corner in America is a woman."
➤ "The nice thing about coaching is that one day you feel like you can play handball against a curb, and on other days you feel like you can fly to the moon."
➤ "The hardest thing in life is to get your first $1,000. The next $100,000 is easy."
➤ "If a guy calls from New York, the third thing he says is why he's calling."
➤ "I only comb my hair if there are four people in the room. And if there are four people, I'm getting paid."

I was such a basketball junkie. Oscar Robertson was playing for the Bucks then. So was Lew Alcindor, later known as Kareem Abdul-Jabbar. Larry Costello was the coach then, and Hubie Brown was an assistant. If I could get in a game, or sneak into a game, or watch a Bucks' practice, I'd do it. I didn't ask to get in. If you asked, then you had a good chance of getting kicked out of the Mecca.

I'd try to be unobtrusive, as unobtrusive as a fat nineteen year old could be. I really believe I got in to see a lot more than I should have because I had that janitor/custodial worker look about me. I always looked like I was cleaning on a crew, like I was born with a mop in my hands. But I watched and tried to learn something. I was fascinated by Costello's commitment to precision and by Brown's teaching abilities.

At Marquette, Raymonds was a very good coach for the basics and fundamentals. And McGuire was a terrific motivator.

Even back then, I had started to sense what each of them brought to the table as coaches and conversely, what they all lacked as coaches. We all lack something as coaches.

I think Al liked me, but I could never figure out why he couldn't call me by my name. He'd always call me Whitey. Actually, now that I'm a coach, I can't remember names either. Last year, my walk-ons were Sluge, Big Red, and a kid that I kept calling Shrimp. As you get older, all these names run together.

McGuire drove a Ford Falcon. No radio. He lectured us about the joys of life. He took the guys to plays. He said there was nothing wrong with being a little cocky and arrogant. He seemed so worldly.

History was my major, with a minor in physical education and education. I later earned a master's degree in guidance and counseling, which was acquired through the help of comp tickets, peripheral vision, and benevolent Jesuits who were avid basketball fans.

I was a good student in courses I liked. But if it was, say, a statistics course, then on test day I had more head fakes than Michael Jordan. I could look left, then right two papers over. It was like that Woody Allen movie where someone asked how he managed to cheat on a metaphysics exam. And he says, "I looked into the soul of the person sitting next to me."

I hated math and anything arithmetical. And I hated courses involving research and statistics; I did that on the Buddy Plan. I often think of all the elaborate cheating schemes we used to have in college. We looked upon tests as a group endeavor. It wasn't just *my* grade, it was really everyone's grade. I didn't mind being on the low end of the bell curve in a class like that.

To this day, there are a couple things that are hard for me to do as a coach. It's hard for me to kick Andre out of the gym. And it's really hard for me to call a kid on the carpet for cheating, especially when I had devised the most elaborate systems of cheating known to man. I could have cracked the German code in World War II in a matter of hours. If we had spent as much time studying as we had devising methods of cheating, I would have never had to cheat. It wasn't really about studying; it was a game for us. It was a code. On the A, B, C, Ds on multiple-choice tests, we had a whole system in place that would have put a navy semaphore officer to shame. Touch the right ear, meant A. Touch the left ear, meant B. Touch the chin, meant C. Touch the chest, meant D. We looked like third-base coaches.

So now when I call a kid in and get on him about cheating, it's a little bit difficult sometimes. I feel a little bit like a hypocrite.

And it's tough, too, when a kid takes some extra equipment. Hey, I was the king of smuggling equipment out when I played. Even then, I really wanted to share Marquette equipment with my friends. And I'd always try to squirrel some away.

There were some classes that I loved. There was a course dealing with John Dewey and his role as an educator and his principles of education. I really liked classes like that.

The Jesuits have a certain method of teaching. They're very fine educators. I got a first-class education at Marquette University, don't get me wrong. And I'm not advocating cheating, but anyone who ever took a stats course in college can understand what I'm saying. It's one of the most boring classes ever invented.

Like most kids, I used to work during the summer. That, and play basketball. For two or three summers I worked at the Pabst Brewery on what they would call the Merry Go-Round. There are seven or eight stations on the brewery line. I worked the third shift, which started between 10:00 and 11:00 P.M. We'd go play in the Hart Park League at night or at the Boys Club or in pickup games, then I'd come to the brewery and, like every other nineteen- or twenty-year-old kid, I wouldn't shower. Even then, I sweated profusely.

So I'd come in and there was some poor guy who would have to work right next to me. These guys would smell me and say, "For God's sake, will you go take a shower!" You could have raised mold cultures on some of those T-shirts I wore. Those guys were amazed when I'd come in for that shift. My shirt was sopping wet with sweat. But my thinking was, In another thirty minutes I'm going to be stinking wet with sweat anyway, so why bother showering?

There were packers. There were closers. There was a job where you and another guy would look at the beer bottles as they came by.

Most of these guys were older guys. There were some young guys working in the brewery, but you had to have some juice to be a young guy and get a job there. Between my father's name and McGuire, I got one of those jobs. For a college kid, they were very, very lucrative. A lot of players worked there.

I was a third-shift guy. You never wanted the second shift. Second shift killed your basketball because it meant working from 2:00 to 10:00 P.M.

I pretty much worked every manual and menial job you could do at a brewery. I worked there three or four summers, all through college. In the Merry Go-Round you had to monitor the bottles as they came out of the pasteurizer. Then they'd go to the labeler. The they'd go from the labeler to the packer. Then they'd go to the closer and then down the ramp.

You'd rotate jobs on the Merry Go-Round every twenty minutes. If you didn't, you'd go nuts.

Sometimes I'd work on the docks and build the pallets of the cases of beer as they came off. Then the forklift drivers would come by and pick them up. Now, driving a forklift, that was a good job. But you had to be lucky to get a forklift job. Someone had to be hurt or sick to get one of those.

We got paid well. It was easily the highest-paying summer job for someone like myself, even better than what you got working construction. We got paid what the regular brewery workers got paid for the most part. Of course, you had to join the union, so I was a member of Local No. 9—Brewery Workers. I had that card for a long time, until someone stole my wallet a few years ago. I always kept that card as a remembrance of hard work, of not wanting to go back.

You met some of the nicest older guys. They'd put their arms around you and say, "Make sure you keep going to school." Or, "Don't let this happen to you." Or, "I've got three kids and got a girl pregnant." That sort of thing.

One of the first years I was at Utah, I took the team back to Milwaukee and I showed the guys the brewery docks. I showed them where I worked. I showed them where the guys would take their breaks and stand outside to get relief from the heat. You've got to remember that none of this was air-conditioned.

We went back and sure enough, guys were taking their breaks in the same exact spots we had taken them. They were real nice guys, but I remember thinking, My God, I've been a head coach at Marquette, an assistant with the Bucks, a head coach at Ball State, and now I'm a head coach at Utah. My life has changed. I've been married. I've got two college degrees. And here are these guys in the same spot and in the same jobs.

I knew I didn't want to work in a brewery for the rest of my life. That was something ingrained in me from the first day I started. But spending that much time there just reinforced it.

Going into my sophomore year, I was easily in the best shape of my life. Somehow our trainer had gotten hold of the Boston Celtics conditioning program. It was a tremendous six-week program. I'd go to the Washington High School track, or the Wauwatosa track and do my running. My next-door neighbor would come with me and time me.

I loved basketball so much. I loved the language of the locker room, the camaraderie, the winning. It felt so good. I would have run around the city of Wauwatosa if you told me I had a spot on the team. I didn't have any great expectations. Just wearing a Marquette practice jersey was a thrill. Running the other team's plays was fun. I knew I wasn't as good as George Thompson or Rick Cobb. But I'd be lying if I said I didn't have dreams of playing in a game or working so hard that one day Al would call me over and give me a scholarship.

> **Says Al McGuire:** *"Guys would call him 'Rick the Pick.' He was more like a pillar in a construction high rise. If there would have been twenty men on the team, he would have been the twentieth. I don't know where he came from. All of a sudden he was there.*
>
> *"He was on the team in some way, and we were playing a warmup game against, I don't know . . . the Denver Truckers, some AAU club. I think we were up twenty points or whatever. Rick wanted to get into the game. That's when I told him I'd put Willie Wampum in the game before I put him in. It brought slight tears to his eyes.*
>
> *"Willie Wampum was our school mascot."*

You know, when McGuire cut me, I knew I wasn't that good. But I was good at loving basketball. That's what I was best at. I remember the two guys who made it: Mike Fons and Jim Cook. They made it and I got cut. What hurt is that basketball didn't mean as much to either one of those guys. Cook was going to be a dentist. He didn't love ball, but he was big. And Fons really liked it, but neither one of them were as committed to it as I was.

Maybe that's one of the reasons why, when I'm recruiting, I look for a kid who loves the game. I really look to see if they're committed. Like Britton Johnsen, the game means a lot to him. With Keith, I could tell the game meant a lot to him too.

> **Says Al McGuire:** *"There was no future in it for him as a player. We were really a dynasty. We had more than enough blue chips. I spoke to him one day. I said, 'Rick, we'll let you hang on, do what you want. If eventually you go to law school, I'll get you on the staff.'*
>
> *"He did go to law school—for about six weeks. He faked me and his father out. Then he gently found his mistress. And his mistress was definitely roundball."*

If I couldn't play, I was going to coach. So I coached some guys from St. Sebastian's High School or coached guys at Neeskara playground, or eventually at Marquette High, where McGuire's son, Allie, was a star.

Says Bill Dwyre, former *Milwaukee Journal* sportswriter, now sports editor of the *Los Angeles Times:* *"I covered the Milwaukee Catholic Conference and the Milwaukee Suburban Conference. I had heard about all these kids at Marquette High practicing all the time, about some guy who took them out to the playground. It was Majerus.*

"I started talking to him. He was really young. He had been cut from McGuire's team. He was a nobody, an assistant high school coach. You can't get any lower than that. But from the very first day I met him, you could tell he knew the game. He had a vision of the game. He'd take those kids out on the playgrounds—it didn't matter how hot or dusty it was—and he'd run them. To look at them, they were a collection of nonathletic white stiffs. But Rick made them into a team. Into a winning team."

I graduated in 1970 and applied everywhere for a graduate assistant's job. Mike Schneider had gone on to West Point and tried out for the basketball team. Don DeVoe, who's now the head coach at Navy, was the freshman coach at West Point back then. Bob Knight was the varsity coach. Mike ended up playing freshman baseball instead, and Knight ended up leaving for Indiana. Desperate at the time, I asked Mike if he'd write a letter to Knight on my behalf. He did, and Knight responded with a very nice rejection notice. I think Mike still has the letter someplace.

In 1972, Al made good on his promise of a full-time assistant's job, but with the understanding that I also would go to law school. Al wanted me to go. My dad wanted me to go. So I went, but not before convincing Mike to take a leave of absence from the army and join me at Marquette. At first, I was pretty excited about going, but it didn't last. It got to the point where my heart really wasn't into it.

Says Mike Schneider: *"Rick tried to do both basketball and law school, but it was an impossible combination. Your first year of law school is very, very difficult. You had to be there to study. You had to devote all your energies to it. But as an assistant coach working for Al, Rick couldn't serve two masters. It was clear that basketball was his master, and he liked it that way.*

"He started to skip classes. In all honesty, he did fade away, not because he couldn't understand the work—he was a very bright fellow—but because he couldn't spend time as a coach and a law student."

I was the third guy on that Marquette staff. There was Al, the free spirit; there was Hank, who was more conservative than a savings bond; and there was me. Al would take me out with him once in a while. Al was the cool guy, which is the last thing people would say about me. He dressed like the movie stars of the day. Meanwhile, Hank dressed like Ward Cleaver. I dressed like a hick.

My salary was $5,000. My responsibilities were less clear-cut. Al had the big name, was a terrific motivator, and a much better coach than people realize. Hank was a great Xs and Os guy. He and chalk-boards were meant for each other. Put Al and Hank together, they were a sensational pair.

What I had to do was find my own niche. I had to worm my way in and make myself indispensable. Stu Inman, a shrewd NBA sage, always used to say, "Pick up the towels, put the water cooler away, open the gym, turn on the lights. Someone will realize you're valuable and you'll have a job." I needed to become invaluable to Al. So I picked the only specialty not entirely covered by our staff: recruiting.

In those days there were no rules about time spent on the road re-cruiting. You could go out 365 days a year, twenty-four hours a day. I recognized that that could be my niche. And I liked recruiting. I thought I could be good at it.

The first time I ever went out recruiting was with McGuire. I re-member meeting one of Jerry Tarkanian's assistant coaches at UNLV. I asked him, "What do you think is the key to being a really good re-cruiter?" I thought he might say something about talent evaluation, a polished presentation during the home visit, persistence . . . something like that. Instead—and I'll never forget this—he looked me in the eye and said, "A big part of it is the threads. You've got to get yourself some fine threads."

Me . . . in fine threads.

I saw a lot of these guys out there when I worked for McGuire. They had the latest fashions of the day. I was basically a blue blazer, short-sleeve shirt, polyester pants guy. I had everything but a plastic pencil case in my shirt pocket.

So I did what the UNLV assistant said to do. I went out and bought some plaid pants, some belted shoes—black with a silver buckle—a long-sleeved shirt, and a blue robin's egg–colored sportcoat. You can see the ensemble in photos from the 1977 Final Four. I look like I'm on my way to see K.C. and the Sunshine Band.

Of course, it beat what I wore in the 1974 Final Four. That would have been the plaid sportcoat with cuffs. I wore this stuff because we recruited New York so hard. I thought the New York kids would be impressed. I was young, I was impressionable, and I wanted to be accepted. I wanted to be considered stylish.

Like everything, there was a learning curve involved. I remember working a camp in Snow Valley, California. There was a coach from Fairbury, Nebraska. A little guy, a really nice guy. We were really rolling at Marquette at the time, and I thought this coach's star player would be a hell of a signing for us. I befriended the coach and I knew the kid liked me.

I got back to Milwaukee that fall and I told Al, "I'm going to recruit this kid from Fairbury."

This went against Al's basic recruiting theory, which was to go after kids in the metropolitan areas. He figured we were an urban school, and we had a better chance at urban kids. But I really liked this player and I thought I could get him.

"Go ahead," Al said, "but you're wasting your time."

I got exasperated. "Well, if I'm wasting my time, why are you telling me to go ahead? Why are you saying this?"

"We can't get him," he said.

"Are you telling me I can't get him? Or you can't get him? Or you don't want to get him?"

"No, I know he's good," he said. "I'm not questioning that. I'm just telling you that kid is not coming from Fairbury, Nebraska, to Milwaukee, Wisconsin, to go to Marquette."

"Well, then I'm not going to go," I said.

"No, you should go," he said.

"Why?"

"So you'll learn that you can't get him," he said. "It's worth it to me for you to spend that kind of money recruiting him. Then you'll realize who you can and can't get."

Al was no dummy. I went ahead and recruited the kid and sure enough, he went right to Nebraska. I don't even know if he took another visit. Probably not.

Al used to pose rhetorical questions to me. He was very Socratic in his methods. He used to have the best lines of all when it came to recruiting. I still use them to this day. He'd tell a kid, "The second-best thing you can tell me is no. Get to the answer quick and if it's no, I'll shake your hand and wish you the best of luck. But that way we're all better off."

Or he'd say, "This is the second most important decision of your life, other than the girl you marry. And the girl you marry will coincide with the decision about where you go to school."

I emphasize that to kids. It is a big decision. It's your academics. It's where you're going to live for four, maybe five years. I always tell Utah recruits, "The location of Utah is not going to change, we're not moving any closer to L.A. The weather patterns aren't going to change. We're always going to have snow. It's always going to be cold in the winter. If cold, snow, and distance are a factor, then don't come. You'll be unhappy. But if you can get beyond the weather, and you want the academics and the basketball, then this is a great place for you."

I challenge them. I'll say, "You tell me the day I'm not the most organized, enthusiastic, energetic guy on the floor. If I'm not that guy, then that will be the day we end practice early and the next day I'll quit. If you can ever say, 'Coach wasn't organized today . . . He wasn't into it today,' then I have a problem. But I challenge anybody to find a Utah player who could ever say that."

Recruiting is such a fickle, weird experience. One time I went into Doc Rivers's home and his mom had her favorite TV show on during the visit. Well, I've got the dean of the Marquette law school with me, because Doc had said he was interested in becoming a lawyer. So here's the law school dean and myself, but she never shut the TV off. She never missed a word, either. She was very smart. But I would have liked to have gone over there and turned it down a little.

Another time I was recruiting a kid named Lloyd Walton. He was from Mt. Carmel High School in Chicago. He ended up playing for the Bucks for five years. Anyway, he showed up for Al's basketball camp and he's scheduled to go somewhere else and Al says, "Let's get him into school." Well, it's Labor Day weekend and school starts at Marquette on Tuesday.

Al tells me to get him in. Well, we can't give him a basketball scholarship, so we're going to give him an Education Opportunity Program (EOP) scholarship. I call the head of the program at Marquette, but it's Labor Day weekend and you have a better chance of finding Dennis Rodman in Brooks Brothers than you do finding a school administrator on the last weekend before classes begin. So I call some girlfriend of mine. I tell her, "Put on a dress. You now have just become head of the EOP program at Marquette."

Back in those days, they didn't have anything like a Kinko's. So I went and had some stationery made up. I buy a stamp and seal. Then I go to the kid's house. The kid was going to go to Jacksonville University. In fact, the coaches from Jacksonsville are circling his block in a car. I told Lloyd, "This is a great deal for you." I introduce him and his mother to this woman who is posing as the head of the EOP. Everything is great. Lloyd signs these fake EOP documents I've had made up. I pull out my seal and stamp and make it look official. Everybody's happy, except the Jacksonville guys driving around the block. They're dying.

According to NCAA rules, I wasn't allowed to drive Lloyd from the south side of Chicago to Milwaukee. So I told him I'd drive him to O'Hare and he could catch a plane up to Milwaukee. It's about a four-minute flight. It's nothing. Nope. Lloyd is afraid to fly. He tells me he's changing his mind; he's going to Jacksonville. Outside the living room window, I can see the Jacksonville guys still circling the block.

I'm desperate. I give my keys to the woman posing as the EOP director. I make an interpretation of NCAA rules and surmise it to be legal for a fake administrator to drive a recruit and his fake EOP documents to Marquette. She takes Lloyd up to Milwaukee, but I'm stuck in Chicago without a car. So I take a city bus down to the Loop and catch the El to the main train station. I couldn't get a hotel room that night (there was a blues festival or something in town), so I had to spend the night in the station and take a train up to Milwaukee the next morning.

By the way, Lloyd got his real EOP documents the next business day.

Lloyd's mother was named Jean Jones. Rumor had it that she used to be a Playboy bunny. Regardless, she was a flat-out knockout. Stunning. She had had Lloyd very young in life.

Al invited her up to campus, figuring she'd never come. Surprise. She decided to visit. Al took her out and I'm sure he had dinner, drinks, and had a nice time. Then she came up again about two weeks later. This time Al told me I had to take her out.

At the time I was about thirty years old. She was about thirty-five, maybe thirty-six. She's dressed to kill. There was no wiggle room in the pants. She has some kind of boa wrapped around her. And it's cold as hell.

Lloyd lived in a dorm right near the gym. I told Lloyd, "I'm going to take you and your mom out tonight for dinner." He said, "Great." But then his mom said she wanted to have a drink while Lloyd was getting ready.

So I took her to a campus bar called the Ardmore, which is where most of the faculty, graduate students, older people, and an occasional

Jesuit on the loose would come to hang out. I walk in the Ardmore with her and she puts her arm in mine. Everybody kind of turns around and you could see them say, "Oooh, look who the coach is with."

We sat down and the bartender asked me what I wanted. I wanted to make her feel comfortable, so I told him I'd have a beer. Then he asked her and she said she'd have a Courvoisier and water. Let me tell you, they've haven't seen a Courvoisier in that neighborhood since the Great Depression. As we were waiting for our drinks she pulled out a cigarette and handed me a lighter. I was a little nervous, so I said, "Uh, no thanks, I don't smoke."

"It isn't for you," she said. "I want you to light my cigarette."

We finally left the bar and it's freezing outside. There's a nor'easter coming off Lake Michigan. It's January. It's five degrees, fifteen degrees below with the windchill. She looked at me and said, "Well, the hawk is out." I started looking around because I thought she had spotted some bird. But she just meant that it was cold out.

She and Lloyd left me laughing. I just gave Lloyd some money and said, "Take you and your mom out to eat. Don't even bring me a receipt. Have a nice night."

I wish I had some sort of sexy story involving a single mom hitting on me, but I wasn't that good looking. My recruiting visits usually involved eating a lot of homemade pie. Nothing sexy about that.

But those were wild days, especially when I was an assistant coach. The NCAA rules weren't as strict, and we were recruiting a different breed of cat.

In those days, you could take people out to dinner and it wasn't against the rules. There was this one recruit—I'm not going to give you the name—and we take the kid and his mom to the Playboy Club in Chicago. Perfectly legal. Then we bring them up to Milwaukee and take them to a fancy place up there. Perfectly legal. Later, the kid's mom gets talking to my mom and my mom tells her how much I love chili. So the kid's mom says, "I'm going to make Rick some chili."

A week or so later, I go to the kid's house and she's in the kitchen making chili. Bless her heart, but there are cockroaches running up and down the kitchen walls and in back of the stove. Plus, the meat is not exactly the ground chuck of the day.

She serves me the chili and I kind of turn sideways. I put the chili in my hankie, put the hankie in my napkin, and put the napkin in my pocket. Then I go to the bathroom and do everything I can to get this chili to disappear. I come out of the bathroom, sit down, and pretend to eat some more. She asks, "How is it?"

I look her straight in the eye and give her the obligatory, "It's great. Better than my own mom's. Can I get the recipe?"

"No," she says, "but here, have another bowl."

So she scoops up some more and hands me a fresh bowl of the stuff. I was dead. I had to eat it.

I was the recruiting setup man. Al was the closer. It was a different time back then. You could take families to dinner, which became an exercise in one-upsmanship. A recruit would come in and I'd say, "Where'd they take you when you visited North Carolina?" And the kid would say, "To a steak house in Chapel Hill." I'd sort of laugh a superior laugh and say, "Well, I'll take you to a *real* steak house. C'mon. And when we get there, I'll introduce you to the cook."

To be honest, I liked to take kids to rib joints, chicken places, the Speed Queen Barbecue, those sort of places. But those days are long gone.

I made my share of recruiting mistakes at Marquette. I could have signed Jeff Hornacek, but I didn't. Hornacek's high school coach begged me to take him. He ended up at Iowa State and has had a wonderful NBA career. We've talked about it since he came to the Utah Jazz, but he never gave me a hard time about it. He understands what happened.

Another guy I misjudged was Hersey Hawkins. I should have signed him when I was at Marquette. But some of the mistakes I made then, I didn't make later in my career. You learn.

Al was a good guy to work for because he basically left you alone. He always used to say that Hank and I were responsible for taking care of the "misdemeanors," the details. Al wasn't a detail guy. Hank did most of the administrative and academic work. In fact, he was almost the de facto athletic director in many ways.

Al wasn't like most coaches. Some people said he was unconventional. Al said he was ahead of his time. He still says he's ahead of his time.

There was an age difference between us, but Al thought and acted young. He rode a motorcycle. One time I was following him and something happened—a car pulled out in front of him, something like that—and he released and rolled onto the street. He was on one side of the car, his motorcycle on the other. I jumped out of my car, asked him if he was okay, and he just said, "I'm fine, Rick. I'm fine."

Al would park his car at a store and throw the keys on the floor mat. "Someone steals this car," he'd say, "and they get the black plague." He was big on the black plague.

If Al was doing a speaking engagement, he'd change into his "soft clothes" as soon as his speech was done. Then he'd find the nearest bus station and go drinking at the closest bar to the depot. He said they had the best country-western jukeboxes.

We went out sometimes. Al wasn't a five-star restaurant type of guy. We'd go to a pizza place, the kind of place where you'd have to bang your fist on the table every five minutes to scare away the cockroaches.

Al understood basketball theory, but he was more concerned about players. *X*s and *O*s were nice, but if your players didn't get it, who cared? He was a terrific speaker. He knew how to handle ballplayers and how to get through to them. He was so positive. He had that whole Al Davis mentality: just win, baby.

I spent six years on Al's staff, and then, when Al resigned after winning the NCAA championship in 1977, another six years on Hank Raymond's staff. During those twelve seasons as an assistant, we went to eleven NCAA tournaments, two Final Fours, and had a 277–76 record. It was a hell of a run.

I knew Al's days as a coach were numbered the year before we won the national title in 1977. We were getting ready to play undefeated and No. 1–ranked Indiana in the NCAA Mideast Regional final in Baton Rouge. We were ranked No. 2, but this was the Bob Knight team featuring Scott May, Kent Benson, Bobby Wilkerson, Tom Abernethy, and Quinn Buckner.

We had some talent too: Bo Ellis, Jerome Whitehead, Lloyd Walton, Earl Tatum, Butch Lee. And we had Al.

Al never came on the court until just before tip-off. I found him in the lavatory and he was shaking. I couldn't look. I turned away. It was obvious that he had reached the point where basketball wasn't fun anymore.

The next season Al made a promise: he was resigning, regardless of what happened in the NCAA tournament. We reached the Final Four, beat North Carolina–Charlotte on a Jerome Whitehead layup at the buzzer, and then beat Dean Smith's North Carolina team, 67–59, in the championship game. Al sat on the bench and cried. It was such a poignant moment for all of us.

But he kept his word. He later said he didn't fool with things that had stopped quivering. For him, basketball had quit quivering.

Al ended up giving away about 200 basketball-related watches to friends and family, including the championship watch he got for winning the 1977 title. He said something that always stuck with me: "The best thing to happen to me is that it allowed me to be called 'Coach.' That's something nonnegotiable. It makes me feel so good."

I feel the same way. It's an honor to be called Coach, just like it's an honor to be someone's friend or to have the unconditional love of a family member.

Says Mike Schneider: *"When I graduated from law school, my wife and I took our kids up to the northwoods of Wisconsin for July Fourth weekend. We had four kids by then, including five-year-old Sonya, who was Rick's goddaughter.*

"We went for a morning hike, came back, and took a nap in the pop-up camper. There was a horrible storm—a tornado came whipping through the campground. A 150-foot tree came crashing down on the camper, killing my daughter Sonya. When I got home, Rick was there. I don't even know how he got in my house. I don't even know what he said. But he was there, and that meant a lot. He's my friend. That's what friends do."

In 1983, Hank resigned from coaching, but retained his title as athletic director. I became the head coach.

Al thought it was a mistake.

Says Al McGuire: *"The Marquette thing . . . there was too much inbreeding. Me to Hank to Rick. There was too much Gipper in it.*

"It was a learning process for Rick, but he didn't know he was going through it. Part of being a success in coaching is to be hung in effigy, to be beat on. Then you close yourself into a little corner, you go into a cocoon."

It wasn't as if the program fell apart. We averaged about nineteen victories during my three years, but we didn't reach the NCAA tournament. We had good teams and we played a killer schedule. We also had some incredible wins. I'll never apologize for what we accomplished.

One of my most memorable games, and one of the classic games in Indiana basketball history, was during the 1984–85 postseason, when the Hoosiers beat us in the NIT.

Both teams were struggling at the time. We played in the third round at Bloomington to see who would go to New York for the NIT Final Four. Steve Alford was on that Indiana team.

We lost in double overtime, 94–82, with four guys on the floor. Five of our group had fouled out. I'll never forget that game. We only had four guys left, and there was about 1:30 left to play. Mandy Johnson, one of our guards, looked over at me during the game, and said, "Box and one still?" I couldn't believe it. That takes five players.

I said, "No, box! Jeezus, we only have four guys!"

To the refs' credit, they would not call a fifth foul on any of those four guys. They would not embarrass themselves and call a fifth foul.

After the game, Knight took the microphone and told the fans, "I'd really like you to give Marquette a hand. This was one of the best games that has ever been played in this building."

He was right. It was a hell of a game.

You know, Del Harris says I might be in the Guinness Book of World Records for basketball coaches. I coached grade school, high school, college, and pro all in the same town.

But looking back, though, Al might have been right. I didn't really know what I was getting myself into. You should never, ever become the head coach where you were an assistant, and especially where you were a student and a player, albeit a walk-on player in my case. Some of the same professors I was dealing with as a peer had had me as a student. They were accustomed to me skipping classes and asking, "Where's Majerus?" and someone saying, "Oh, he and his buddies went to Arlington Racetrack today." So that was difficult.

The players don't look at you the same, at least, not initially. The truth is, you're never afforded the respect and the consideration you deserve as a head coach. For instance, it's a little thing, but when I was named head coach at Marquette, they didn't print a new set of photos, they simply crossed out the word *assistant* on the original set.

I wouldn't recommend that scenario to anybody. I think Joey Meyer got victimized by the same triple whammy. He played at DePaul, was a longtime assistant coach at DePaul, and then succeeded his father at DePaul. Ultimately he got fired, partly for expectations his father helped create years earlier.

I was always fighting those battles, for an academic advisor, for cars for my assistant coaches. And they'd say, "Well, you didn't have one." No, I didn't get a car, but I would have liked to have had one. So I had to go behind their back and get cars for my assistants.

I was following McGuire, and that was hard. I don't care what anyone says, none of those legendary figures want their records to be broken or matched. Al could have given me more help. I don't think he meant it personally, that's just human nature. I'm not mad about that. And Hank was older than Al, and was bitter that he didn't get this. Then

I got a shoe contract, and Hank never got one. Al never got one. But shoe contracts weren't around in their day. I didn't have a basketball camp at Marquette, so that didn't help my situation.

Al and I had a real good relationship. But I'm telling you, subliminally and in the recesses of his mind, he wasn't pulling for me to eclipse his accomplishments. I'd probably be the same way. Nobody wants that. Lombardi didn't want the Packers to do as well after he left for the Washington Redskins. That's just human nature. You're proud of what you did. It's just the way we're built.

At Marquette, there was tremendous pressure on me. That's fine. That's how the business works. But there were so many daily battles to fight. At Marquette you'd go in and say, "We need a strength room." And Hank would say, "Well, I didn't have one." Or I'd go to the administration and it would say, "McGuire didn't have a strength room."

They didn't understand that you needed something like that to stay competitive. You wanted to tell those people, "By the way, there was no Big East Conference a few years ago, but there is now." You needed new equipment and facilities to stay competitive with those emerging conferences.

I'm sure Joey Meyer had the same problems at DePaul. You noticed as soon as they fired Joey and hired a new coach, DePaul suddenly upgraded its facilities.

One time Brother Mike Wilmot, who was an assistant on my 1983–84 staff, and I went out to the University of Nebraska and visited Boyd Epley, the guru of strength and weight training. He turned Nebraska into the mecca of strength programs. They had a strength museum there and one of the featured artifacts was a Universal machine, which is kind of this one-piece, old-time pulley-and-plate weight machine that you find in someone's garage. It was roped off, like it might fall apart if you touched it. I guess they thought it was sort of the Gutenberg press of strength machines.

I looked at Brother Wilmot and said, "My God, that's our strength room."

It was, too. We had a Universal machine and it was in their *museum*. After that trip we eventually put in a weight room, kind of half-assed, but we didn't hire a strength coach.

So it was a combination of things. Frustrations over scheduling. Fighting to get academic advisors. And I got tired of the recruiting. It was a difficult situation, and I knew it wasn't going to get any better.

Back then we used to call ourselves "The Big Four." It was us, Notre Dame, Dayton, and DePaul. We were four independents trying to survive in a basketball world that was becoming more and more conference-oriented. Now that I look back, I'm the only guy still coaching. Don Donoher at Dayton was a hell of a coach, a great coach. I thought Digger Phelps was a good coach at Notre Dame. And I thought Joey Meyer did a very good job at DePaul. But that's another reason why I eventually left. Without an affiliation, it was becoming harder and harder to succeed.

We could take the Big East on when I was at Marquette as an assistant. We could still go in and compete against Syracuse when they were an independent. But when the Big East began to assert itself in scheduling and TV and all those things, it became very difficult to recruit against a Syracuse or Georgetown or Villanova or whatever. Kids would say, "Jeez, I want to play in the Big East. Look at the TV. Look at the schedule. Look at the exposure."

I got caught up in all those frustrations.

I was the head coach at Marquette for three years. We had three NIT bids and we had some real good teams and yet, the expectations were still '77 the national championship, Al McGuire. But Marquette hadn't moved forward. I couldn't even get a basketball camp there. But much worse, there wasn't a direction at Marquette, relative to academic advising, recruiting monies, perks for assistants. I made as much from New Balance at the time as I did with Marquette; the money from my New Balance shoe contract was exactly the same as from my head coaching contract, and I had been at Marquette as an assistant for thirteen years.

I don't fault Marquette. I was young and I didn't know how to politicize it. I didn't have a benefactor and there was no vision or direction. It was like Loyola under George Ireland or DePaul under Ray Meyer. A mom-and-pop shop. Successful, but still a mom-and-pop shop. At Marquette, it was a seat-of-the-pants operation. And since McGuire had done it in '77, Marquette thought it could happen again regardless of the circumstances. But what nobody realized—or what nobody would accept—was that '77 was the culmination of everything with McGuire. But the culmination was also the beginning of the end. If you'll recall, we had had the most losses (seven) of any NCAA championship team, a distinction we owned until 1981, when Indiana won the title with nine regular season losses.

But I think Al could see some things coming too.

Knowing what I know now, I still would have taken the Marquette job. But I wish I would have gone to Xavier later on. At one point I think I could have had the Xavier job, and I know I had the Wisconsin job. I stayed at Marquette, but when I look back, I think it's better to get out and go to a place where you come in and you're the head coach. You're not viewed as the assistant coach or a walk-on or a student. You have a head coach identity.

I tried so hard at Marquette. I tried almost too hard. I don't think I could have worked any harder or put in more hours than I do now. But sometimes when you want it so much—like I did at Marquette—you press too much. I think one thing that always hurt me was not having a wife who could be part of the deal. I think Al's wife, Pat, was a terrific asset to him with players and recruiting. I think she was a great asset to him in other aspects of his life.

It would be great to have a counterbalance, someone you could go home to and who would say, "Hey, look, they're only freshmen" or "Look, is this as important as your health?"

I spent every second at Marquette trying to make that program better. Plus, I was trying to emerge from a giant shadow—the shadow of Al.

It also didn't help that we had some drug problems on that team. We had some kids who did drugs. Even to this day, I'm amazed by how many people are willing to compromise on marijuana, as if it's the Clinton "I didn't inhale" scenario. We had some guys on it, and I wanted to drug test for it. Someone would tell me about it, or I would just know, and then I'd go confront the player and he'd say, "No, I'm not smoking dope." So what could I do?

Now, it's different. One of the things I enjoyed about Ball State and also about Utah is that I'm going to test for drugs. The players know it going in. I'm very up front about my policy. I tell them, "If you test positive, I'm going to suspend you for the rest of the season. I'm going to get you counseling—and I think you do need counseling."

And here's why I'm the king of counseling when it comes to this: nobody has ever gone and done cocaine first. You know how smoking and drinking are gateway drugs? I believe marijuana is definitely the gateway drug to cocaine. And marijuana itself isn't good.

I thought Bill Russell had the greatest line of all when it came to drugs. He said he wanted to see in "real time, at real speed." You can't see it in real time if you're on drugs.

So that was another reason why I left. And Marquette was very political. And quite frankly, some of the frustrations that led to Al leaving were very similar to why I decided to leave.

I also tried to get academic advisors for the players, but Marquette told me it didn't want to give special treatment to the athletes. That's the kind of thinking I encountered. But providing players with an academic advisor isn't the same thing as providing them with a car. It isn't a bad thing. It isn't an illegal thing. It isn't an extra benefit. For some of the players, it was a necessity. But Marquette didn't see it that way.

Look at Dayton right now. Dayton has the premier basketball center in the country—the Don Donoher Center. I visited it last year and it is cutting edge. Ohio State is going to have a new facility. Cincinnati is going to be left behind if it doesn't do something. It's like an arms race. That Dayton facility is going to attract players. There's no facility like it.

The same thing applies to cutting-edge strength rooms and academic advisement programs. They're not as splashy as a state-of-the-art basketball arena, but they make a difference in attracting and keeping good players. When I was at Marquette I could see everyone else around the country going into weights, going into academic advising, and we couldn't keep up. In some instances, we didn't even try to keep up, or if we did, we did so on a minimal basis.

I know we didn't go to the NCAA tournament, but we did average nineteen wins a year at Marquette. So even with some of those problems, we did pretty well. But we could have been better. The basketball program could have been better if we'd had more support from the administration. And I'll be honest with you, I didn't really have anyone I could depend on. Hank Raymonds was very nice, but he and Al were from a bygone era. They were great in their era. But I could see guys like Jim Boeheim from Syracuse and these Big East guys beginning to assert themselves nationally. And part of why they were able to do it is because they had conferences, TV exposure, ready-made schedules, facilities, support, and a hundred other little things that make a difference. I'll guarantee you this: their weight room equipment wasn't on exhibit in Lincoln, Nebraska.

At the end of the three years, I had had enough. A wonderful little school in California—St. Mary's—had called about a job, and I wanted to go out there and interview. So I asked Marquette to release me from my contract. The job at St. Mary's was mine if I wanted it, but Marquette wouldn't release me. Yet I was bound and determined to leave. I didn't feel like they would change things, and I was frustrated. The frustrations were from a combination of sources, and some were of my own doing.

Another thing that might have hurt me was this: I saw the world according to McGuire and Raymonds. Although I went out of my way to go to Indiana and California for summer camps, and I traveled extensively and I read books, I had grown up in Al and Hank's system. And we were no longer going to get the inner-city kid from the East. We had to start looking elsewhere. Al used to say, "If they have grass in front of their home, we're not going to recruit them." But we had to get some guys who had some lawns. I wasn't used to dealing with that, nor did I have a recruiting network for that. Plus, our recruiting network was the East. It was Pennsylvania, New York, and New Jersey. As soon as the Big East came along, those recruiting areas dried up for us. Marquette, Notre Dame, Dayton, and DePaul haven't been the same since.

We used to practice at the old gym at Marquette. I tried to get new backboards and rims. It was as though I was asking for construction materials tantamount to building a new on-campus facility. All I wanted was a rim and a backboard.

You know, McGuire really did win with mirrors. He did it the way I do it now in some ways: he did it with friends. Friends with recruiting referrals. Or he did it with buddies he'd meet along the way.

One thing that was difficult for me is that I was young when I got the head job. I was in my early thirties, and I was dealing with a booster club with a median age of about forty-five. They didn't really relate to me, and maybe I didn't relate to them.

For years Loyola lived in '63. Marquette lived in '77. Dayton in their Final Four year. And DePaul in their glory years. When I leave Utah, I'll feel bad for my successor because he's always going to be held accountable for our playing in the national championship game. But our playing in that game was really more of an aberration. If you looked at the last decade and said, "Which school doesn't belong in the top ten?," you'd circle Utah.

I don't want to sound entirely negative about my Marquette experience. I enjoyed Marquette. I'm proud to say I coached at Marquette. There are some very nice people there. There are some Jesuits to this day that I still consider good friends. I invited some of the fathers to come sit on the bench at the Final Four.

I think what happens, too, when you get the job and you come up the ranks like I have, there is a lot of envy and jealousy from within. I was victimized a bit by that and my naivete about it. But there were many more good people and nice people at Marquette than there were vindictive types.

There was a guy named Mike Price, who was the head of the school of journalism, who would have done anything he could have to help a kid academically and, by doing so, further the cause of the basketball program. You need those allies. Don't get me wrong. He didn't do anything illegal or unethical, but he was willing to make an extra effort for a player if the player was willing to commit academically.

I don't think I could ever coach at Marquette again. I'd always like to live in Milwaukee for a part of the year. I'll probably go back at some point in my life. I love Milwaukee. My accountant is there. My dentist is there. My lawyer is there. My bad investments are there.

In a way, I was complicitous with the problems at Marquette. I should have gone out and left. You can stay at a place too long and I did exactly that at Marquette. When you stay at a place too long, you become blinded by the problems. You're not even aware of them until you get an outside perspective.

Not long ago, my high school named me the Alumnus of the Year. Two years ago, Marquette named me the Liberal Arts Alumnus of the Year. When they did, my first thought was, I wonder if they want money?

That's the McGuire in me.

3
Post-Al, Pre-Wasatch Mountains

By the end of the 1985–86 season, I wanted out of Marquette. I had averaged about nineteen victories and worked as hard as I could have possibly worked, but it wasn't good enough for those people still trapped in the McGuire time warp. They didn't realize Marquette's program had inherent problems that could not be solved by staring at a ticket stub from the 1977 Final Four.

I was frustrated with everything at Marquette. The recruiting. The skirmishes with the athletic department and administration. The lack of heat in the gym. The little drug problem on our team. The wild expectations. The politics. Almost all the same things Al was frustrated over.

I needed a change, and Don Nelson was the guy who made it possible.

Nellie and I saw each other on occasion. He was the head coach of the Bucks, I was with Marquette. I'd run into him at practices or games, and we'd talk for a few minutes here and there. He was always great to me.

At some point during that 1985–86 season, Nellie mentioned the possibility of joining his staff as an assistant. I told him I'd be interested, but didn't really pursue it. He offered it to me again, but he made it clear he wouldn't ask a third time. That's the way he is. He said it would be a great situation for him, and for me. And he was right, though I think it was better for me.

So I went to Marquette and told them I really wanted to work for the Bucks, that it was a great opportunity for me. The starting salary was about $25,000, but money wasn't an issue. This was a quality-of-life decision.

This time, unlike when I interviewed with St. Mary's or Xavier, Marquette released me from my contract. I wasn't forced out by any means.

As it turned out, moving to the Bucks was the best thing I ever did professionally. That's because I got to see how somebody else ran a practice, how somebody else put together a game plan. There are so many decisions in pro ball and I got a chance to be exposed to all of them. It also gave me an opportunity to see my mistakes and catalog what things I would want if I ever went somewhere else as a head coach.

Nellie was really a terrific coach, a two-time NBA Coach of the Year who had great relationships with his players and staff. I had heard great things about Del Harris, too, and had read his book on zone offense. Del wrote if not the best book then one of the best books on zone offense. Del was also a first-year guy on the staff (he replaced Mike Schuler; I replaced Garry St. Jean), but he was a former NBA head coach and a guy I knew I could learn from. That was exciting to me.

One time I was sitting with the late Jimmy Maloney of Temple at the L.A. Summer League. I had just taken the job and we were going over the Bucks' playbooks.

"Jeez, Jim, look at all these books," I said. "What do you think?"

He said, "Rick, you are in a great situation. If you can just tap into Nelson and tap into Del, those guys are really basketball guys."

And they were. It was a perfect situation.

Says Del Harris: *"In November of 1974, I went to finish out the season as an assistant to Jerry Pimm at the University of Utah. In the process of all the recruiting calls, Jerry and his other assistants were always talking about—or talking to—Rick Majerus. It seemed like so many sentences began with, 'Majerus says . . . ,' when they were evaluating prospects. I knew Rick was a young assistant at Marquette. I had never met him, but I just had this image in my mind of this slick guy with a briefcase, wearing a suit and tie, with long, slick-backed hair, and some jewelry hanging down from his neck. Kind of a cross between a lawyer and a pimp. That was the typical college recruiter look of the day.*

"It wasn't until 1977 when Marquette went to the NCAA finals that I actually saw what he looked like. It totally blew my mind as to how wrong I could have been with the image of Rick that I had. And it wasn't until about ten years later that I actually met him.

"I'll tell you one thing about him. For all the notoriety he had gained in the Milwaukee area, he treated me right from the start with such respect. He and I were the assistant coaches, but he always treated me with the same respect he did Nellie. He would often say, 'Yeah, I'm working for Nellie and Del.' He wasn't working for me, but he just had that way of making everybody feel good."

I was young and I was enthusiastic. I got to work with Scott Skiles, the team's top draft pick from Michigan State, and Jerry Reynolds. I got to work with those guys every day. Coming off of screens, reading screens, that sort of thing. I got to work with Randy Breuer, sort of our project center. Nellie said Breuer was my guy. That became one of my main responsibilities, to work with the bigs, the centers. I also did game preparation and scouting.

After practice, we sometimes would play three-on-three. I'd get on a team and do whatever it is I do. I'm a good screener, a good passer, and I understand spacing and I know how to play the game. My problem is, I'm not a great athlete.

Says Del Harris: *"I will tell you for a fact that I don't think Rick ever lost a game. Whoever would team up with Rick would win. I don't care what Rick might have looked like in comparison to an NBA athlete, he absolutely understood how to play basketball. He would pass to the open guy at the right time. Or he would set a double pick. He was a double pick himself. He would get the other guy open, and all the other guy would have to do is make an open shot. They called him 'Rick the Pick.' I called him 'Rick the Double Pick.' "*

I brought a little something to the table as a coach, but Nellie really knew his stuff. He was a master of the clock and terrific with dealing with the players. He was great at role definition, where every player knows exactly where he fits in with the team. To this day, there are lessons I learned from him relating to personnel.

One time I was working with Ricky Pierce, trying to get him to go left off the dribble. Nellie came up to me later and said, "Look, you have to learn to look at a player and determine what he can do, rather than dwell so much on what he can't do. It'd be nice if Pierce had a left hand, but he's got a great curl game to the middle, and he has a nice shot when he fades it. We want to use those. That's our job: to put him in a position where he can be successful."

I remember that like it was yesterday.

Says Don Nelson: *"That was the first thing that you noticed about him, how enthusiastic he was, how excited he was when he learned something new, how respectful he was."*

The whole Bucks experience was refreshing. It was a whole new terminology. The game was faster. You had to make more decisions.

Those were the old days, when you had two-a-days during training camp and the coach had the stick. He had some power. That was the beginning of the era when the coach was just starting to lose his grip on the hammer. There weren't as many teams. There were fewer players. The contracts weren't as guaranteed. A coach was still a coach.

Nellie had some good tricks. He called Skiles in once. I was in the office next to his and his door was open. He said to Skiles, "You know, last night in your apartment?"

"Yeah?" said Skiles.

"And you know that party you had and all that noise you were making? How many people did you have at that party?"

"Just a few friends from Indiana."

"What did that go to, about two, three o'clock?"

"I guess so," Skiles said.

Well, turns out that Nellie really didn't know if Skiles had had a party that night. But he did know that Skiles had had a horseshit practice, and that Scott needed a porter to carry the bags under his eyes. So Nellie called him in and, in a very clever and shrewd way, pulled the truth out of Skiles. Skiles, a rookie who needed the lesson, ended up confessing to the whole thing.

Nellie got on me too. He was always on me about my weight and my diet. We were in Sacramento and I was in the coffee shop drinking a milkshake. Out of the corner of my eye I saw Nellie coming, so I immediately hid the milkshake behind some flowers and a menu. As soon I saw him it was as if I were squirreling away cocaine. To look at me you would have thought I was hiding illegal drugs.

Says Don Nelson: *"We were both trying to lose weight at the time, and we were both on strict diets. I hadn't strayed from the diet for three or four weeks.*

"I saw Rick sitting in the coffee shop that day, so I waved and went over to join him. As I was walking over, I could tell he was trying to hide something in the middle of the table, behind the flowers.

"We started talking and I pretended I hadn't seen a thing.

" 'So, Rick,' I said, 'you sticking with the diet?'

" 'Oh, yeah,' he said. 'Sure I am.'

" 'No, you're not,' I said. 'You're cheating, aren't you?'

" 'No, why do you say that?'

" 'Because you've got a chocolate shake mustache, that's why.' "

Nellie and I both struggled with our weight. During the summer of 1986, he raised money for his Nellie's Farm Fund by dropping fifty pounds. For every pound he lost, Nellie pledged money to the program, which helped financially strapped farmers in Wisconsin.

I was also a gofer sometimes. We got Jack Sikma in an off-season deal from the Seattle SuperSonics, and Nellie told me to pick up Jack at the airport and take him out to eat. But I wasn't just a chauffeur. Nellie wanted information too.

"And ask him where he likes to get the ball, and when he gets it, what move he likes to make," Nellie said.

You know, that was a hell of a smart thing on Nellie's part. Sikma was a key player for us. He was the first legitimate center the Bucks had had since Bob Lanier retired. Nellie was already trying to find out what worked best for Jack. That's one of the reasons he's a player's coach.

I'll tell you something else Nellie told me, and he doesn't even remember saying it. He used to say, "You know what the five most important minutes of a game are? It's the five minutes in the press conference after the game."

I learned that from Nellie. You know what? As diametrically opposed in coaching life as Al and Nellie are, there are great similarities between the two of them when it comes to dealing with the press. Each of them will walk into a room and to this day, they'll each pick up the dinner tabs for reporters. Or they'll buy a round of beers, something like that. They weren't sucking up; they were being regular guys.

Nellie used to say those five minutes with the media were so important because it was the only time you could put your spin on a game. It's your five minutes to talk about how a game went, or to throw a bouquet in a certain direction. At Utah, the press was so enthralled with Van Horn that I would sometimes use those five minutes to berate Keith's defense. I would say, "Yeah, sure, Keith's a hell of a player. Obviously he made some big shots tonight or we wouldn't have won. But he's got to understand he can't score enough points to make up for bad defense."

Nellie had won at least fifty games each season with the Bucks since 1979–80. And now he had an actual center in Sikma.

But our season was affected by injuries. Lots of them. John Lucas played in only forty-three regular season games. Marvin Webster played in just fifteen games. Paul Pressey twenty-one games. Sidney Moncrief, a poster person for class, appeared in thirty-nine games.

The rest of the roster featured, at one time or the other, Terry Cummings, Craig Hodges, Dudley Bradley, Paul Mokeski, Keith Smith, Junior Bridgeman, Skiles, Webster, Hank McDowell, Don Collins, Jerome Henderson, Mike Glenn, Kenny Fields, Cedric Henderson, and Chris Engler. Needless to say, we had some turnover.

A year earlier, Nellie had squeezed fifty-seven victories and a sixth consecutive Central Division title out of this team. They beat New Jersey in the first round of the playoffs, and then Philadelphia before being swept by the Celtics in the next round.

But the 1986–87 season would be more of a struggle, both on and off the court. The team was one of the oldest in the league. Sikma was thirty-one. Lucas was thirty-three. Bridgeman was thirty-three. Webster was thirty-four. A lot of guys were nearing the end of their career. We were going to have to grind to reach fifty wins.

So we ground. Nellie kept tweaking the roster to keep us competitive, and he coached the hell out of the team.

When guys would come in, one of my jobs was to pick them up at the airport, take them to the gym, and then run them through the plays. A lot of times I'd have one of my buddies along to help me.

Bridgeman had a friend who was a minister and a coach. When we picked up Junior in the middle of that year, the minister came with Junior. In fact, I called a buddy of mine at a bar and begged him to help me out that night.

"Bill, we just acquired Junior Bridgeman and I need a fifth guy to run through some plays," I said.

So Bill came right out of the bar, reeking of cigarette smoke and beer, and came over to the gym. I had Junior, the minister, Bill, myself, and Skiles. Some group. But we ran through all the plays.

One of the best things about being on Nellie's staff was the lack of fashion pressure. I really appreciated the fact that he was such a bad

dresser. He wore those ugly fish ties and black tennis shoes. Mr. Black-
well would have had a field day.

We were easily the worst-dressed coaching staff in the NBA. Del
Harris said we were the worst-dressed NBA staff in the last twenty years.
I had my ensemble from the wardrobe that time forgot. Del actually had
good fashion taste, but he didn't have any money to buy clothes because
he went bankrupt from investing in Texas oil, gas, and real estate. He
was broke, divorced, and had three kids in college. In fact, he wore some
hand-me-down clothes from Nellie. But Del was one of those guys that
you could put a serape on him and he would look good.

Nellie gave us a couple of those fish ties, but we never wanted to
wear them. We at least had some fashion principles, compared to Nellie,
who had none. The scary thing is that Nellie thought he looked good
in those ties. He would come in before a game and say, "We're all fish
tie-ing it tonight." And if we won, we'd have to wear a fish tie for the
next game. But if we lost, the fish tie was history. That was the one
consolation of losing.

Del, who had coached a 40–42 Houston Rockets team to the
1980–81 NBA Finals, sort of looked after me at times. He knew the
league, having spent four years with the Rockets and three more as a
part-time scout with the Bucks. We were down in Atlanta one time and
I said something to a referee, which is rare for me. But against the
Hawks that night I got upset because I thought Moncrief got screwed
on a call. You have to understand: I had a soft spot for Moncrief because
he played so hard and was so competitive.

Jess Kersey was the ref that night. After he blew the whistle, I yelled,
"No way on that call!"

Kersey came over to the bench, stood in front of me, and said, "I
don't know who you are or what you're doing here, but the next time
you say a word you're not only off the bench, but you're out of the
building."

So Del, bless his heart, stuck up for me. He told Kersey, "Who do
you think he is, Jess? You think he's some guy who just came down and
decided he was going to sit next to us and call a play or two?"

What a scene. Kersey, who's no longer in the league, had a real
arrogance about him. I could understand why he didn't want to take
grief from an assistant, especially this assistant. But I'll never forget Del
sticking up for me.

There's a rite of passage in the NBA. Del and I used to work out
the players on an individual basis. We also worked up a pretty good

sweat, so we took a shower after the practice. So there we were in the shower, along with these twelve players who were built like Adonises. And here's Del and I in the shower. I was never so self-conscious about my private parts, not to mention the rest of my body, in my whole life. It was one of the longest showers of my life. I said, "My God, I'm waiting these guys out. I'm not getting out of the shower until I have to."

I was so self-conscious that I kept turning my back to them. I looked like a raisin in the sun after that shower.

Nellie and Del were seven-days-a-week, twenty-four-hours-a-day basketball guys. That was one thing I really did like about pro ball. I enjoyed being able to just focus on basketball. But I also love movies. One time, when we were in Seattle for a game, I brought Nellie with me to a movie. Del was going to meet Tom Chambers for a drink, and Nellie said he wanted to come with me. I said, "Nellie, trust me, you won't like the movie."

He said, "Yeah, I will."

"Nah, Nellie, you won't," I said. "It's real long."

"What are you trying to say to me?"

"Well, Nellie, I'm just trying to tell you it's not your kind of movie."

The movie was called *The Mission*. Robert DeNiro was the star and it was a great movie. It was a very poignant movie about man's treatment of man, and the Catholic Church, territorialism, and geopolitics.

But Nellie isn't really a geopolitical type of movie guy. He's more of a John Wayne-kicking-everyone's-butt kind of guy. Nellie thought the Duke walked on water.

Anyway, we're sitting there in the Varsity Theater in the University of Washington District and, at that time, they were serving wine and cheese at the movie. It was very much an adult, professorial crowd. Not Nellie's type of crowd.

Part of DeNiro's penance in the movie was that he had to carry a bag of implements that were symbolic of his sins. He was carrying it up this waterfall and it was a telling moment in the movie, very quiet.

Well, Nellie had had a few too many wines and DeNiro had been carrying this bag of implements for a long time. Nellie looked over to me and said real loud, "See that? That's me carrying Kenny Fields around all day. I know how he feels."

Kenny was not having a memorable year and would, by season's end, be sent to the Los Angeles Clippers.

The people in the audience, these very serious people, weren't pleased by Nellie's outburst. They kept telling him to be quiet. First of all, they didn't have any idea who Kenny Fields was, and they were aghast that this guy would even think of comparing himself and his stature in life to this priest character paying penance for his sins.

I should have learned my lesson, but I didn't. I took Del and John McGlocklin with me to go see *Hoosiers,* when we were on a road trip in Phoenix. Del and John ruined that whole movie for me. Del was from Indiana. They would say things during the movie like, "Jim didn't look like that" . . . "The baskets weren't there" . . . "They didn't wear that color uniform" . . . "There was no principal like that."

I kept thinking, Jeezus Christ, give me a break.

People were exiting the movie as though it were a fire drill. Del and John killed business that day; they argued and critiqued during the whole movie. They didn't understand poetic license. They wanted those gyms and that team to be just as they remembered. But did they have to do it during the movie?

As the season progressed, it became obvious that Nellie and new owner Herb Kohl, now a U.S. senator from Wisconsin, weren't always in agreement on team issues. In turn, it became a problem for me because I was friends with both Herb and Nellie.

I first met Herb when I was at Marquette. He used to hang around with Coach McGuire, and he loved ball. I just introduced myself to him, and over the years we got to know each other. When I was a graduate assistant at Marquette, my seat on the bench was right next to Herb's seat in the stands. So we'd spend part of the game talking to each other.

Later, when I became the head coach at Marquette, Herb would always make a point of coming over and saying hello. He would do that during my years at Marquette, tell me I was doing a nice job. He was very nice. He knew my dad and mom, and sometimes we'd talk some politics.

Our friendship continued to grow. In fact, I went to his ranch in Wyoming for my honeymoon. He was a guy I could call on occasion and ask for advice. I respected him for a lot of reasons.

Herb gives a lot of money to charity, and he does it anonymously. He used to run this thing called the Milwaukee Foundation. He never got credit for it. He used to call me and tell me, "I'll give them money if they don't use my name, and if they don't have a dinner for me." He gave without restriction, and he gave a lot.

I used to enjoy seeing him and McGuire battle to see who could pay the dinner check. Al had more fakes than Oscar Robertson. And Herb could do a disappearing act faster than Houdini. They used to get the biggest kick if they could stick the other guy with the bill. In fact, I think they hate it when I pick up the bill, which I do every time I'm with them. I could never repay the debts I owe those guys. But I think it pisses them off because they're like the guys from *Grumpy Old Men*—it's more fun to stiff each other. I take the fun out of if for them.

Years later, I brought my Utah team to Milwaukee and Herb let us work out at the Bucks' facility. He's always been very fair to me. It was like, "Whatever you need. If you and your team want to go to a Bucks game, here's a box for the game, here's tickets."

But Herb and Nellie didn't get along as well. I don't want to call it infighting, but it was fractious. Nellie had almost a father-son relationship with the previous owner, Jim Fitzgerald. But Herb had a different management style, and there was tension between him and Nellie. Nellie could see the writing on the wall, and he started to consider the possibility of coaching elsewhere, possibly for the New York Knicks.

It became an awkward situation for me because I found myself caught in the middle. And to be honest, I was beginning to miss the associations you could build with college players. I didn't miss the Marquette experience, but I did miss the variety of the college game. I kept thinking that's where I belonged. Plus, it was difficult to go from being a head coach to an assistant. Not difficult from an ego standpoint—that was never an issue—but difficult from the standpoint of running your own program. And anyway, it wasn't as if I were qualified to be a head coach in the NBA.

It was about that time that the Ball State job became available.

Says Del Harris: *"Rick asked me, 'What do you know about Muncie, Indiana?'*

"I said, 'I know a lot about Muncie, Indiana. I'm from Indiana. Furthermore, I know some people who can help you if you want that job. I'll call and help you with it.'

"He said, 'Yeah, I'd like you to do that.'

"So I called someone I knew there. The guy I knew had a number of associations with board members and was highly connected with Ball State. He made a couple of other calls to people who knew the athletic director and the school president. Rick ended up getting an interview there and was able to sell himself."

There were a lot of decisions to be made. First of all, Ball State offered me the job. Plus, I was going to get married, and I knew my dad wasn't doing that well. I was offered the job at Nevada-Reno and I came back from that with some decisions to make. My father lived in Detroit at the time, and I knew he had had some health problems. So that eliminated Nevada-Reno. That's partly why I took the Ball State job, so I could be closer to my dad and my mom.

It was a little bit of an awkward situation because the recruiting season was underway and I'm sure Ball State was hoping I could start right away. The Ball State athletic director never pressured me to do that, though. In fact, he was very good about the whole situation. But I knew it didn't help Ball State's recruiting to have me sitting on the Bucks' bench.

I went to Nellie and Del to explain the situation, and they were terrific about it. I told them I'd stay the rest of the season if they wanted me to. They said to go ahead, that they'd be fine. They knew I was ready to go. As much as I loved the pro experience, and as much as I learned from Nellie and Del, they knew I was more a college guy than an NBA guy.

The Bucks finished 50–32 that year. They beat Philly in the first round, but lost a seven-game series to the Celtics. Nellie resigned after the season, and a year later was coaching the Golden State Warriors.

Meanwhile, I had moved on to Ball State, alma mater of David Letterman.

Of course, Al didn't think it was the right move. I remember the words he used: "Tap city . . . suicidal . . . kamikaze." Maybe he was right. Maybe that's why once I arrived at Ball State, I became more consumed by winning and the team than I did with nurturing my marriage. I didn't really handle the marriage well. I didn't understand marriage. I was very immature in that regard. You know, I don't even know how old I was when I got married.

I try not to remember the bad things in life. Like, I don't remember the day my dad died. I know it was in December, during my first season at Ball State . . . maybe around December 15, 16, 17. But my mother remembers that day.

My dad was sixty-three when he died of a heart attack in Milwaukee. I still miss him so much.

I remember certain days of my dad's life, certain moments with my dad. I remember hitting a home run in a rec league baseball game and my uncle and dad were there, and how proud my dad was. I remember making the team at Marquette and beating Syracuse in the Milwaukee Arena, and how happy my dad was. I remember how sad my dad was when we'd lose. I remember my dad with my friends. Guys would sleep over at my house and he'd get up and cook breakfast. He'd walk among us and over our bodies as we slept on the floor in the morning. He loved to make omelettes. He would sing in the morning—life was wonderful. I remember him and my mom driving to Muncie to see some of those Ball State games. I remember what kind of person he was, what kind of dad he was, and the impact it made on me.

Says Mira Panella, longtime friend: *"There is so much of Rick's dad—his compassion and caring—in Rick. It was Christmas Eve of 1987 and Rick and his wife, Deor, were at our house for dinner. I made all this Italian food that night, and when we were done eating we sat around the table and talked about how fortunate we were, how blessed we were.*

"Rick looked at how much food we had left on the table, how many presents we had under the tree, and he started talking about the poor and the homeless. He said, 'I wonder what their Christmas is like?'

"My daughter Tiffany was there that night, and she said the homeless were probably in shelters. Rick said no, that some of them lived on the streets. And then he had an idea.

" 'You know,' he said, "I've got all these blankets and all these clothes, and you guys have all this food. Why don't we try to help some people out tonight.'

"So my husband, Rich, and Rick drove over to his old place and picked up a bunch of clothes, Marquette sweatshirts, gloves, and blankets he had. We wrapped up the food, packed up everything, and then drove to downtown Milwaukee. It had to be about 1:00 or 2:00 A.M. by then.

"We were driving near one of the freeway entrances, maybe around 11th and Michigan, and the city had a Christmas tree there. It was decorated with ornaments, and under it were two big boxes. They weren't boxes like presents. They were boxes with homeless people inside. The homeless were sleeping under the Christmas tree.

"Rick and Rich approached the boxes, and all of a sudden a man came out yelling and waving a stick, telling them to get away. He must have thought Rick and Rich were going to hurt them, or take their boxes.

"Rick said, 'Look, I'm sorry. We just wanted to share some of our Christmas with you. We have some extra things and we thought it would really be a shame not to share it with you. We have some clothes, some food.'

"So they brought the stuff over, and as Rich and Rick were walking back to the car, the homeless person said, 'Hey, guys, do you have something for my buddy next door?'

" 'Sure, we do,' Rick said.

"They brought more food and clothes for the person in the other box. And then, just before they came back to the car, you could hear the four of them say 'Merry Christmas' to each other.

"That was probably the best Christmas of my life. It was a gift. It was like living a Christmas card. All because of Rick wanting to do this for these people."

I love to remember the good things. I don't like to remember or dwell on negative things. Sometimes it's hard not to. I still remember when I coached at Marquette and we lost to Notre Dame at the buzzer. After that game, I sat out in the cold, even though I was so sweaty and overheated. It was like five degrees. I sat there for about twenty minutes, just thinking about how they tipped it in at the buzzer to beat us at their place.

Then there was the time David Rivers made some half-assed shot to beat us at the Mecca. I had crushing defeats to Notre Dame.

Marriage was something altogether different. I was married to Deor for about two years, and I would say the majority of that failed marriage was my own fault. She was a very nice girl and a very good person. But I'd go into a zone during the season. I still do. I know it's not healthy, but I almost can't help it. I can almost feel myself going into that zone. My only respite during the season is on Sundays. That's when I'll try to go see a movie and forget about basketball for two hours. It's like a little treat to myself. We've played two games during the week and now it's quality time for me. But that's it: two hours.

I'm plagued by not having done that drill or this drill. Call it Catholic guilt . . . whatever. During this past off-season, I was determined to learn a zone defense we could use here. Something I could sort of hang on to. We're mostly a man-to-man-oriented team here, but we need a zone defense we can use on occasion.

Once the season starts, you have to make a total commitment. You can't do things half-assed. If you do, you usually lose. But there's a danger to making basketball the center of your existence. Duke's Mike Krzyzewski didn't sit out most of the season a few years ago because he had a hangnail. The game, the responsibilities, the pressures take their toll on you.

I used to tell my assistants the same thing I told myself: schedule nothing. Keep twenty-four hours a day, seven days a week open. Because you don't know when we're going to practice. Now when it comes to family obligations, hey, I'm the king of saying, "Go home and take care of it. Don't worry about it." I rarely call my assistants at home, and I'll even take the younger guys on Sunday nights and work with them. That way the assistants can spend Sunday nights with their families.

Part of the reason my marriage ended was because I wasn't willing to give up enough basketball to make it work. Part of it was an immature thing. My wife was a wonderful person and very kind-hearted. She was more mature than I was. At the time, she went back to school, to Indianapolis Tech. She had to take some courses and I told her, "What are you, nuts? You don't need to take those courses. You've got life skills in that. Let me call those guys up and talk to them."

That was how I was. I was going to intervene and fix things. I was used to doing that. But all she wanted was someone to talk to about it. I realize that now.

Other times I would bring guys home. I did that all the time. I wouldn't even call. I'd just show up with a couple of buddies. Deor would be mad because I hadn't called, or the house was a mess. I'd say, "They don't care what the house looks like." I realize now that *she* cared what the house looked like. I never understood that then.

As I write this book, I feel bad in some ways that my life has been filled with such passion for a game. But I take some solace in the fact that I've become involved in certain charities and have tried to do a good job. I'm always good for raising a few bucks for somebody. I care about those things. I probably should be even more involved.

I've traveled all around the world with dear friends. I've coached games and conducted clinics on four continents. I've had life experiences. But there is a part of me that isn't completely fulfilled. You make choices. I've had an unbelievable career, considering where I started. Like, I don't think I was one step above the manager, I *was* the manager.

Now it's amazing to me when I walk into a camp where there will be four hundred campers sitting at attention. I go back to where I was running McGuire's camp and I was squeegeeing the water off the court or visiting the vacuum cleaner filter guy for the pool or calling the parents of the kid who had cigarettes in the dorm or overseeing twenty fingertip pushups. Grunt work. And then, years later, to walk into that San Antonio environment for the Final Four with my Utah team, that was the culmination of a dream.

But it came at a cost. And one of the costs was a marriage.

Says Mike Schneider: *"I was his best man at his wedding. It was a hot, humid Milwaukee day and he was as nervous as a cat. I've seen people sweat* *through a shirt, maybe even a coat, but he was sweating through his tie. It was so soaked in sweat, he was trying to dry it with the blower from the air-conditioner. I've never seen him so nervous.*

"In the end, his marriage became a test between wife and basketball. His wife wouldn't accept him in a part-time role as husband. Basketball won out again, like law school and everything else.

"Basketball is the center of his universe, but it's not all of his universe. He's more than one-dimensional."

Says Mira Panella: *"It was a difficult time for them. But they were still so giving.*

"We had a family crisis—our daughter Tiff had a very serious problem with her boyfriend at the end of her senior year in high school—and Rick was absolutely phenomenal. I can't tell you the crisis he helped us through. At the time, we couldn't get through to her, so we packed her up, and Rick came and got her, and she stayed with Rick and Deor for about a week at Ball State.

"They were so much help. Tiff used to call Rick, 'my Continental buddy,' because Rick traveled so much. She rose from this adversity and later married a wonderful man.

"Rick is now the godfather of her son."

There was a lot of work to be done at Ball State. The program had never won an NCAA tournament game. It had never had a first-team consensus All-America. It had never finished the regular season ranked in the Associated Press poll.

We finished 14–14 that first season. In fact, one of my toughest losses ever was going to Purdue and losing to them against all odds.

I called a timeout with about two minutes to go, and we were down by about forty-six. I didn't call a timeout to embarrass our players or to embarrass Purdue. I respect the game and the other coaches too much to do something like that. But I called my team together and I said, "Look, let's set a goal. We're not getting beat by fifty. You guys have been working your asses off here. I don't want you quitting in these last two minutes, and letting it really get away from you."

Being behind by forty-six points was bad enough, but I wanted them to understand there are all sorts of small victories. Purdue wasn't trying to run it up against us either. We were just that bad.

I can't remember the exact score, but we kept the final margin under fifty points. Then the next year we beat Purdue, which was one of the most satisfying wins I've ever had. We went from losing by nearly fifty points, to winning by fourteen points the next year.

Says Rick Hall, former Ball State player: *"Every player had a role in the game. It didn't matter if you sat the bench, you had a role. Each player had to know a specific play from the other team. As soon as the other team started to run the play, our guys on the bench were supposed to shout it out. They might have a lob play where they run an alley-oop for a certain player. Our guys would be able to identify it by the way the team set up on the court.*

"I remember how proud he was that the last guy on the end of the bench recognized a certain play, and that we were able to stop it. He'd say, 'Brian Slick, that was a great read by you. That was really key.'

"Brian was a walk-on for us who sat the bench. But Majerus recognized his contribution."

There weren't a whole lot of lighthearted moments that first year, but at least I discovered a new fashion comfort level.

In the NBA, you had to wear a coat and tie every night. Luckily, Nellie was such a bad dresser, it didn't make any difference if I was too. And the only guys who were wearing Armani suits back in those days were Pat Riley and Chuck Daly. Most guys didn't get paid enough money to afford those kinds of clothes, especially assistants. It wasn't a haberdashery contest.

When I got to Ball State, I was coat-and-tied out. I remembered a guy named Bill Mulligan, whose Cal-Irvine team had played against my Marquette team during a Christmas tournament. Mulligan wore saddle shoes, a sweater, cotton pants, and no socks. I liked the look.

I was through wearing ties. I hated wearing ties. Sportcoats were so confining, but I knew I didn't want to take my sportcoat off and expose my body. I took a lot of criticism for my rotundity. So I decided I'd do a Mulligan, and start wearing sweaters. It was Ball State . . . who cared, right?

I had a shoe deal with Avia and they gave me some nice sweaters to wear. But then Avia got a little too daring with its sweater patterns. Some of the worst pictures you'll ever see of me is when I wore a red-and-white horizontal-striped Avia sweater. I looked like a target balloon for aliens.

Our program was similar to other mid–Division I programs. We usually got the second- or third-echelon type player. A lot of the kids we had were inner-city kids from Detroit, and later we signed some junior college kids. But we also tried to get some of the better kids from Indiana. You always do that in your own state.

Says Dick Hunsaker, former Ball State assistant, now Utah director of Basketball Operations: *"We were going to Richmond,*

Indiana, to recruit a kid named Woody Austin. Austin was the No. 1 player in the state that year.

"Rick wasn't sure there would be food there, so he made us stop so he could get a quick sandwich before the home visit. We got back in the car, but the other assistant coach overshot the town on I-70. Rick told the guy to pull over and he got behind the wheel.

"By the time we got to the school, we were about forty-five minutes late. Everything was dark. The lights were off. The doors were locked. Nobody was in sight.

"Rick got back into the car and started driving on the school sidewalk, in between every building, down the alley, over the pathway. It's pitch dark. Just as we were driving down this one sidewalk, Austin's coach came out of the door and Rick almost hit the guy. It was within an eyelash.

"Rick bumbled out of the car, he was rubbing his head, trying to apologize. But the coach told him we were too late for the visit. We missed the appointment, and that was that.

"Rick told him about the wrong turn on I-70 and pleaded for a second chance. The coach finally relented.

"We got to the house a little before nine. We were supposed to be there at seven, so the family had been waiting almost two hours. Rick turned on the charm, and by the end of the visit, even the coach thought Ball State was the best place for Woody to go.

"Woody ended up going to Purdue. But think about it: we went from being two hours late, having the visit canceled, almost killing the coach . . . to just missing on the kid. We weren't even in the picture with this kid, and in the end it came down to us and Purdue.

"That's Rick."

Entering the 1988–89 season, we had nine new players who had never played together. We opened at Minnesota, but a week before the game we had yet to have a single practice where the entire team was in attendance. That's because at least one person always had academic commitments.

As much as I wanted everyone there, the academics were more important. They always are. If a kid has a class or needs to study for an exam or has too much schoolwork, all he has to do is tell me. I'll let him skip practice, no questions asked.

By the way, we beat Minnesota. We were the only non–Big Ten team to beat a Big Ten team on their own floor that year.

Despite having so many new guys, we started winning games. Even the voters in the polls noticed us. We had some big victories—the wins against Minnesota and Purdue—but we also had some letdowns.

Says Rick Hall: *"We were 25–2 during the regular season, with losses to Ohio and Toledo. But maybe the most upset I saw him was after a game we won. We beat Central Michigan, 66–65, in Mt. Pleasant, but Majerus felt we didn't perform very well. He threw a tirade after the game.*

"The next day when we came into practice he was still wearing the same clothes he had worn the night before. He had spent the whole night in the office watching film. And that was after a six-hour drive back to Muncie from Central Michigan.

"He used to watch game film and say, 'I'm so fired up, we've got to go out and practice now.' He was that excited."

Rick Hall was one of the reasons that season was so special. He had barely played his first two years, was a starter for me as a junior, and then became a reserve as a senior. But he never complained. He was a team guy, and he wanted to win.

Rick was similar to Drew Hansen at Utah: a brilliant student, a player with a modicum of basketball talent. He recorded straight As during his freshman and sophomore years, and a single B as a junior, and a B as a senior. But grades aren't always enough. I told him, "You're a very bright person, but unless you can communicate your thoughts to other people, the thoughts are worth nothing. You need to go out and develop skills as a public speaker."

And Rick did that and became a confident speaker. He also spent the summer between his junior and senior years working in the office of Indiana Senator Richard Lugar. To this day, Rick says it was the best summer of his life.

With his grades, his majors in political science and accounting, and his basketball backround, Rick was considered for candidacy as a Rhodes scholar. He later was selected to receive the prestigious Walter Byers Award, a postgraduate scholarship that Rick used to go to Northwestern Law School. He's now an attorney at Barnes & Thornburg, a large law firm in Indianapolis.

Our 28–2 record and Mid-American tournament championship guaranteed us three things: an automatic invitation to the 1989 NCAA tournament, the best winning percentage of any Division I school that year, and one of the biggest win-loss turnarounds in Division I history.

This was my first NCAA tournament appearance as a head coach. We were seeded No. 9 in the Midwest Regional and faced eighth-seeded Pittsburgh in the first round.

It was a strange, unpredictable tournament. Princeton almost beat Georgetown. Siena, which had not played in front of a crowd for five weeks because of a measles quarantine, shocked Stanford. And this was the tournament in which interim coach Steve Fisher led Michigan to a national championship.

We had our moments too. We beat Paul Evans's Pitt team, 68–64, and I'm guessing most people couldn't name one starter from our team (Paris McCurdy, Shawn Parrish, Curtis Kidd, Billy Butts, and Scott Nichols).

No. 1 seed Illinois didn't have the same problem. That was a team with at least four future NBA players: Nick Anderson, Kenny Battle, Kendall Gill, and Marcus Liberty. Illinois didn't have a player taller than six foot seven, but few teams could match their overall athleticism. They beat us, 72–60. "They just jumped us," I told reporters after that game. "They took us right out of what we wanted to do."

Says Don Donoher, owner of 437 Division I career victories:

"I'll tell you what kind of guy Rick is. I was fired by Dayton and it was announced on a Monday. One of the first calls I got was from Rick, and he was insisting I meet with him on Tuesday. His team had just been knocked from the NCAAs that weekend, but he was more concerned about me. We met in Indianapolis, drove down to watch Bobby's team practice—Indiana was going to the regionals—and then spent most of the evening together. Rick was being interviewed for jobs at the time, but that didn't matter to him. He was ready to roll up his sleeves and help me any way he could."

Still, it had been a remarkable season for us. I don't think anybody picked us to win twenty-nine games or reach the tournament or certainly win a tournament game. In fact, I would say to this day in the state of Indiana, I cannot pull over to take a pee or wash my hands at a truck stop or get an ice-cream cone without being approached, if not inundated to a certain extent. And all because of Ball State and the appreciation those people have for what we accomplished.

But I'm equally proud of what some of the kids did academically. Rick Hall, for instance. I also derived great satisfaction seeing a kid named Keith Stalling get a degree. That meant a lot.

Despite the professional success, it had been a difficult two years for me. My dad had died. My marriage had ended. I kept thinking that maybe it was time to start over.

That's when I heard about a job opening out West.

Utah.

4

Welcome to the Hinterlands

McGuire told me not to take the Utah job. So did Billy Packer. So did Bobby Knight. They were the most vehement. They said it would be too hard to recruit against Brigham Young University, that it would be too hard to win there. All those were legitimate points. Utah is a long way from any talent pools. The talent pool you do have is comprised of a lot of Mormons, and they usually went to BYU, which is just up the road in Provo. And then there were the Mormon missions to deal with. It was a difficult situation, especially for a non-Mormon coach.

But I was interested enough to use Del as a reference. He had coached at Utah, and was nice enough to offer his help.

Says Del Harris: *"As I understand it, the selection committee boiled down the list of candidates to two names: Rick and Ron Arrow, then the coach at South Alabama and a good friend of mine. Ron used me as a reference too.*

"One of the people involved in the selection asked me who I'd hire. Well, I was on the spot. I was closer to Rick, but I certainly did not want to hurt Ron Arrow. So I said, 'Well, I think you've done a great job with your list.' But they pushed for an answer. I thought Rick's personality, his background, and his coming from Wisconsin, would make it easier for him to acclimate better to Utah. So I said, 'I would pick Rick Majerus.'"

Says Dr. Chase Peterson, then University of Utah president:

"Chris Hill, our athletic director, had sort of scoured the country for likely names, and Rick's name kept coming up. I did not know a great deal about him, quite frankly, just that he was an attractive candidate. We had talked with several other coaches, including Tim Floyd, who was at New Orleans, and, I believe, Fred Trenkle.

"Rick was bright as blazes. He was focused, and he was believable when he talked about the academic progress of the kids being important. He seemed to be an astute technician.

"At that point, the man looked awfully good. But first impressions are not always accurate. We talked to secretaries, other university presidents of his, and coaches. But I also thought it would be interesting to talk to his players. So I said, 'Tell me the name of the player at Ball State who played very few minutes. I'd like to talk to him.'

"He gave me Rick Hall's name. So I called. Rick, who was a very interesting fellow, said that, yes, he had been a starter his junior year, and then had played very little his senior year.

" 'And how did you feel about that?' I said.

"He said, 'Next to my father, Coach Majerus is the most important man in my life.' "

I took the job because I wanted to go West. I thought it was a beautiful place to live. The people were nice. There was a little bit of Ward and June Cleaver atmosphere, but that's not all bad. It was a tremendous school academically. Tremendous undergraduate preparation for law and medicine. A tremendous law school. A great dance school, though I don't sign a lot of players who want to be dance majors. Everything here is really superb academically, with the exception of its not being the place to write the Great American Novel. It doesn't have the classic liberal arts curriculum. I tell kids that. I mean, you have to be honest about it.

But if you want physical therapy, premed, prelaw, law, engineering—it's at Utah. And yet, there's a spot for a kid such as Andre Miller, and I don't say that disparagingly. There's a spot for kids who might not have the highest SAT scores or whatever, but if they're willing to work hard, they can achieve and succeed here.

Utah isn't Stanford. We don't want to be; that's not our purpose. I liked it because it wasn't so elitist academically that it felt snobbish. I also really liked Chase Peterson. Great guy.

There were other factors. I thought the Western Athletic Conference was a good league. And they love their basketball in Utah.

All things considered, Utah is probably the third- or fourth-best job in the WAC. BYU is a hell of a job. We probably have every Mormon player on our team that they should have.

The second-best job is New Mexico. It's the only game in town there. They've got the Pit. And the local media covers them as if they're the Lakers.

The third-best job could be Fresno. They're the only game in town, and it's a very wealthy community.

We're next. We're the academic school of our league.

At Marquette and Ball State, I had a plan when it came to recruiting. I had the same plan at Utah: evaluate the existing roster and try to fit in the missing pieces every year. First, I would try to get the best player that we could get, regardless of position. I've always gone for the best talent. I can work around positions. If you get a hell of a talent, you can always move a guy over to another position.

But Utah was different because of the Mormon factor.

I knew recruiting Mormons was going to be a real challenge the first time I went down to visit Shawn Bradley, which was the day after my press conference at Utah. Bradley was a center, and one of the top recruits in the country. He was also a devout Mormon.

I drove to his hometown, which is near Provo, and met his coach. The coach's dad owned the gas station, and there were a couple of good ol' boys there, great guys, actually. But they were Mormons, and they weren't sitting around the gas station having a beer. And they didn't bet on the weekly football pool. On Sundays they were in church from one o'clock to four o'clock.

I was down there to introduce myself to the high school coach, to let him know we really wanted to sign him. "He's seven foot four, and I'm good with big men," I said.

A lot of good it did. In fact, I knew that day it was going to be hard to sign Shawn. The coach told me it would be hard—and he liked Utah. Shawn's dad liked Utah. But in that state, you're either a Mormon for Utah, or a Mormon for BYU. There's no in-between.

Shawn signed with BYU.

During my first few years there, I was told on occasion, "Hey, you're an out-of-stater, you're new here, you're not Mormon, you're at Utah, you don't have a chance." For the first three or four years we tried to sign Mormon players, and we usually got the players BYU didn't want. That's just how it was. But one thing about Mormons: they're committed to the conduct of life and how you live your life. Academics, family—those are the cornerstones of the religion. And that's good. Being Mormon is really a way of life.

But here's what I told parents then, and here's what I tell them now: "I'm going to care more about your son's education than you will."

And I mean it. I've called in guys with 2.7 GPAs and 3.1 GPAs. I'm serious about it. I think academics and conduct are the two most important things in a program. And that's just not a convenience, so I can retreat to the moral high ground if I lose. I really believe that's what people should be in school for, and that's what we're about at Utah.

I think the big thing with breaking the Mormon recruiting barrier was word of mouth. The Mormon guys who played for me recommended the program to other Mormons. I can tell parents whatever I want, but if word gets out that I don't keep my promises or I'm not committed to their educations or I don't come to practice every day committed to making them better players, then none of it matters.

I inherited some good Mormon players when I got there, including Josh Grant and Keith Chapman. But I also had a plan in mind about rebuilding the program.

The first thing I had to do was assess where the academics were, where the discipline was, and where the problems lay. When I first got to Utah, guys weren't graduating, there were some drug problems, and there wasn't enough emphasis placed on academics. There were also some problems with the basketball side of it. Like, the weight coach would come in and say, "Nobody comes to the weight room."

Once I addressed those issues, I began to put together a staff. I hired Donny Daniels from Cal State–Fullerton, where he was an assistant coach. I also hired Jeff Judkins, who was born and raised in Salt Lake City, starred at the U, played in the NBA until 1985, and was in private business when he joined the staff initially as a part-time coach. Joe Cravens was the other full-time assistant.

Says Donny Daniels: *"He brought me in for an interview. We met in the hotel lobby and he said, 'C'mon, we'll get a bite to eat and talk.' As we were driving around town he kept pointing out restaurants and commenting on them like a food critic. 'That one has great Italian' . . . 'There's a place with* *great barbecue'* . . . *'That one has the best Mexican food'* . . . *'Best Chinese in town.'*

"*He must have pointed out ten restaurants. I'm thinking, This man has been here less than a month and he's already eaten at all these restaurants? I just couldn't believe it.*

"*I didn't know a lot about him. I knew he had done a real nice job at Ball State. I also remembered him being named Player of the Game by NBC for the coaching job he did in a 1986 loss to North Carolina when he was at Marquette. But I was surprised he called me. I had actually applied first to BYU.*

"*I knew I wasn't his first choice. But I came in, we had a good talk, and then I didn't hear from him for a month. He brought me back out. It was a Sunday, June 3. He called that afternoon and offered me the job. I'll never forget it.*"

Says Jeff Judkins: "*Coach probably doesn't remember this, but I first met him when I was fourteen years old. I was at a basketball camp at the U, and he was my counselor. He was a grad assistant at Marquette at the time—I didn't have any idea who he was—and he was on me the whole week. I'd go home and tell my parents there was this coach at the camp, and he just hates me.*

"*On the last day of camp, he pulled me out into the hall and he said, 'Jeff, you're going to be a great player some day. Keep working at it.'*

"*When he offered me a job he said, 'Jeff, you were a great player, but sometimes a great player isn't a great coach. I'm going to make you the part-time coach. I want you to learn how to recruit.'*

"*At the time, I was kind of let down. But now, I see he was right. One of the first things he told me was, 'If you spend an hour and a half on recruiting each day, you'll get players.' I'll always remember that. And he was right.'*"

To be successful at Utah, you have to get the best Mormon players in the state. But there were probably some bitter feelings among the top Mormon players because Utah fired Lynn Archibald, who had a terrific relationship with a lot of those recruits.

It also wasn't easy getting out-of-state kids to come. It still isn't. It's especially hard to get black kids to come to Utah. That's because there are some misperceptions about the place. People back in the kid's community will say, "Utah? Why do you want to go there?" or "There's no blacks. All those Mormons are there." That sort of thing.

Granted, there are few black members in the Mormon church. There are almost none in the hierarchy of the church. There are only 14,000 black people in the whole state and fewer than 300 black students at the U, which is less than 1 percent of the entire student population.

Meanwhile, some of the California kids I've tried to recruit couldn't believe it could be that cold. I've literally had some California players stammer and stutter at the mention of the word *snow*. It's so different in California.

It's quiet here. It's not the happening spot. There's not a club or restaurant or significant campus hangout.

I tell recruits and their parents three things: the most important thing is education. I'll say, "Here's the number of every parent of every player on my team. Call one, call them all. If you talk to one parent and they say their son's education has not been the most important consideration of his career with me, then you shouldn't come to Utah, because I've lied to you."

But I know the parents of my players won't say that. They can't say it. I know what classes each of my players is taking. I get a weekly report on every kid. I'm keenly aware of their respective academic situations.

We don't convene as a team without talking about academics. It's discussed ad nauseam. It's highlighted every day. A coach's commitment to a kid's education is paramount to academic success. It coincides with that coach's willingness to understand that a player is also there as a student.

Sometimes I'll hear coaches say that a kid signs with a school, not a coach. To me, that's a pure cop-out. The coach determines the program. The coach selects the players. Nobody else selects the players or nobody else *should* select the players in his program. If the coach is foolish enough to abdicate those decisions to his assistants, then he deserves what he gets. A lot of coaches do that too.

Second, I'll talk to recruits about basketball—my commitment to them, and their commitment to me. And if they have NBA potential, I tell them, "Do you want to come to Utah, where we play tough man-to-man defense—which is what they play in the NBA—or do you want to go someplace where they play zone, and maybe you'll win?"

And then I talk to them about the social aspect of Utah. I come right out and tell them, "Look, if it's a social experience you're looking for, and your decision is based solely on activity and nightlife, then this is not the place for you. It is what it is."

That's why evaluation is so important. When I'm looking at a player, I look for guys who love to play. My first year at Utah I offered a scholarship to Jimmy Soto, a little guard. I wasn't worried that he was only five foot seven. I knew the game meant a lot to him. I knew that if the U sign on the mountain near campus wasn't blinking after a game (it blinks after wins), that Soto was feeling as bad about it as me. And he turned out to be a hell of a player, by the way.

I look at guys who have a feel for the game, a sense of the game. That's very hard to find. Things like making the simple pass or letting the game come to him. I look for guys who can fit in with other guys. If you get too many guys who are score-oriented, then it's hard to blend as a team.

I'll look at guys whose teams win. I look for improvement, for physical maturation. If a guy is really well coached, then sometimes he'll have a talent ceiling. You've got to spend a lot of time looking at their best games, but also at their worst games, to see how they react to adversity.

I always ask certain questions. I ask them what they shoot from the foul line. If they start the sentence with the word *about,* then they're probably a poor shooter, and second, they might not be committed to foul shooting and its importance.

I'll ask them whose game reminds them of their own. That's a big NBA question to college kids.

The most important thing I do is go to a kid's school. As I walk around the school, I'll stop a student and ask where the coach's office is located. Then I'll ask the student about the kid I'm recruiting. I'll ask if he's a nice guy, that sort of thing. Those students usually tell you the truth about a kid. And those answers are as important to me as anything else I do.

I pick up on little things. I watch how a kid responds to his parents. I watch how a kid deals with his high school coach. I watch how they are during timeouts. I try to get to practice early and watch them. I don't like guys looking over at me when I'm watching them. I can understand them being nervous, but I don't want them to be more worried about me than basketball.

If someone asked me for recruiting advice, I'd tell them they have to know their market and know their school. You don't want to waste time. The worst thing you can do in recruiting is come in second. You've got to know when to cut your losses.

For instance, I'll meet with my assistants and ask where we are with certain kids. If we have a chance, then we'll stick with it. But if we don't have a chance, then what's the point?

You have to determine how a player will fit into your system. The most pivotal spot is point guard. The next spot is the four spot, the power forward. That's the spot I pay the most attention to because I like to play the middle less congested. I want my four-man to be able to go on the floor, shoot, and stretch the defense.

I don't know if I'm a good recruiter. I know I'm a hard worker. I'm diligent. I spend a lot of time on the road. I'm a good evaluator. But your proficiency comes through repetition. I always say, "You've got to kiss a lot of frogs to find a prince."

We made mistakes on kids. We passed on a kid named Byron Ruffner when I first got here. It was my fault because I didn't go look at the kid play. Guys told me about him, but I didn't make the effort to see him. Completely my fault. He signed with Utah State and was an all-league player as a freshman. But I'll tell you what: we haven't made a mistake on a local kid since then.

The other factor in recruiting at Utah is accounting for players taking Mormon missions. They're gone two years. When the missions started hitting me, there was a little of, My, God, what have I done?

There was a nucleus of pretty good players when I got to Utah. Josh Grant and Keith Chapman. Walter Watts was a junior. Byron Wilson and Tyrone Tate were sitting out the year because of Prop. 48. Paul Afeaki was at junior college ready to come in the following season. Phil Dixon was being redshirted. Larry Cain was a freshman.

There were some adjustments to be made—by me, my coaches, and my players. After the first practice, Jud, who's Mormon, came up to me and said, "Uh, Coach, you said about ninety-eight swear words in practice."

I started laughing. "What, you counting them?"

My language, at times, has been an issue with some people. But you have to remember several things. When I first came to Utah, I was only a few years removed from the NBA and going into the locker room at halftime and seeing Nellie smoke, Bob Lanier smoke, Lloyd Walton smoke. And the operative word there was the F-word. The F-word had become noun, pronoun, adjective, adverb, dangling modifier, preposition, conjunction. You name it . . . in syntax, out of syntax. It was there. I think that's part of the reason I used profanity on occasion.

Part of it was working four summers at the Pabst Brewery, where every other word was "F-ing beer," "beer F-word," "bottle F-word."

I really don't swear that much. If I've got to get a message across, I'll sometimes use profanity. I have a degree of vulgarity and profanity in me. I don't know too many coaches who don't.

Now if I get mad during practice, yeah, sometimes I say a few swear words. But Senator Orrin Hatch once told me, "If you ever want to do anything politically, run for office, you've got a friend here." So I guess I haven't offended a lot of people if he's going to make that kind of offer.

P. J. Carlesimo, Rick Pitino, Mike Krzyzewski . . . they swear. But they do it very discreetly. I would feel sad if my players and people associated with the program would remember more my occasional swearing than they would all the other things I try to do.

Says Tim LaComb, former Utah team manager: *"After I got out of school, I moved to Austin and started a business. During Keith's senior year they played SMU, so I went to Dallas for the game. There were tickets waiting for me at Will Call and a message from Coach Judkins: 'Coach Majerus wants you down on the bench.'*

"I went down to the court and there was a seat on the bench for me. Coach Majerus saw me, but he didn't acknowledge me. He acts as if he doesn't know your name when you're a manager.

"After the game, I was talking to some of the players, and Majerus came over. I thought he was going to say, 'Get the hell off the floor.' But instead, he said, 'I'd like to talk to you after I get done with the media.'

"He got done with the media and started asking me how things were going with my business, with my life. I had married, started a family.

" 'Great,' I said. 'Really good.'

"Then he put his arm around me.

" 'Hey, it was hard for me while I was kicking your ass every day to let you know how I felt, but you're like a son to me. And you're the best manager I've ever had. If there's anything I can ever do for you in life, you make sure you let me know. Keep in touch with me.'

"I was just stunned. I couldn't believe it. That meant more to me than anything. That's the real Coach Majerus. He even got on the postgame radio show and said the highlight of the night was to see me and talk to me there. That was neat."

We started the season 2–1 and were getting ready to make a road trip to Washington and then Oregon. Before we left, I went over to the

East High School track, which is near the U, and did my usual jogging. But this time I started having some shortness of breath, even some mild chest pains. I thought it was indigestion.

We made the trip to Seattle, beat Washington, and then flew to Eugene for the game against Oregon. I had some time during the day, so I started jogging along the river. I didn't get very far before I had difficulty breathing again. I called my doctor.

"Can you get back here after the game?" he said. "I'll get you in tomorrow morning. Just come on in and let me take a look at you."

We played, we lost, and the next day I reluctantly went in to see my doctor, Kent Jones. He did an examination and ran some tests. The results: severe blockage of the arteries. Surgery was scheduled for three days later.

Before the surgery, I talked with my lawyer. I didn't tell him to draw up a will, but I wanted to make sure everything was in order. Everything was supposed to go to my mom and sisters. I also had some money going to charities.

I also called Bobby Knight and asked if I could get Bo Schembechler's number. Schembechler, the legendary football coach at Michigan, had undergone a heart procedure and recovered nicely. Knight said he'd get Bo to call me, which I thought was really nice on his part.

Schembechler called and it was really good to talk to him. He took a lot of time with me. He said the recovery period would be painful, that it would require a lot of hard work, but that I'd be okay. He said if I wanted to come visit him after the operation, I could.

That was a really nice gesture on his part, and I've never forgotten it. In fact, I've done the same for other coaches who also have suffered heart problems.

McGuire didn't call. That's not his style. He told a reporter a few years later that he had hoped I would be okay. But if I had died, he wouldn't have gone to the funeral. He said, "I don't go to funerals because I bought you a drink while you were alive. Anyway, the crowd at a funeral is governed by the weather."

Typical Al.

Utah was wonderful about the whole thing. Here I had coached only a few games, and now this. But Chase Peterson, who's a medical doctor and who now teaches at the med school, was great. He really looked after me. He got me second opinions and just said, "We'll see you when you come back." That was it. No pressure.

Says Donny Daniels: *"I was on the road recruiting at the time. I think I was in Kansas. Coach called and said he was going to have open-heart surgery, that he was probably going to be out for the season.*

"I flew back and visited him in pre-op. I knew he was scared as hell. His mom, his sister, his ex-wife were there. The guy could die. He was looking at death.

"So he tells me he'll be back in January. I said, 'What? January? No way.'

"It was time for me to leave, so I went over and said, 'Coach, you take care of yourself, okay?'

"He said, 'You've got to do me one favor. Promise me one thing.'

"I leaned over. Maybe he wanted me to look after his mom or call somebody back home.

" 'Yes, Coach?' I said.

" 'Promise me you'll get me some players.'

"Incredible. They were about to crack his chest open and he's asking about getting him some players.

"But I know he was worried. You could see it in his eyes. He started to cry and his voice cracked when he told the team he couldn't coach them that season."

Sure, I was scared when I had the surgery. Who wouldn't be? It was septuple coronary bypass surgery. I tell people, one artery for every major food group.

The surgery was complicated. They took veins out of my legs to repair my heart. They use a vein to go around your heart and bypass it. They've got to crack open your sternum to do it.

Says Jon Huntsman, longtime friend: *"I went up to his room and waited outside the operating room during part of the surgery. The next morning he was in intensive care and just coming out of anesthesia. I had taken with me a very dear friend of mine, who has since passed away—a man by the name of Elder Marvin J. Ashton. Elder Ashton was one of the Twelve Apostles of the Mormon church, and a man who had great admiration for Rick, and what had been done historically before his coming to Utah. He tracked the University very carefully and he loved basketball. I had taken this man—he was a little bit older, this gentleman . . . white hair, dark blue suit—and asked him if he would go over to the hospital with me because I thought Rick ought to be coming around soon. Although I didn't know Rick very well, I wanted to be there when he came around just to tell him how much we loved him, appreciated him, hoped that he felt better.*

"Rick flipped his eyes a few times, looked up at us. We had a great chat. He knew at that moment that I really cared about him. From that point on, I think Rick has been an everyday event in my life. He's clearly the dearest, most trusted friend outside of my own family that I have on the earth today."

I tell people about that visit all the time. I woke up and I saw two people standing there. I recognized one of them as Jon Huntsman. I heard that he could perform miracles. But I thought the other guy was an undertaker. I thought Jon had brought the undertaker to cart me away. He was tall, had on a dark suit, had white hair, looked very serious. So I closed my eyes and pretended to go back to sleep.

Joe Cravens coached the rest of the season. We finished 16–14, and tied for sixth in the conference. I probably could have come back by February 15, something like that. But I didn't think it would be fair to the team, to me, to the coaches. Instead, I ended up watching the team at the WAC tournament in El Paso. I didn't coach another game that season.

Says Don Donoher: *"I was with Bobby Knight the year Rick had the bypass surgery. Rick came out to IU [Indiana University] twice. Rick had spent a lot of time with Bobby when he was at Ball State.*

"One day, Bobby was asking Rick to sort of critique the team. It was a young team, and it was having trouble in the Big Ten.

"You have to understand that Rick had lost his own team for the year, and he was just wanting to be involved in something basketball related. So he interjected a couple of things, probably one more thing than Bobby wanted to hear.

"Bobby kind of went off on Rick. 'Hey, Rick, we're trying it. It's not like we're not trying,' Bobby said.

"Rick felt so bad. We went out to dinner, and Rick still thinks he offended Bobby. I told him not to worry about it.

"I got home from dinner and Bob calls. 'Is Rick okay?' he said.

"Rick was worried about Bobby, and Bobby was worried about Rick.

"But the next morning, we were back in the office and Rick walked in. Knight went right after him, just needling him. 'Hey, Rick, did you come up with some more things? Maybe four, five more things to work on?'

"Rick was so apologetic about it."

Our breakthrough of sorts came the next year. We won twenty of our first twenty-one games, won the WAC, beat South Alabama and Michigan State in the 1991 NCAA tournament, but lost to UNLV, the

defending national champions, in the Sweet Sixteen. Josh was our leading scorer, leading rebounder, leading shot blocker, leading free throw
shooter, leading steals guy. Tate was our assists guy. Dixon was our best
three-point shooter. Watts was our power guy inside.

Says Dr. Chase Peterson: *"As you know, the rules allow a player who
is eligible in the winter term of his senior year to also be eligible for the spring
term. There's a one-term lag, so to speak. We were starting the spring
term—and on our way to the NCAA tournament—when I received a copy of
a letter Rick had addressed to one of his players. This same player had had
academic difficulties in the past, but Rick had forced him to come to grips
with it, gotten him help, and the kid had become a very adequate student.*
"The letter to the player began,

> *You know how proud I am of the progress you've made academically and
> on the basketball court. You've become a fine young man.*
> *I am distressed to learn you have failed to keep your academic
> responsibilities in class. It is my understanding you failed to complete a paper
> in time. As you know, this will result in your automatic loss of scholarship
> and your separation from the team.*
> *I hope will you do something in the next day or so that will give me
> assurance that you can take care of this matter. I have a lot of faith in you.*
> *Sincerely,*
> *Rick Majerus*

*"The paper was written and submitted within two days. Only then did
Rick allow him back on the team.*
*"We could have not won one game in the tournament without this
player. How many coaches would have risked that? Theoretically, the kid
was eligible and could have played."*

Something else also happened that year, something I'll never forget.
We were getting ready to play University of Texas–El Paso at the Hunts-
man Center, and shortly before tip-off I went over to say hello to Don
Haskins, one of my coaching heroes.
"Boy," he said, "do you know why I coach?"
"Because you love it," I said.
"Boy, I coach because I don't have any money. You take care of
yourself."
And then he walked away.
I've come to know Haskins very well, and I regard him as one of the
finest coaches ever to walk a sideline. I've said it before, but that 1966

national championship victory against Kentucky was perhaps one of the most socially significant wins in the history of sports. Every coach in America owes him a debt of gratitude.

One time Don Donoher and I were driving to the El Paso airport after beating UTEP. We were listening to Haskins on his postgame call-in show and someone asked him about the loss. Haskins said, "We lost to Utah. But we lost to the best coach in the United States."

Another time he came up to me after a game and said, "Son, you played defense the way we used to."

That's one of the biggest compliments I've ever received.

I'm not repeating these stories to be boastful, but to hear Haskins say that about me meant so much. I mean, here I was riding in the same car as Don Donoher, one of the great coaches in the game. My team had just beaten a UTEP team coached by Don Haskins, one of the great coaches in the game. And then there's me. Those were remarkable things to hear, especially for someone who wasn't any good as a player. I don't belong in the game.

Now, if it had turned out that I became involved in Democratic Party politics or became a great jurist or a social leader of the community or a labor advocate, that wouldn't have been totally out of the question. After all, my dad was involved in many of those things, and I did get a meaningful education.

But absolutely no one—and I mean no one—would have ever predicted that I would be recognized as a top college coach. I'm not saying I'm the best, because I'm not. In my mind, there's an elite three or four in that group of real legends: Dean Smith, before he retired; Mike Krzyzewski. Bobby Knight. And Haskins.

That 30–4 season was also the year the media discovered my fondness for hotels.

I didn't come to Utah saying I was going to live in a hotel. I got the job, and there were so many things to do. I was busy recruiting. I was going through a divorce. I still had to finish up my Ball State basketball camps. It just sort of happened that I ended up at the University Park Hotel. I needed a room, a place to put my stuff.

Huntsman actually offered me a nice condo in Park City. He even has a cook there. He said the cook would make all this low-fat food for me. Or I could go to Jon's home in Park City and stay in a 40,000-square-foot place.

But the hotel is two minutes away from the arena, and it's convenient. If I was in Salt Lake City every day, I wouldn't live in a hotel. I'm not there year-round. It's not like I greet people at the door.

In fact, being single and living in a hotel sometimes can be a liability in recruiting. If I could have a wife—like George Karl, Rich Panella, or Scott Layden do—I'd win the national championship. I mean that. If I could depend on someone else who could help me recruit, it would make a difference. I'd be able to bring some families and recruits to a home, instead of a suite.

There's probably not another Division I coach who lives in a hotel. It's unusual, but not unprecedented. Herb Kohl used to live in a hotel for a number of years. Jerry Sloan lived in a hotel when he was an assistant coach with the Jazz.

I have a nice suite, and it's all the room I really need. I don't pay utility bills. If the shower doesn't work, I call maintenance. I mean, how many people have five televisions in their room? I do. Three in the main room, one in the bathroom, one in the bedroom.

Last year, the hotel became a Marriott property. So the hotel general manager asked if I'd say a few words at the ribbon-cutting ceremony. No problem.

It was an amazing sight that next morning. There were a lot of people in suits, and there was a very nice breakfast buffet, and management had arranged for several cheerleaders from the U to come over and do . . . I guess, Marriott cheers. I told those cheerleaders that I hoped they didn't mind, but I couldn't quit staring at their belly buttons, mostly because I hadn't seen my own in years.

This ribbon-cutting thing was a big deal. They even had an ice sculptor carving out these huge, ornate statues. I thought that was pretty strange. We've got ice sculptures, but no ice machines on the hotel floors.

As part of my deal, the hotel uses me in some of their advertisements. And Marriott grandfathered me in their Honored Guest Rewards system. I don't know exactly how many Marriott points I have—something close to 2 million—but I've been told no other member in the program has more than I do. They say if I turned my points in I could live for free in any Marriott in the world for months.

Since I started staying at the hotel, I've gone through three Stairmasters, four university presidents, three BYU coaches, more than 6,000 mints, 2,000 bars of soap, 730 bottles of lotion, and 4,000 bottles of mouthwash—those are the hotel's figures, not mine.

Jerry Garcia stayed at the hotel once. He had a gig in town, but I didn't really know much about the Grateful Dead or the Deadheads. I wouldn't know a Deadhead from the night of the living dead. I'm an Elvis guy. But one of their guys in the band recognized me and invited me down to a band party after the show. So I walked in, and there was Jerry Garcia sitting in a chair, smoking dope, and eating Cherry Garcia ice cream. It was obvious he didn't want to be bothered, so he just shot me a peace sign and then went back to eating his ice cream and smoking his dope.

There were other celebrities. Ellen DeGeneres stayed at the hotel. I think she was in the next room. Lyle Alzado, the former NFL star who died a few years ago, threw a party for the ages. And I swear I've seen every movie star who's ever been in one of those *Halloween* movies, the ones with Freddie Krueger. They filmed those movies in the Salt Lake area, and the casts stayed at the hotel.

Magic Johnson stayed here when the NBA All-Star game was in Salt Lake City. I was in the shower and I heard somebody knocking on the door. So I got out, wrapped a towel around me, and cracked the door open. Standing in the hallway was this knockout blonde.

"Hey, you're not Magic," she said.

"How do you know?" I said. "Give me a try."

I think I'm also responsible for mentally scarring several hotel maids. I was having problems with my back one time and this masseur, sort of a big Grizzly Adams type, was in my room trying to help get the kinks out.

If you've ever gotten a massage, you know you don't wear a whole lot. The masseur was sort of behind me, adjusting my back when one of the hotel maids walked in. She mumbled something, dropped her head in embarrassment, and nearly left contrails, that's how fast she got out of the room.

I didn't think much about it until a couple of days later. The elevator door opened, I got in, and that's when I heard giggling. It was a couple of the hotel maids. They were laughing at me. I guess the massage story had made the maid circuit.

People have tried to find my room. People from out of town, kids, fans. I've had people knock on the door for an autograph. Of course, everything is prefaced with, "I hope I'm not disturbing you." Hey, if I'm out and about, I don't mind signing autographs and posing for photos. But if it's 7:00 A.M., and my Do Not Disturb sign is on the door, then it's probably not a good idea to knock.

Someone once asked me if there was such a thing as a Majerus groupie. Not that I know of, and if there was, I'm not sure I'd want to see her. Once, a middle-aged woman sent me long, heartfelt letters detailing an imaginary life we had together. We'd run through fields together, hold hands, teach her kids how to hunt and fish. She said she adored bald, overweight men. Very strange.

The 30–4 season also marked the end of my one-sweater policy. I'd wear the sweater, get it cleaned, wear it again. Donny used to look at me like, "Is he ever going to change that sweater?"

I retired the sweater after that season. It's in our basketball office, never to be worn again.

A few years later, when I renegotiated my Reebok contract, I asked them to give me some logo sweaters and I'd wear them on the sideline. They gave me some, and I think they're tasteful looking. Ever since then, I've been in a one- or two-sweater rotation.

We ended the 1991–92 season 24–11, which wasn't bad considering Josh had to sit out the year because of a knee injury. That was a team that featured one of my favorite players, M'Kay McGrath, and Craig Rydalch, Soto, Byron Wilson, Afeaki and Phil Dixon. We missed out on the NCAA tournament, but reached the NIT Final Four. Notre Dame beat us in the semifinals on a questionable call. By three.

The next year was better. Josh was better. We had a 24–7 record, a first-place tie in the WAC, an NCAA tournament win against Pittsburgh, and then elimination at the hands of Kentucky. Who knew that three of our next five seasons also would be ended by Kentucky?

Larry Cain was a senior captain that year, along with Josh, Soto, and Wilson. Larry wasn't the best player we had (though he led us in field goal percentage in 1992), and up until his senior season I was always evaluating whether he should quit the game. But he was a bright kid, an academic All-WAC pick three consecutive years, and he never let me give up on him. It's incredible to think we won the conference with this spindly, gangly, Ichabod Crane–looking center.

Larry wanted to study medicine, but he wasn't sure he could make the commitment. I tried to tell him to set goals, to dream. He ended up going to med school and, at last check, was interning in a hospital in Pocatello, Idaho. To me, that was more important than any win that season.

Despite our success, we were still having trouble signing the best Mormon players in the state. Most of those kids were still going to BYU. It was frustrating, and maybe there was a part of me that wondered if we'd ever get one of the elite LDS (Church of Latter-Day Saints) kids.

However, there was a non-Mormon kid in southern California who committed to us in the fall of 1992. Tall. Gangly. Haircut from hell.

His name was Keith Van Horn.

Donny had given me the scouting report on Keith. He said he was, "Made for TV." About six foot ten . . . a dunker . . . long arms . . . could run the floor.

Keith played at Diamond Bar High School, which is about thirty miles east of Los Angeles. What first attracted me to him was his passion for the game. This was a kid who would play in a late-morning tournament and then get in his car and drive 115 miles to play in an afternoon tournament. He was totally committed to the game, maybe even a little obsessed by it. Just like me.

I went to see Keith and his family. At the time, there were rumors about me looking at other jobs. I remember sitting downstairs in the bar with Keith's dad, Ken. Ken said, "If you're going to be there, we want to be there."

"Okay, well, I'm going to be there," I said.

Keith had a brother and a sister, but there had been some problems.

"I really didn't know how to do this thing right until Keith came along," Ken said. "I made some mistakes with the others that I don't want to make with Keith."

Ken was so intent that everything go well with Keith. He wanted the very best for Keith. He wanted to atone maybe for sins of the past—not egregious sins, but sins of not knowing, sins that every parent makes.

Keith and his dad came for the campus visit the Friday before the fall quarter started. He went out with our players and seemed to have a good time. On Sunday he flew home.

Donny followed him back. We knew we were on Keith's short list, and that his dad liked us, but you're never sure until you get the word.

Says Donny Daniels: *"I fly in, check into the Fullerton Marriott, and call Keith. I tell him if he has any questions, to call. Not in my wildest dreams do I think he's going to call me.*

"At eleven-thirty that night, the phone rings.

" 'Hey, Coach, it's Keith,' he says. 'Me and my parents thought it over. I want to come to Utah.'

" 'Really?'

"I couldn't believe it. Arizona State and Cal were on him, and I was worried about him changing his mind. The official signing date wasn't until the middle of November. But his dad says, 'Once Keith gives his word, he holds to it.'

"Now I have to find Coach Majerus. I call Salt Lake and wake up Tina, one of our basketball secretaries. She says Coach is in Roswell, New Mexico, recruiting.

"I call the hotel. Coach is dead asleep.

" 'Coach,' I say, 'Keith Van Horn just committed to us.'

"That woke him up."

We got Keith, but that 1993–94 season was filled with heartache and struggles.

We won seven of our first eleven games, but only seven of our last seventeen games. Dixon suffered a career-ending injury. Darroll Wright quit the team after seven games because of suspensions. Another player, Ed Johnson, was kicked off the team for smoking marijuana. He was a good player, too, the kind that could have made a difference. Suddenly we went from a six-foot-eleven guy at the center spot, to six-foot-six Doug Chapman.

I don't think there were any blacks on that team. We looked like the Utah ski team and, at times, played like it too. We had no depth. We were playing walk-ons. Mark Rydalch did a nice job for us at guard, but it was not a good team.

Ma Jian, a kid we signed from China, added about eight points and four rebounds per game. But he liked to shoot too much and even worse, he took bad shots. Drew always tells people that Ma had more physical skills than Keith, and maybe he did.

He was a nice kid. But I'd remind the team that there are a lot of guys you want to go out with on Friday night, but there are only a few you want on your team.

As a freshman, Keith led us in scoring, rebounding, blocks, field goal percentage, and free throw percentage. In fact, he led us in scoring, rebounding, and free throw percentage in each of his four seasons at Utah. He was the WAC Freshman of the Year, as well as a first-team All-WAC selection.

But in the wee hours one morning, I got a phone call from Keith's mom, May. Keith's dad had died of a heart attack. Would I go to Keith's dorm room and tell him the news?

It was about 2:00 A.M. when I knocked on Keith's door. He later said that when he heard my voice, his first thought was, I'm in trouble. Is it my defense?

We ended up going to an all-night cafe and trading stories about our dads. He told me about the time he ruined the transmission on his dad's boat, and how he promised his dad he'd graduate from college. It was sad in a way, but it was also good to talk—for both of us.

Says Keith Van Horn: *"I was in shock. But Coach Majerus was great through the whole process. We just talked, and he got me set for going home the next day. He knew what it was like, and how to deal with it. His own father had passed a way a few years earlier."*

The biggest temptation for me to leave might have been after the only bad year we've had, and that was that 14–14 record during Keith's freshman season. But I know one thing: I would have never left after Keith's dad died. They could have given me the state of New Jersey and I wouldn't have left.

I went to the funeral, and I remember listening to the minister. I remember looking at Keith. And I remember watching his mother.

In many ways, Keith was on his own. As I stood in the cemetery that day, one of the thoughts that kept going through my mind was, Well, you're at Utah for sure now with this kid. No matter what happens, you can never abdicate that responsibility.

In Keith's case, I just blocked out everything for the next three years. I didn't know how good Keith was or how good he could be or how good our team would be, but I knew Ken Van Horn had made a promise to me: "If you're going to be there, we want to be there."

Now it was my turn. If Keith was going to be at Utah, I was going to be there with him.

After a 14–14 season, it was clear we needed players. Soto was gone. Wright was gone. Johnson was gone. Cain was gone.

There was more bad news. Rydalch, who would have been our starting point guard, tore an anterior cruciate ligament during the summer, the second time that had happened. Seriously, what are the chances of a kid tearing ACLs in each knee? He wasn't expected back until January, at the earliest.

Silas Mills, who wanted to re-sign with us after leading Salt Lake City Community College to the national junior college tournament, was ruled ineligible by the NCAA. He was a helluva talent and a kid who had turned his life around.

Andre Miller would have been a nice replacement for Rydalch, but he was ruled academically ineligible.

So I went from having Rydalch, Mills, and Andre, to having none of them. Plus, the only senior I had on the team—Ma Jian—couldn't speak fluent English.

But at least we had Keith, whom I knew had a chance to be a special player. Keith still needed lots of work on his defense. He had played strictly zone in high school, and hadn't come close to perfecting the technique and exerting the effort it took to play man defense. If he questioned my assessment, which he rarely did, I'd say, "Do you want me to get Nellie on the phone?"

We also had signed one of the best juco swingmen, Brandon Jessie, and one of the best players from Utah, Al Jensen. Michael Doleac and Drew Hansen were also coming in, but hardly anybody had heard of them. In fact, I was thinking of redshirting Doleac.

That might have been one of the most hectic off-seasons of my career. I had issues regarding my own team, but I also had committed to be an assistant coach on Nellie's Dream Team II staff. A promise is a promise.

As you might expect, Dream Team II was the overwhelming favorite to win the World Championships in Toronto. We had our share of bad boys on that team, guys like Derrick Coleman and Shawn Kemp. We also had Steve Smith, Shaquille O'Neal, Dominique Wilkins, Mark Price, Kevin Johnson, Reggie Miller, Joe Dumars, Dan Majerle, Alonzo Mourning, and Larry Johnson.

The assistant coaches were guys I knew: Don Chaney and Pete Gillen.

Looking back, the only guy on the team who was difficult to be around was Coleman. There were some embarrassing moments and some immature actions, especially by Kemp. But some other things were sensationalized beyond what they really were.

Dream Team II wasn't really a showcase of super-competitive basketball. The best two teams in the tournament scrimmaged every day in practice—USA vs. USA. That was just the reality of the situation.

Nellie did a good job of keeping things simple. He really tried to play everybody. He agonized over each player's playing time.

The competition in the tournament was solid. In fact, when I got back to Utah, we actually put in an offensive set I stole from the Russians. Basketball espionage. It was a high-low offense that I had never seen before. Del Harris was intrigued with it too.

Nellie involved all the assistants. I had zone offense responsibilities, and I had something to do with presses. But you should have seen us when it came to working the electronics stuff. There was me, Nellie, Chaney, and Gillen, and I don't think any of us knew how to work the VCR machines. We had a meeting one time and nobody could figure out how to turn the damn thing on. It had about a hundred switches and buttons on it and looked like something you'd find at NORAD. Reggie shook his head in disgust, asked for the remote control, and pressed the on button.

We had scouted the other tournament teams and made some break-down films to show the guys, but it wasn't very intense stuff. It was nothing like what I do with my own team. But I really thought we did a good job in terms of preparation, given our situation. Then again, we really didn't have to do that good a job. Our playing talent was so much better. It wasn't really close.

Nellie was apprehensive about the World Championships because we were expected to win. But as we watched the teams play, we pretty much knew we were the best team. In fact, I don't even remember who came in second. People always say nobody remembers who comes in second place, and they're exactly right.

Nellie did a classy thing during the tournament. He never ran up the score. Look, it's hard to tell guys not to score, especially with the shot clock. But I think for the most part, we conducted ourselves well.

I left that team with a great appreciation for certain players. Reggie was great. Dumars is the best. He's professional and he handles himself so well. A wonderful human being, gracious and classy.

Steve Smith was a great kid, a kid who donated a lot of money to Michigan State.

Price was a nice kid. If you don't like Price, then there's something wrong with you. I think he prayed before, during, and after meals. He is a very religious guy. He had his family with him and some of the guys on the team were laughing, saying they couldn't believe he did that. Some of those guys figured this was a chance to be sort of footloose and fancy, if you know what I mean. Price wasn't a footloose and fancy kind of kid.

Shaq was a really nice guy. To be so young and have so much money, and yet handle himself so well. That's tough to do. In fact, Shaq gave me a watch one day. He came into the locker room and said, "Maj-erus" (he always called me that), "I want you to have this." I don't know what kind of watch it was, but it was expensive, I know that. I don't think Shaq walks around wearing a Day-Glo Timex. Anyway, it was a really nice gesture on his part.

Mourning gave me some basketball shoes, which was nice. A couple of the players gave me shoes for some charity auctions.

For the most part, it was a pretty relaxed atmosphere, and I'm glad

I was part of it. It was also a learning experience, and I try to share some of those things with my own teams. For instance, I told them about Dumars, what a class guy he is. I told them about Dominique. Dominique scores a lot of points, but he had poor shot selection and he didn't have strong practice habits. He was older than most of the guys on the team, so his legs weren't always fresh. Some of the players called him "Antique."

Unlike Dream Team II, my Utah team was an overwhelming favorite to win nothing. But we doubled our wins from a season earlier, won the WAC, and made it to the second round of the NCAA tournament.

I didn't redshirt Doleac. Instead, he made his Ute debut in Hawaii against Knight's Indiana team. He was seventeen. And we won the game.

Rydalch was a turned ankle from never playing again, but he came back from the knee surgery and was steady for us. Keith was WAC Player of the Year, and Brandon was first-team All-WAC.

Drew didn't play much, but I could already tell he was going to be invaluable as a defensive stopper.

Says Drew Hansen: *"He always stressed that: if you don't play defense, you're not going to play. But he was so intense. We beat UTEP at home by fifteen points, but when he came into the locker room I thought we had lost the game. I thought UTEP had hit a sixteen-pointer at the buzzer. He said, 'Van Horn, we're back to a whole new world with you and your defense. And Drew, you couldn't be worse. We didn't play that game tonight.'*

"He thought we should have beaten them by thirty."

Al was very good. He was a greyhound out there. He shot 58.8 percent from the field and gave us quality minutes, rebounds, and toughness. He was our best defender. After the season, though, he decided to take his Mormon mission. I wouldn't get him back until the 1997–98 season.

With Al Jensen in the lineup, I would have taken my chances against anybody that next year. But as it turned out, we won another twenty-seven games, earned our fourth league championship in six years, and reached the Sweet Sixteen in the NCAA tournament before losing once again to Kentucky.

But the year wasn't without its difficulties. There was a preseason shoplifting incident involving Andre and Jessie. Both players had to learn from the experience.

Ben Melmeth, a kid we signed two years earlier from Australia, missed the first five practices and three games of the season because he had played in the 1994–95 WAC tournament, and had done so despite being two credits shy of the NCAA mininum. Obviously, had I known that at the time, he would have never played.

Plus, we were criticized for recruiting Richie Parker, a kid from New York who later pleaded guilty to charges of sexual assault.

And there was Al's decision to take his mission.

We handled the Andre and Jessie situation internally, and Melmeth wasn't allowed to return to the court until after the third game. Parker eventually signed with Mesa (Arizona) Community College and later transferred to Long Island University.

Andre, back from his Prop. 48 year, gave us the depth we needed at point guard. Rydalch was tough, but there were days he couldn't practice or could barely play because of the pain in his knees.

Ben Caton was a juco (junior college) kid who came in and replaced two-guard Jimmy Carroll, who transferred. We opened against Kansas, and Caton scored fourteen. In his second game, this one against Texas, he hit the game-winner with 2.5 seconds. He scored twenty against BYU, and twenty-two against Kentucky in the tournament.

Keith won WAC Player of the Year again, and clearly was one of the top forwards in the college game. But there were games we let slip away. The one that bothered me most was a last-second loss to Fresno State at our place. Dominick Young hit a thirty-foot three-pointer to beat us as he was falling down and out of bounds.

Afterward, I talked to the team, to our local beat reporters, and then went to our meeting room to look at the film. We watched it as a staff until 4:30 A.M. At one point Donny said, "Coach, if he misses that shot, we're in bed right now."

But he hadn't missed the shot. I let the assistants go home, but I kept replaying the tape until sunrise. I just couldn't believe it.

One game that didn't slip away that season was the 1996 Midwest Regional Semifinal against Kentucky. We got beat by 31.

Says Tim LaComb: *"It's the first time I've ever seen him speechless. He wasn't pissed off at anybody because I think he knew we were up against one of the best college basketball teams ever assembled. He got on one knee, kind of looked up at the ceiling, and said, 'Boy, this is tough. Okay, let's just see if we can get it down to thirty by the next timeout.'*

"It was so amazing. He was deflated beyond what I've ever seen him. He couldn't even say two words."

Says Keith Van Horn: *"That 1995–96 team could have been our best team ever. It was probably the best team we had when I was there. Jessie was there. It was Andre's first year. Mike was really starting to come on. Drew was so good on defense. I just think we ran into Kentucky a little too early. Kentucky was loaded with six NBA guys, and they just cruised to a national championship. But if they hadn't been in our bracket, I think we could have been in the Final Four that year."*

Keith had a decision to make after his junior season: stay at Utah or turn pro.

During his sophomore year, his girlfriend gave birth to daughter Sabrina. The labor lasted more than nine hours, plenty of time for Keith to sit in the delivery room and finish a take-home exam in health education.

The topic: Personal Resiliency.

Baby and final exam did just fine—in fact, Keith cut the umbilical cord and aced the test. And Keith and Amy eventually became engaged and were married a few months before his senior season began.

But in March, months before the marriage, Keith had to decide between instant wealth and the NBA or a fourth year of being a college kid.

This is a guy who had a little daughter, a wife-to-be, a Nissan pickup truck with 101,000 miles on it, a modest apartment, a sweet disposition, a pro game, and lots of reasons to leave early.

We met at the Bagelry, a favorite place of ours to have heart-to-heart talks. We sat at a corner table. I brought a notepad and did just as the Jesuits taught me: consider each issue, consider the pros and cons, and make a decision. Or in this case, a recommendation.

I asked Keith to give me his wish-list of material things. He said he wanted a Lexus SC400, a home with a pool, enough money to put Amy through nursing school, and a stroller that Sabrina couldn't escape from.

With the exception of the stroller, I couldn't see how he was going to be able to afford any of those as a college senior living off a scholarship and student loan. So I told him to go to the NBA. I figured he'd at least get a three-year, $6 million deal.

But as each day passed, more and more underclassmen added their names to the draft list. I also asked David Falk for his evaluation.

Says David Falk, consultant and eventual agent to Majerus and Van Horn: *"We talked to Rick at the end of Keith's junior year. I* *wrote him a six-page letter with my strong recommendation that Keith stay in school for another year. I explained to him our view of the market.*

"Rick initially recommended that Keith leave early, but we recommended that he not. I went through the same exact situation with John Thompson and Patrick Ewing as a junior. I think we understand it better than coaches because we're in it every day. But it's a risk to them. I think Rick was making the recommendation out of fondness to Keith. He felt he had accomplished a lot, would go high in the draft. I think the coaches who really care generally want them to come out because they think it's risky to stay for a another year.

"But I think it was a great thing for Keith to stay."

Says Keith Van Horn: *"I hadn't made up my mind. I was going to listen to Coach and then decide. But my heart was always to stay in school. Anyway, to me money has never been that big a factor. It can give you a little freedom, but it's not going to make your life any better or any worse."*

Keith stayed, but I wouldn't have blamed him had he left. That said, I'm glad he stayed from the standpoint that I think he developed more as a person, developed more sense of self.

I've said this before, but I think the college game is in better shape than the professional game, and I'm a big fan of pro ball. I like to watch pro ball.

But you get these guys coming out early who can't live their own age, and they're not ready for the lifestyle. Kids like Tracy McGrady, a high school kid . . . they make a deal with the devil coming out early. Yes, you will get a lot of money in your life. But then, after money, what else do you have? You don't know how to deal with it. You don't have friends. You don't develop a sense of self. You compromise your self-esteem. You see yourself as a basketball player only, and not something beyond that.

As much as Keith loved the game and was driven by the game, I really wanted for him to be more than just a player. And he is. As wonderful a player he is, he is even a better person.

Our 1996–97 team was sort of a table-setter for the following season. Keith was among the best players in the country. Andre had established himself as a budding star in the league. Doleac still needed to board better, but he was improving every day. Ben Caton was a terrific offensive player, very good defensively, and very tough. Drew was becoming one of my favorites.

We had good players, but we were young. This was the season

David Jackson, Jeff Johnsen, Ashante Johnson, Jordie McTavish, and Hanno Mottola all made their debuts.

Caton and Keith were our captains, probably two of the best captains I've ever had. Caton was twenty-five, married, and had recently adopted a baby daughter, Kelsey. Keith was recently married and expecting a second child. These were stable guys, and their maturity and calmness was a wonderful balancing force on a team with so many newcomers.

Caton was an honor roll student, a husband, a father, a good player with a terrific work ethic. He was a basketball junkie, enough so that he worked three jobs just so he could save enough money to work as a counselor at Michael Jordan's summer camp.

Ben's nickname on the team was "Grandpa." Everybody respected him, and respected his devotion to his family. We even changed our practice time on Super Bowl Sunday so the Catons could have Kelsey christened earlier in the day. The players missed some of the game, but nobody seemed to mind.

His wife, Angie, worked part-time for a local housing developer and the family lived on her salary, a housing allowance, and a $5,000 student loan. But you never heard them complain about a thing.

Ben had already been on his Mormon mission, a two-year stay in Slovenia. Slovenia was part of the former Yugoslavia before civil war ravaged the country. He spent six days a week trying to convert people whose new republic was 96 percent Roman Catholic and 1 percent Muslim. On the seventh day, Ben would try to play basketball or keep in shape by doing sit-ups or lifting satchels filled with textbooks.

He learned the language. He said he even dreamed in it. He also learned a passable Serbo-Croatian.

It must have been very different to come back to Utah. He went from tanks and barricades and sandbags placed around government buildings to the peacefulness of Salt Lake City. His biggest new concern was making sure Kelsey wore Utah red to games.

I really wanted it to be a good season for everybody on the team, but especially for Keith. I knew how much it meant to him.

Keith was more interested in winning than in numbers. On February 22, we beat Tulsa at their place on a last-second shot by Andre. I got the game ball and immediately handed it to Keith, who gave me this puzzled look. "Just hold on to it," I said.

That night Keith had broken Bill "The Hill" McGill's all-time scoring record at Utah. McGill led the nation in scoring during the 1961–62 season, and held the Utah all-time record for the better part of four decades. But I don't think Keith's record will be broken, at least not in my lifetime, or Keith's.

Drew didn't break any scoring records, but he continued to play the kind of defense that wins games. We were in New Mexico in late January, and I called a team meeting at the hotel ballroom. I'm not exactly sure why I did it, other than to make a point, but I said, "Do you know why I love Drew Hansen?" And then I dove headfirst and spread-eagled on the ballroom floor. I just laid out, just like Drew did when he dove for loose balls or when he took a hard charge. "This is Drew Hansen," I said.

I think they got the point.

We entered the WAC tournament winners of fifteen of our last sixteen games, including a twenty-point regular season–ending victory against New Mexico. We were on a roll, right?

Instead, we needed a last-second tip-in by Keith to beat Southern Methodist University in the first round, and another last-second shot by Keith to beat New Mexico in the next round. The WAC championship was less dramatic—we beat Texas Christian University by twenty-one.

Says Keith Van Horn: *"Coach called the play that we used to beat SMU on the buzzer beater. Andre was going to take the ball out and I was going to line up directly with him. When the ref gave Andre the ball, I was supposed to hook my guy and spin free toward the rim. Then Andre would pass me the ball and I'd try to make the shot.*

"But SMU made a huge mistake. I don't know what the heck they were thinking. There was only .3 seconds left on the clock. There's no way you can pass it in and shoot it with .3 seconds remaining in the game. It's impossible to do.

"Coach had one guy on one corner, another guy on the other corner, and a third guy at the three-point line. Andre was the in-bounds guy and I was near the basket. At first, SMU had two guys on me, and a guy on each of the corners and at the three-point line. But then—and I still can't believe how dumb this was—one of the SMU guys on me decided to run to the corner and guard our player. He didn't realize we didn't have enough time for our guy to catch and shoot.

"Andre got the ball, I spun free of the guy fronting me, and then Andre lobbed it toward the basket. But the pass was too long. Had it been a little shorter I could have dunked the ball. Instead, it was too long and it took all I

had just to get my hand on it. When I first tapped it, I didn't think there was any way the ball would go in.

"Instead, the ball practically swished through the net and we won the game. I couldn't believe it. I started running to the other end of the court. I was semidelirious. I had no idea what I was doing. I was running by myself and my teammates were running after me so they could celebrate.

"When we finally got to the locker room, Andre called a quick players-only meeting. In fact, he pulled us into the shower area, so the assistant coaches couldn't hear us. We started talking about how we needed to focus and play better, how we couldn't let something like this happen again.

"When Coach got to the locker room a few minutes later, he wasn't in the mood to celebrate. He was pissed. He was mad because we had played horribly and because it should have never been that close of a game. And when he saw us come out of the shower area after our meeting, he just assumed I was the one who called it. He started yelling at me. He said, 'You know, we don't need to wait for last-minute shots. You guys don't need to call any meetings.'

"Afterward, the players were laughing because they knew I wasn't the one who had called the meeting. But as usual, I was the guy who caught the heat.

"Now, the New Mexico game was a different story. Coach was happy then. I made another game-winning shot at the buzzer and the place went nuts. I've seen the replay a hundred times. There's me hitting the shot. There's Coach leaping for joy. Well, maybe leaping *is the wrong word. He jumped about three inches off the ground."*

We were seeded second in the NCAA West Regional. The No. 1 seed? Kentucky.

The first two rounds of the tournament were in Tucson, home of Lute Olson's University of Arizona program. Very nice facilities. Their locker room was like an Ethan Allen showroom.

Our locker room at Utah is very spartan, very basic, very Third World. There's no carpeting. The lockers are lousy. But I don't really care about that.

Then you walk inside Arizona's locker room, and it's nicer than any home I've ever lived in. If I ever had a locker room like theirs, I'd just live in it. Forget the hotel. They've got leather chairs, plush carpeting, and a real nice TV. My players said they wanted one just like it. I told them maybe Keith could buy us one when he gets his millions.

We beat Navy in the first round and UNC–Charlotte in the second round to advance to the Sweet Sixteen in San Jose. One problem: we didn't have any way of getting there.

As only our athletic department could do, nobody had made any provisions for travel. All of sudden we get a chance to become an Elite Eight team, maybe even a Final Four team, and we don't have plane reservations to San Jose. No one from our school had made those arrangements. It was almost as if our school was shocked that we were winning. I mean, we really have a small potatoes mentality sometimes.

Jon Huntsman helped us out by sending his plane to pick us up. But what an embarrassing situation.

We played Stanford in the regional semifinal, and needed overtime to beat them. But Kentucky was too good for us. They were too good for everyone, except Arizona, which beat the Wildcats in the Final Four championship game.

We finished 29–4, won another WAC title, and I think Keith enjoyed the season. I think he helped himself in the NBA draft. He was the No. 2 pick in the draft by the Philadelphia 76ers behind Wake Forest's Tim Duncan and was later traded to the New Jersey Nets.

Keith certainly left a lasting impression on our program. We won three consecutive WAC titles and advanced to the NCAA second round, the Sweet Sixteen, and the Elite Eight during his three years. Not bad for a kid who wasn't on some top 100 recruiting lists out of high school.

When Keith left, I told him life was going to be different. He was going to have money and new friends. He was going to be away from home for the first time in years. I told him it was going to be a difficult adjustment.

I wanted him to know that his best friend wasn't the Lexus dealer trying to sell him a car (by the way, he never bought the SC400). I wanted him to know that pro ball isn't like college ball. We were so close as a team, but I've seen the Knicks in the Marriott restaurant in Salt Lake City, and there's four guys sitting at four different tables.

I also said I was going to give him advice, whether he wanted it or not. I said I was looking forward to going to his first training camp, sitting there with my legs crossed, and telling him, "I told you so."

Most of all, I wanted him to know how fond and proud I was of him. His work ethic was infectious and exemplary. It was so much fun to coach Keith. He loved every day. He might not admit this—maybe now he will—but I think he liked me getting on him. I accommodated him and he accommodated me.

He truly is a better person than he is a player. He dealt with so much—the death of his father, the birth of his daughter, marriage, the question of turning pro early, the pressure of carrying this team—and handled it with aplomb, maturity, and class. He was an All-American in so many ways.

5
Want to Be a Ute?

It was a courtesy call, really. A favor for a West Point classmate. That's what Mike Schneider told me the day he called to half-heartedly suggest I take a look at a kid from Central Catholic High School in Portland, Oregon.

"I went to school with his dad," Mike said. "He has this six-foot-nine or -ten son. I think he called Mike Krzyzewski and asked him to call Bob Knight. Then he called me, and I told him to go ahead and call you."

"I haven't heard from him," I said. "What's his name?"

"Phil Doleac," Mike said. "He's a retired army colonel. A dentist. His son's name is Michael. I don't know much about him, but he's probably not your kind of player anyway."

It was the summer of 1993. We had finished the season 24–7, tied for first place in the WAC, beaten Pittsburgh in the first round of the NCAA Tournament, and then, in what would become a postseason trend, were eliminated by Kentucky. I'm always interested in bigs, so I decided to check out this Doleac kid. All it would cost was a plane ticket and a day's worth of time. And if he stunk, maybe I'd see somebody else worth looking at.

Doleac was playing in a tournament at Wilson Junior High in Long Beach, California, and there wasn't another college coach or scout in the gym. I checked. Actually, Doleac was doing more sitting than playing.

I got there early to watch warmups. I like seeing how a kid conducts himself while doing the pregame fundamentals. Does he take it seriously? Does he screw around? Does he show good form?

Just by watching Mike in warmups, I could tell he had a real nice shooting touch, which is something you usually don't see in big men. And Mike was big. He had a Baby Huey look to him. Fleshy, but not fat. Thick, but not oafish. I loved his attitude and his enthusiasm. Some kids sleepwalk through warmups, but Mike treated each drill as if it were the game itself.

What I really noticed about him were his hands. If you're going to play in the low post for me, you've got to be able to catch the ball on the feed. Some of Mike's teammates threw him some bad passes during warmups, and he caught every one of them. A big guy with soft hands. I was intrigued.

Mike didn't play much, maybe three minutes, tops. But there was something about him that I liked, so I went back to the tournament the next day and invited him to my basketball camp. Mike seemed interested, but Phil Doleac wasn't so sure. Phil isn't obtrusive, but he is protective. He said he was worried the camp might be a waste of money.

"Phil," I said, "I'll give you the same money-back guarantee I give every kid who comes to the camp. If at the end of the week you don't think Mike has learned more ball or progressed to your liking, come on in and I'll refund your money on the spot. Fair enough?"

"Okay," said Phil.

We break our camp down by positions. Mike was with the bigs, and I really liked his potential. But what I really liked was his willingness to learn. He was like a Handi-Wipe towel, soaking up anything and everything about the game. His retention level was terrific, and he had an insatiable appetite for ball. We had these early-bird sessions at 6:15 each morning. Attendance wasn't mandatory, but Mike came to every one of them. He was smart enough to take advantage of the special attention; smart enough to realize we were offering private tutors for post play.

Midway through the week, I knew what I wanted to do. I told my staff, "I'm going to offer this kid a scholarship." Nobody disagreed. Mike wasn't a polished player by any stretch of the imagination, but you could see how far he had come in a single week. And even if Donny or Jud had objected, it wouldn't have mattered. I had a feeling about Mike. As long as I was the head coach, he was going to have a scholarship offer.

On the third day of camp, I grabbed two folding chairs, went outside the Huntsman Center, and positioned them just so. From the northwest vantage point you could see the mountains and valley and the beginnings of a beautiful sunset. I had never taken as much care with propositioning a woman as I had setting the scene for my meeting with an incoming junior in high school. It was like a marriage proposal. About the only thing missing was a bottle of champagne, romantic music, and maybe a nice appetizer.

I called Mike out, sat him down in the chair, and said, "I really like your game and I just want you to know you've got a scholarship here."

Mike looked at me in stunned amazement. "You're kidding me," he said.

"No," I said, "I really want you."

He looked as if he needed to be treated for shock. I don't think he quite believed anybody would want to offer him anything, especially a Division I scholarship. This is a kid who had probably spent more time fishing for halibut than working on his drop step. He was cut as a high school freshman and barely made the team as a sophomore. School came easy for him—he had straight As through his junior year—but playing ball was pure work. I always tell people that Mike doesn't have a basketball jones like me, or Keith, or Andre. He's a Renaissance man. His whole life has been a lesson in diversity. He's a sportsman, but he isn't consumed by sports. He's like a big sheepdog. A six-foot-eleven sheepdog.

Says Mike Doleac: *"I didn't really even know what a scholarship was when he made the offer. I was never into basketball, or in sports big time. My dad was in the military so we moved all over the world, from San Antonio to Kansas City, to Frankfurt, to Fort Hood, Texas, to Fairbanks, Alaska, to Portland. And I played whatever sport was in season. I played Little League baseball, Little League soccer. When we lived in Alaska I skied and played volleyball. We did a lot of camping. I was never a guy who was in one place, watching the NCAA tournament, making that my goal to get a basketball scholarship and become a star. You have to remember that during most of high school I rarely even played. I never expected to go to college to play basketball. When it happened, it was a complete surprise."*

By the end of the week, Mike had basically committed to us. That's when it got interesting. I called his dad to tell him about the scholarship offer and he said, "Well, we've really got to make sure this is the right thing to do." Like I said, Phil was a little on the protective side. What he had forgotten was that Mike hadn't even started on his high school team. I was offering a scholarship to a kid who wasn't even a starter, who couldn't even get any minutes in a summer tournament in Long Beach.

Mike was very smart. He was a National Honor Society member at a very well-respected high school. He had a lot of scholarship opportunities, relative to academics. But we were the first to offer him a basketball scholarship, and I think that meant something.

By the end of his senior season, it was obvious that Mike could play Division I ball. He averaged seventeen points, nine rebounds, and led Central Catholic of Portland to the state championship. He was also named the Oregon Player of the Year by *USA Today*.

That fall, Mike and Phil came to Salt Lake City for an official campus visit. But to be honest, I think Mike's mom, Marge, was the real rock of this whole thing. By then, Stanford might have nibbled a little bit, but only because Phil was soliciting calls. Oregon invited Mike to be a walk-on, but that was about it for offers. It was us and a full ride or nothing.

Needless to say, none of the recruiting services hailed the signing as a watershed moment for Utah. To them, Mike was a big body, nothing more. To me, he was Baby Huey with a big upside.

Even then, Mike had a calmness about him. He was so even-tempered, and in some ways that became a problem for him as it related to basketball. But all things considered, that sort of disposition is probably more of an asset than a problem. He's really a well-balanced young man. He has a great sense of self. He loves to golf. He loves to fish. He loves to camp. The problem—if you can call it that—is that basketball is not a passion for him. Not when he was a no-name kid at a summer league in Long Beach. Not now in the pros. He plays the game hard. He practices hard. But he doesn't have the obsession with the game that Van Horn or Andre have. And I think that's good. This is a guy who, when his playing career is finished, is going to be a doctor. I'd rather him obsess about surgery or curing diseases.

As big as Mike was, he wasn't really the enforcer type of player. He played tough, but the toughest kid on the team was Andre.

The first time I saw Andre was in Los Angeles. I went to the gym and I saw this woman yelling at anything that moved. At Andre. At the refs. At the coaches. At the other players. She was storming up and down the court as if she had a bet on the game. She was yelling, "Take him, Andre! Take him!"

During a long break in the game, I leaned over to Andre's coach and said, "If there is a god in heaven, tell me that isn't Andre's mother."

"Sorry," he said, "that's Andre's mother."

I was impressed with Andre, but all I could think about was his mother. I told my assistant, "We can't have his mother doing that at our games. We'll run right into each other."

Later, the coach's wife told me what a wonderful woman Andre's mom was. "You're really going to like her," she said.

She was right. Andrea Robinson is a remarkable woman. But no one worked the court harder than she did that day.

I had never heard of Andre until Donny handed me a list of guards with Miller's name on it. "He's worth looking at," Donny said. So I flew to Los Angeles and went to see him play at a gym near LAX.

My original plan was to watch him play an AAU game at 2:00 P.M. and then fly back to Salt Lake City in time for a big Pioneer Day barbecue that night with my girlfriend, Betsy Hunt, and some friends. But the more I watched, the more I wanted to see more of Andre. I was spellbound by the dynamic of Andre, his mother, the coach, and the coach's wife.

Andre didn't stand out, but he did make a couple of very nice passes. I didn't know what to do. I wanted to stay, but missing the barbecue wasn't going to be a real popular decision.

"What time is your next game?" I asked the coach.

"We play at seven," he said.

I thought about it for a minute and then said, "I'm staying."

"But don't you have assistants for that?" the coach said. "What about the barbecue?"

"No, no," I said. "I want to see him."

So I stayed, and Andre really showed me something with the way he passed the ball. After the game I told the coach, "This kid's got a scholarship."

"He does?" said the coach.

The coach pulled Andre's mom over and said, "Andrea, this is the coach of Utah."

"Don't forget me," I said. "I'll be in your home in September." That's when I could make an official home visit.

I know it was only two games, but I could see that Andre had great court vision and court awareness. He didn't see one teammate, he saw four. And what I liked best was his great enthusiasm for the game. He wasn't a pretender.

With Andre, you literally had to kick him out of the gym. And he is so competitive. He's like John Stockton in that regard: a very, very nice guy who will do what it takes to win. Andre would turn out to be my most competitive player.

As a point guard, the most important thing is that you have a feel for the game. You also have to get your team into the offense, as well as get other people shots. Andre could handle the ball well, he could really see the floor when he played. He had sort of a soft, doughy, un-buff body, but he could play tough. He learned how to play physical against the gang-bangers in L.A. There were some good players in those gangs, kids with raw skills, but kids who were going a different way than Andre. Andre didn't do drugs, didn't flash colors. He played basketball, and the gang members respected that and left him alone. It was like a code of ethics with them.

Andre also knew how to post low. That's because he was the second-biggest guy on his Verbum Dei High School team.

Plus, I started to understand what made Andrea Robinson so special. She and her husband raised a family in the tough Compton area, which you're not going to find on any Hollywood map of the stars. She worked for the Department of Veterans Administration and scraped enough money to send Andre to private schools. And unless he was sick, she didn't let him miss a day of school. She made him do his chores, and if he didn't, then he couldn't play basketball. One time, he forgot to do his work and Andrea went to the gym and pulled him off the court. It didn't matter if he was in the middle of a game or if all his friends were watching. I liked that kind of discipline.

Andre and his family knew unconditional love and tragedy. His brother, Duane, died of encephalitis when he was eleven, and that must have been a tremendous heartache for that family.

The more I got to know Andrea, the more I realized someone ought to write a motherhood how-to book based on her life. Everything revolved around her kids. She works every day from March to October so she'll accrue enough days off to watch Andre during the season. The two of them talk at least once a day on the phone. It is a beautiful, loving relationship.

Andre had solid grades in high school, but his standardized test scores weren't good enough for NCAA mininum requirements. There's absolutely no doubt in my mind that the SAT and ACT are culturally biased, but that didn't change Andre's predicament. To be eligible to play Division I basketball as a freshman, his SATs or ACTs had to improve.

I was willing to take a chance. In fact, one time I told him a story about a point guard named Raymond Lewis. Lewis was an L.A. legend who played with Donny at Verbum Dei and later signed with Cal State–Los Angeles. As a freshman in 1972, he scored forty points against a UCLA freshman team that featured future Bruins stars Dave Meyers and Pete Trgovich. CSLA won, 94–86, and broke UCLA's twenty-six-game freshman win streak. Lewis also scored seventy-three points against UC–Santa Barbara's freshman squad. As a sophomore, he scored fifty-three points against Long Beach State. He outscored Larry Bird, 39–25, when CSLA played Indiana State. Lewis was the second-leading scorer in the nation that year, averaging 32.9 points. But like I told Andre, Lewis was also one of the biggest quitters I'd ever seen in my life. He later went hardship and was taken by the Philadelphia 76ers as the eighteenth pick in the first round of the 1973 NBA Draft. He never played a minute in the pros.

"Andre, Raymond Lewis never got his degree," I said. "That will never happen if you come to Utah. Now, you might not have the best social life, relative to the latest dance craze. In fact, the dance might not even hit Utah in the four or five years you're there. You might not ever go to parties where everyone is dressed to kill. But you'll never end up like Raymond Lewis, either."

Not long after I told him that story, Donny and I went to see Andre play. And damn if we don't get out of the car and who's at the gym? It's Raymond Lewis, and he hits Donny up for some money. He tells Donny he needs the money to get out to the airport and interview for a job.

We went inside the gym and afterward I told Andre, "We just saw Raymond, but we didn't want to embarrass him. But another guy also saw him and told us, 'I gave him that same twenty dollars a month ago.'"

I thought that was a very telling story. The sad truth is I see too many Raymond Lewises, guys who had athletic talent, but not academic commitment. Or maybe they were sort of interested in academics, but they didn't have a support group to push them and force them to see it through. I wanted Andre to know he would always have a support group in place at Utah. Plus, he'd have me acting as his Andrea. After all, I'm the king of academics.

I think all that had a lot to do with him coming to Utah. But despite some nice stats (he averaged twenty-four points and seven rebounds), Andre wasn't that good a player when we signed him. He had talent, but people weren't knocking down his door to get him. He didn't look like a prototype guard. He was mushy.

It also didn't help that his ACTs and SATs weren't high. The possibility of him becoming a Prop. 48 scared away a lot of schools. But this was a kid who made his high school dean's list and honor roll.

Says Andre Miller: *"There were a lot of people who thought that since I came from South Central, I couldn't do well in school. They looked at the ACTs and the SATs and decided I couldn't succeed in college. But I had a 3.0 grade-point average coming out of high school. I knew I could do college work.*

"I was recruited by Oregon, Long Beach State, the University of San Diego, and Utah. Long Beach State and San Diego were a little too close to home. I thought about Oregon, but Coach Majerus is the one who came to my house and guaranteed me that I would graduate. And once I came to Utah, he made sure I went to class, that I went to tutors, and that I was on top of my studies."

Drew Hansen never needed help with his studies. He was a National Honor Society member, the editor of his high school newspaper in Tooele, Utah, an academic all-state, a regular poster boy for higher education. He was the kind of kid mothers hope their daughters marry. You want to make him chocolate chip cookies and pour him a cold glass of milk. He's too good to be true.

Drew averaged twenty-two points, eight rebounds, and five assists as a senior, and he was named to the all-state team. But he had exactly one dunk during his entire high school career. I'm not sure anyone else was looking at him except Brown and the Naval Academy.

Jimmy Soto's high school coach is the guy who first told me about Drew. He said, "You'll really like this guy. He's your kind of guy. He really loves to play the game. He's tough."

I vaguely remembered Drew from our camps. He came to one after his freshman year at Tooele and one of our coaches said he was a hell of a defender. So we had him guard a kid we were recruiting and Drew shut him down, even stripped the ball from him.

Richie Smith came with me to Tooele for the scouting trip. So did Kent Jones and Jeff Jonas. We watched him play, and on the way back they were really getting on me about Drew. They weren't impressed. They thought I had wasted a night. They had nothing against Drew personally; they just didn't think he could play for Utah.

If you judged Drew by traditional basketball methods, they were probably right. You didn't watch him and go, "Wow!" He was a blender. A complementary player. His shot was okay, but he didn't look very athletic. He wasn't your classic-looking, veins-popping-out-of-calf-muscles athletic.

But I could see how hard he tried. In fact, I told these guys, "He'll be a great eighth man, maybe sixth or seventh man. He likes me. He wants to come to Utah. He likes the Utes. He works his ass off. We can't pass a kid up like this. He's a role player."

They weren't convinced.

We were driving back to Salt Lake City, and there was a Utah Highway Patrol car in the distance in front of us. I saw the cop car, but I was so involved in my heartfelt defense of Drew that I kept hitting the gas on the Explorer and passed him going about ninety. They thought I was nuts. Nuts about Drew. Nuts about passing this cop. They thought I was just screwing around or that I knew the cop. I didn't know the cop.

Well, it took about two seconds for the cop to hit the blue lights and pull me over. The cop walked up to the window and he probably didn't know what to think. I mean, what kind of person purposely passes a Highway Patrol car on the highway?

He looked at me, recognized the face, and his eyes kind of went wide in surprise.

"Coach," he said, "you've got to slow down."

He was almost apologetic.

He said, "I didn't know it was you, but have a safe day. Just slow it down."

That's not the first time I've come near to cracking the 100-m.p.h. barrier. One time I was driving to Hyrum, Utah, to see a kid, and one of my buddies said, "Uh, Rick, does this car have airbags?"

I started laughing.

"Hey, if we crash, *I'm* your airbag."

I've been lucky with state troopers and cops. I've got a badge from the governor in Utah that carries a little weight when it comes to nudging past the speed limit. I've got a badge from Indiana. In most places, the cops will cut you a break if you're a coach. Now I'm not talking about doing a Jeff Gordon or running gin across state lines. But there are a lot of cops out there who like basketball and who will give a coach a free pass maybe on a small speedometer violation.

I had my own feelings about Drew's potential, but what really convinced me to offer him a scholarship was when I talked with his coach, the recently retired Clyde Alquist. Alquist was a good coach and I respected his opinion. He crystalized everything for me when he said, "Coach, Drew doesn't care what position he plays. He doesn't care when he plays or how much he plays. He doesn't care if you redshirt him. He only cares about playing for you, playing for the University of Utah, and getting a Utah degree. That's it."

Says Drew Hansen: *"They had signed Doleac, Alex, and Greg Barratt, and I knew they wanted to sign Andre. Eventually, Coach Judkins came to my house and asked me to wait until the spring before I made a decision. He said there might be a scholarship available. I thought he was pulling my leg.*

"Meanwhile, Don DeVoe, the coach at Navy, wanted me to commit. He was a great guy, but for some reason, I couldn't tell him I was coming there. I wanted to go to the U.

"Somehow a scholarship came free and Coach Majerus invited me to watch them play Colorado State. They lost, but afterward Coach said he was 90 percent sure he was going to offer me a scholarship. Then he came to one of my games, but he didn't get there until the fourth quarter. That was lucky for me because I had a really good fourth period. Then he saw me play a couple of days later and I did well. Not long after that, he offered me a scholarship. I couldn't say yes fast enough. But I always thought if I had played poorly in those games, he would have never made the offer.

"Looking back at it, Utah was probably the only top-twenty-five team I could play for. With my physical skills, I could never average ten points. And if I did average ten, the team would be terrible. But what Coach did was this: he let my mind be a factor. I could play defense, and I could play smart."

I think I'm a good evaluator of talent, but if you would have told me Drew Hansen would start as a small forward on an Elite Eight team that was ranked No. 2 in the country for most of the season, or that he'd start as an off-guard on a team that went to the national championship game, I would have said you needed a breathalyzer test. But someday Drew is going to be a great NCAA basketball trivia question. Quick, name the kid with four conference championship rings, four NCAA tournament watches, a Final Four ring, and maybe the best NCAA tournament winning percentage of any senior in recent years.

And the answer is . . . Drew Hansen. Remember that. You'll win a lot of free beers.

Alex Jensen could have played for a lot of programs. I'd never heard of him until a friend of mine, Bob Henderson, dropped some film of Alex in an AAU game at the front desk of my hotel. There was a note attached: "Rick, I want to show you a guy you're going to love."

He was absolutely right. I watched the tape and then told my staff, "This kid has a chance to be a pro."

One of my assistants looked at me and said, "What are you, nuts?"

"I'll tell you something," I said, "this kid plays really hard. Watch how good he plays defensively. Look at his instincts."

Al was only a sophomore at the time, but he had good size and strength. He also had a nice way about him, a nice feel for the game. But his high school coach had the same problem I did: Al didn't like to shoot. He loved being a complementary player. He was such a neat guy. It was almost as though he didn't want to be really good. Al's the kind of guy who wins the lottery and is embarrassed that he won and someone in the cancer ward didn't. He is really a genuinely good person. I remember when he was a freshman, we had a handicapped manager with a bad arm and leg. I didn't know this until really late after a game one night. I went down to look for some film and there was Al carrying all the equipment bags for the manager. That's Al. That's how sweet he is.

Al is my favorite. The players know that. He's my favorite because he plays such great defense with a modicum of talent. He's such a great warrior, without a warrior's body.

I didn't waste any time with Al. I offered him a scholarship during his sophomore year. I think he thought I was nuts too. But I knew this kid had what it took. I told Al's dad, Jerry, "Look, I love your son. I like his attitude. I like his toughness, his sense of team, and the fact that he does all the little things on the court. I want you to know he has a scholarship waiting for him, but I'm not going to pressure him."

And I didn't. Al didn't sign until late in the recruiting season. BYU was in the picture, as was Arizona State. I also knew there was a chance—probably a good one—that Al would take a Mormon mission in the next couple of years. I used to joke with Al that I'd become LDS if he wouldn't go. But if you're going to recruit LDS kids, you have to deal with that possibility.

Says Al Jensen: *"One of the reasons I liked him was because he'll straight out tell you what he thinks. He came to my home (in Centerville, Utah) and he didn't guarantee that I'd start, like some coaches did. And he said there were going to be times when he yelled at me. But I learned that he'll praise you just as quick as he'll rip on you. I respected his honesty."*

As it turned out, the recruiting class of 1994–95 would become the core of the Final Four team: Alex, Andre, Drew, Mike. Drew and Mike probably weren't on anybody's Blue Chip lists. Andre was a Prop. 48. And my own assistants didn't want me to sign Al.

Hanno was the fifth piece. He signed in time for the 1996–97 season and let me tell you, that was some recruiting courtship.

I first heard about Hanno from a guy who books some of our overseas exhibition games. Someone sent me film of Hanno and I really liked the way he played. So I told Hanno's coach I was interested in coming to Finland.

"Many coaches call," he said, "but not many come to Finland. If you come here, that will mean a lot to me and to Hanno. It will show you have a genuine interest."

I said that was fair enough. But before I made the travel arrangements, I needed to know two things:

Was Hanno at least six foot nine?

Would Hanno be allowed to leave Finland, even though he had a military obligation to the country?

The coach assured me there would be no problems. Not with Hanno's height and not with his military situation.

Says Hanno Mottola: *"I'd never heard of him or the U. A lot of schools were recruiting me. The only thing I knew about Utah was the Utah Jazz. But I kind of figured out there must be a school there."*

The flight to Finland takes forever. I left New York at 5:00 P.M. and didn't get there until about eight o'clock the next morning. I think it's the longest flight from New York to a European country. Whatever it was, my five o'clock shadow had a five o'clock shadow of its own.

On the same flight was a former player from Butler University. He was on his way to play for a pro team in Europe. We talked a little bit and I wished him luck.

The most terrifying part of the flight had nothing to do with the occasional air pocket or the dreadful airplane food. Instead, I was worried sick that I'd get off the plane, and there would be Hanno. All six foot four of him. It's happened to coaches before. A guy flies to Europe and then discovers his foreign recruit shrunk in the wash. What happens is that the foreign coaches sometimes fib about size and height. Same thing happens in the States.

When we finally landed in Europe, I was a wreck. All I wanted was a hot shower, a decent meal, a change of clothes, a Hanno who was at least six foot nine, and then lots of sleep. I went to baggage claim and saw the kid from Butler heading toward customs with his luggage. Later, my red Reebok bag tumbled onto the conveyor belt.

I went to customs and here's what they found when they opened my bag: Afro-Sheen, Doc Marten boots, a hair dryer, and assorted clothes that wouldn't fit me in 1,000 years. The kid from Butler had my bag and apparently had been whisked through customs. I had his bag—an almost identical Reebok bag—and no change of clothes. Worse yet, I barely had time to check into my hotel and then go see Hanno and his brother at a YMCA gym in Helsinki.

I took a shower, but is there anything worse than having to put on the same dirty, grungy clothes you wore for a trans-Atlantic trip? I sure as hell didn't need any Afro-Sheen or a hair dryer. The Doc Martens didn't fit, nor did the other clothes. The guy from Butler had a size 15 neck, size 38 sleeves, and he had a great affection for safari jackets and silk shirts. Not my size and not my style.

When I finally got to the YMCA, I could barely keep my eyes open. I felt like I was being rope-a-doped by Muhammad Ali. I was just hanging on for the count. I was so tired that I actually fell asleep while I was talking to Hanno and his brother. I could feel myself fading into sleep, but I was helpless to stop it. It was like watching one of those old detective movies where someone slips the guy a Mickey. That's how I felt.

I hadn't shaved. My clothes smelled. I couldn't stay awake. I looked like a sewer troll. But Hanno and his brother, Matias, were extremely nice. So was the coach. They knew I was trying. And they knew I was serious about Hanno.

The big discussion mostly had to do with Hanno's ties with the Finland national team. The coach wanted to know if I would let him come back and play for Finland in international tournaments. I said I understood how important it was to play for your country, so I offered a deal: Hanno could come back anytime during the season except during the WAC tournament and the NCAA tournament.

I kept that promise, too. During Hanno's first year at Utah, I let him leave two or three times to go play in European tournaments. He missed several regular season games because of those tournaments. But a deal is a deal.

Later, the Finnish coach and I reached a basketball accord. Hanno wasn't doing himself much good by trying to play in these tournaments; he wasn't doing Utah much good playing in the tournaments; he wasn't doing the Finnish team much good playing in the tournaments. No more tournaments during our season.

But before Hanno could actually sign with us, we had to get clarification about his military obligations. At first I was told he could play. Then it looked like he was going to have to stay because of military duty. Then they said he could leave.

Hanno was a very worldly guy, especially compared to most kids in the States. He had spent time as an exchange student in San Antonio. He had played with several Finnish teams that traveled all over Europe. But he didn't know much about Utah, which is understandable. There are kids in the States who don't know much about Utah.

I told him Utah was very much like Finland: very cold, overcast, with a great deal of snow during the winter. He had a friend who had played at BYU, so he knew something about the climate and the basketball environment.

I liked Hanno enough that I took two trips to Finland to recruit him. The cuisine was interesting. Lots of fish. Reindeer meat. Vodka. You know what they say, "When in Helsinki . . ."

I might have been sleep-deprived the first time I saw him practice, but you could tell he was a player. He was every bit of six foot nine and once I saw him shoot, well, it was a no-brainer. He was very enthusiastic about the game. Plus, Hanno was a very nice guy. He always took extra steps to make sure I knew where I was going when I visited him. He didn't want me to get lost. He was very proud of his country and very determined.

We weren't the only school to recruit him. Kansas was interested, and so was Illinois State and Cal-Berkeley. As usual, I told him exactly what was going to happen if he signed with the Utes. I told him how we were going to play. I told him how I was going to play him. I said we'd develop his inside game, his outside game, and if he worked hard, I said he was going to have a chance to play in the NBA. I don't say that often, but with Hanno, I thought with his size, his touch, and his instincts, he had a legitimate shot to play pro ball in the States. I also told him—as I tell every recruit—that sometime during his career at Utah, we would play in his hometown, or in Hanno's case, in his home country.

"I will coach you every day," I told him. "I'll show you everything I know. Together we can make this dream happen. We need you to have a good team, and you need us to play on a good team."

I think a big thing to Hanno was that I had a reputation for coaching bigs, and that I had coached in the NBA. Playing in the NBA was really a big deal to Hanno. That's why he wanted to come to the United States, so he could position himself for a shot at the NBA. Whereas Doleac didn't really give much thought to the NBA, mostly because he never thought he'd play in the NBA. Telling Doleac he was good enough to go to the NBA was like telling him you could have a baby if you had sex. It was like an awakening. In fact, until his junior season at Utah, he didn't believe it could happen. The NBA, that is.

I kept in touch with Hanno, and I made sure Donny and Jud did the same. We called when allowed, and I even sent Jud over there once.

When it came time for official visits, Hanno narrowed it down to Cal-Berkeley and us. If ever there were two radically different programs, campus environments, and physical plants, those are the two. Everything about the two places spoke to opposites. But in the end, I think Hanno really liked our players, liked our program, and liked what we were building.

Not only did we sign Hanno in that recruiting class, but we got Nate Althoff, a big from Delano, Minnesota. We got David Jackson from Portland. David was a fourth-team *Parade* All-America, and I liked his athleticism. We got Jeff Johnsen, a two-time Utah Player of the Year. And I signed Jordie McTavish from Salmon Arm, British Columbia.

In 1997, we added Jon Carlisle, a center from Salt Lake City who originally had verbally committed to BYU, but changed his mind when they fired Roger Reid. We signed Trace Caton, whose brother Ben played for me. Trace was worried about following in his brother's footsteps, and almost signed with Colorado State. And we got Britton Johnsen, Jeff's younger brother, the first McDonald's All-American I've ever signed, and part of the fifth set of brothers I've coached in my career. A lot of people thought Keith was one of those kids, but the closest he ever got to McDonald's was the drive-thru lane. You couldn't find Keith's name on some top-100 recruiting lists.

It was only natural that Britton was compared to Van Horn. And in a way, I agreed with the comparison. Entering the program, Britton had the same bad body that Keith had, and the same lack of commitment on the defensive end. But I wasn't complaining.

Britton could have signed anywhere. Bad body or not, he was a bona-fide top-ten, top-twenty recruit. He also was a nice kid, got good grades, and could play three positions.

Britton visited Syracuse, Connecticut, and us, and canceled his visit to UCLA. It was such a long, drawn-out process, and there were so many other things going on with the team and in my own life, that when he finally said he was coming to Utah, it was like, "Okay. Great."

Says Britton Johnsen: *"I first met Coach when he was recruiting my brother Jeff. The Utah coaches came to our house and they asked me if I'd want to come in and visit Utah too.*

"What'd I think? I thought he was big. I thought he was a totally nice guy. He really knew his Xs and Os. It's funny. A lot of coaches who came in to recruit Jeff kind of told him how good they were. But right away he started telling Jeff what he needed to work on. He didn't say anything about himself. He didn't say anything about his record, or how good of a coach he was. He just started telling Jeff, 'You need to work on your jump shot. I think I can do this with you. I think I can do that with you.' I thought that was pretty cool.

"I won't say any names, but the night before, a different coach from a different part of the valley—I'll put it that way—had, uh, a different approach.

"When it came time to make a decision, it wasn't that hard a choice. I took a couple of visits—one to Syracuse and one to Connecticut—but I pretty much had my mind made up.

"The Syracuse visit was pretty interesting because of what happened when I met with Coach Boeheim. I really think Coach Boeheim is a good guy, but when I was in his office, he pointed to a ball he had from the Final Four and he told me, 'You see that ball? You know, you can go play for Utah and you'll probably be a good player there. And Coach Majerus is a good coach and Utah is a good school. But I'm telling you, you'll never get the chance that we just did. You'll never reach the Final Four.' This was the year after they went to the Final Four.

"I even kind of believed what Coach Boeheim said. But I wanted to stay close to home and I really liked the program here."

So this was who we were: Doleac, Andre, Drew, Alex, Hanno, Britton, Dave, Jordie, Trace, Nate, Barratt, Carlisle, and Adam Sharp. Including walk-ons, we had fifteen players. We were the ultimate blended family: seven Mormons, one Finn, one Canadian, two African-Americans. There were my longtime assistants Donny and Jud, my new assistants Brock Brunkhorst and Jeff Strohm. And there was me and a dream.

6

The Best Move
I Never Made

I didn't really have an off-season. Instead, I had a job offer from the Golden State Warriors. Then I had reporters constantly calling about the job offer from the Warriors. I had an Under-22 USA Basketball team to coach in the World Championships in Australia. I had my own team to worry about. I had recruiting concerns. I had a personal schedule that didn't allow for a day off. And in a strange way, I loved every minute of it.

The Warriors job was extremely tempting. I had been approached in the past about coaching at other college programs, but I never seriously considered leaving Utah. However, this was different. The offer from the Warriors really turned my head. The money was beyond belief. The Bay Area is one of my favorite places in the world. And I really liked the owner, Chris Cohan. He was a great guy, and he was honest and really up front. In fact, I was more attracted by his honesty and his directness than I was about the financial side of the deal.

The Warriors were a mess, mostly because they were prisoners of their past personnel decisions. Their record was terrible and the roster was on the thin side. But to his credit, the owner didn't put a happy face on the situation.

"Look," he said, "we're really bad. We've got problems. We've got salary cap problems. We've got attendance problems. I'm offering you a seven-year deal because no human being can right this ship in less. I just want your enthusiasm and energy and your commitment."

I loved that approach. And again, even more than the money, I loved that area. I think the Bay Area is a great place to live. Plus, he was going to get me a home or get me a condo suite in a beautiful hotel up in the hills in Oakland. And I'm not going to pretend the money wasn't important. It was mind-boggling: seven years, $23 million. For a guy who used to work at Pabst Brewery, that was more money than I could ever imagine.

Says Don Nelson: *"He was offered so much money at Golden State, I actually thought he should take it, work his way through that bad situation there, and see what happened. That was an incredible offer they made to him."*

Everybody told me to take it. But you know what? I would have never traded $23 *billion* for the experience of a Final Four year.

There were some other considerations. To be honest, I wasn't sure how I'd feel about pro players. I didn't know how the pros would accept teaching. And I didn't want people saying, "Van Horn left, now he's out of there too."

Nobody would have blamed me had I left Utah. It was difference-making money, and it was the NBA—there aren't many of those jobs in the world. And it was in San Francisco. But the truth is, I really like my guys. It's hard for me to tell them that. I'm like a German father: joy through work . . . never pat you on the back while you're on the job . . . save all the hugs for Senior Night. That's how I am.

Cohan was really passionate about his team. The team would have a new arena and new uniforms. I remember he was so excited when he showed me the new team logo.

I turned him down, not because I didn't think I could coach in the pros—I could. I turned him down because I didn't think I would enjoy it. I wasn't sure about the players. I wasn't crazy about the constant travel.

Before I made my final decision, Richie Smith flew out to L.A. to see me. I was there doing analysis of the Jazz-Lakers series for one of the local Salt Lake City TV stations. I showed Richie everything I had: the Warriors players' salaries, the salary cap numbers, the deal Cohan was offering. Richie looked at it and strongly encouraged me to take the job. He was the only person from Utah telling me to take it. He said the offer was too significant to turn down.

I met with Cohan one last time. It was a Sunday. That's when I told him. Afterwards, I went out to my rental car and called Richie.

"It's over," I said. "I'm sitting in Chris Cohan's driveway. I'm not taking it."

"Are you sure?" Richie said.

"I really am," I said.

Richie asked why I turned it down. That's when I read him a pair of letters I had with me.

Says Richie Smith: *"He had a letter from Keith Van Horn's mom, May. She had written to him to express her appreciation for everything Rick had done with Keith, what a positive influence he had been on her son. Then he read me a letter from Larry Cain. Rick inherited Larry when he took the Utah job. No one took more abuse from Rick than Larry Cain.*

"Larry's whole goal was to go to medical school. But during his senior year, Larry almost gave up on that dream because of a personal situation. Rick jumped on him just as hard as if Larry had missed a block out. Larry ended up going to medical school and becoming a doctor. He wrote Rick during the Golden State courtship.

"So Rick had these letters and he's saying, 'Do you think there's a player on Golden State who's going to write this kind of letter?' That's what he based the decision on. Not money, but if he could enrich a person's life.

"After I hung up with him, I told my wife, 'The world doesn't know what a wonderful guy this is.' "

I could have taken the job for the money. Even if I had failed, I think I would have been able to go back to college ball. College ball would have been a great security blanket. And certainly there was the financial security blanket. It was like, Voilà, here's a couple of million dollars. I would have never had to work another day in my life.

But I didn't get into coaching because of money. I make plenty of money, enough to keep me happy. Del Harris and I were talking about this a couple of years ago. I never got into this business to be famous or to be rich. I never thought I would be paid and compensated like this. I realize it's a fairy tale.

I made $5,000 for my first nine-month contract at Marquette. I made $40,000 as the Marquette head coach and got another $30,000 from New Balance. At Ball State, I made about $60,000.

When I was making five grand a year, I thought that was all the money in the world. Now I can write a $25,000 check to the Huntsman Cancer Institute. I don't do it for publicity. In fact, nobody except Jon Huntsman knew about the donation until now. My biggest dream would be to hit it big and give something in my dad's name. That's something I'd really like to do.

The point is, money only means so much. If money was my driving force, I'd be the coach of the Warriors right now. Or the Milwaukee Bucks.

Says Keith Van Horn: *"He definitely has the knowledge to coach in the NBA. But I don't know if he'd be able to put up with the players. They're definitely not the type of players he's used to. He's used to players who are willing to accept roles. And some of the players have pretty flamboyant lifestyles. So I don't know if he'd want to put up with some of the stuff that goes on in the NBA. I don't know if he'd really like it."*

Says Drew Hansen: *"For me personally, I didn't think he would go. I don't think he's a coach who could accept sixty losses a year."*

P.J. Carlesimo eventually got the job. He also got Latrell Sprewell's hands around his neck.

With the Warriors romance behind me, I started to concentrate on coaching the Under-22 team. It was important to me, which is why for only the second time in my career I didn't go out recruiting during the summer months. I let my assistants at Utah handle it. The only other time I made that promise was when I was with Nellie's Dream Team II staff.

I enjoyed coaching the Under-22 team, but it was frustrating at times. When USA Basketball selected me as the coach, I thought I'd get guys like Raef LaFrentz of Kansas, Paul Pierce of Kansas, and Vince Carter and Antawn Jamison of Carolina. But none of them came to the tryouts. They were in summer school. I also thought I'd get Mike Bibby, but he was on an overseas trip with his Arizona team.

USA Basketball had a committee that helped pick the team, but I had a lot of input. The committee was very fair. Terry Holland, the athletic director at Virginia and a member of the NCAA tournament selection committee, headed that group. They basically gave me who I wanted. Anyway, it wasn't the committee's fault that certain players pulled out at the last minute.

We could have really used a kid like Robert Traylor from Michigan. You know the guy: Tractor Traylor. He's a load in the low post. He's very physical, which is important in international play. And he's quick enough with his feet to defend perimeter big guys and strong enough to defend anyone inside. He also could score on anyone inside. I've always been very high on him. In fact, I think he's potentially a very good NBA player, if used the right way.

At the time, Steve Fisher was still the coach at Michigan. Our practices began July 6 in Newport Beach, California. Fisher called the night of July 4 and left a voice mail—as if we're all going to check our message machines on July 4—and said Traylor would be a no-show. He said Traylor was going to summer school.

Now that begs the question: Didn't Fisher know Traylor was going to summer school before July 4? And if he did, why would he wait two days before our tryouts began to tell us?

USA Basketball let me have camp anywhere I wanted, so I picked Newport Beach. I love California. We could have had it in Salt Lake City, but I didn't want to host a Fan Night every night, you know what I mean? The fans in Salt Lake are great, but it would have become too much of a distraction. It was the exact opposite in Newport Beach. Nobody cared if we were there or not. It was as if we didn't exist. Southern California is like that. Here we were, the USA's representative for the Under-22 World Championships, and you would have needed the FBI to find us in the local sports pages. It wasn't like people jumped out of their pools, toweled themselves off, and said, "Hurry up, honey, let's go watch Majerus coach the Under-22 team." People didn't even know we were around. We were the stealth team.

As part of our preparation for the World Championships, we played in the L.A. Summer Pro League. That's when I had a minor problem with Scott Padgett, a six-foot-nine junior forward from Kentucky.

I guess I kicked him off the team. It depends on how technical you want to get. He quit and then he changed his mind, but by then it didn't matter. I thought he had a bad attitude and wasn't worth the trouble.

What happened was this: during halftime of a game, he started yelling at Corey Brewer, a kid from Oklahoma. That didn't last long.

"Take a seat and shut up," I told Padgett. "You don't yell at a teammate. He's trying just as hard as you are."

Padgett said something back to me, so I said, "Look, if you don't like it, leave."

Well, he took me up on it. After the game he came back in and apologized and said he'd like to come back. But my mind was made up.

"No, but I wish you a lot of luck," I said. "I'm not going to sit here and dwell on this. But you're not coming back."

And that was that.

To this day, I still don't know who was the best player on that Under-22 team. If you called my assistant coaches on that team—Jim Crews of Evansville, Lorenzo Romar of Pepperdine, and Dick Hunsaker, who's now on my staff—they'd all have separate picks. The NBA guys also used to ask me to name the best player on the team.

If pressed, and I say this with a little bit of prejudice, I'd go with Andre. We pulled him out of summer school and he didn't even know he was coming. He hadn't done anything for two weeks because he was immersed in the summer school program. But he played very well.

Crews, Romar, Hunsaker, and I used to debate which player would make the best pro. That seemed to be the fairest way of picking a top player. You could have made a case for Minnesota's Sam Jacobson or Texas Tech's Cory Carr. Pat Garrity, the kid from Notre Dame, was mentioned, but none of us were sure how his game would translate to the pros. I thought Nebraska's Tyronn Lue was probably the best over-all talent, but he got hurt. That's when we moved Purdue's Chad Austin over to point, and eventually brought in Andre.

We had a good team, but we didn't win the World Championships. In fact, the very best college players from the USA would have been challenged to win the Under-22 title. Even if I would have had Bibby, LaFrentz, Carter, Jamison, and Traylor, I'm not sure we would have won it all.

First of all, the level of international competition has improved dramatically. There are a lot of good players around the world.

Next, you have to deal with the trip to Australia. You've got a thirteen-hour, or sixteen-hour, or whatever-it-is time change and it takes its toll on the body. Going to Australia is like the ultimate road trip. You think going from Salt Lake to Honolulu to play Hawaii is a tough trip. But multiply that trip by two and you've got Australia. You also have to allow for the time zones.

Now if it sounds as if I'm making excuses, I'm not. We got beat . . . not that anyone knew what had happened. People back in the States said you could barely find our results on the agate pages of sports sections. You could poll 100,000 basketball fans, and only ten of them would know we were playing in that competition. But I knew we had lost, and I felt like I let people down. They gave me the head coaching job and I didn't come home with the gold medal. I felt bad about that.

Even the Melbourne papers didn't consider the Under-22 tournament a big deal. Australian Rules Football received the marquee coverage.

I was really intrigued by Australian Rules Football. You've seen those guys on ESPN or FOX Sports. The games are always on about 3:15 in the morning and every players looks like he ought to be a bouncer at a bar on the south side of Chicago. They're tough, physical, athletic, and talented guys.

I went to some of their practices and games, and I really picked up some good things to use for basketball conditioning. We're going to have a leather tamborine, if you can visualize that—a steel rim with leather stretched over it—and make the players box against it for thirty, sixty, and ninety seconds. That's what they do over in Australia. The tambourine is about the size of a small, circular dinner table, or a big war drum. And I'm going to tell you something, you've got to be in great shape to keep hitting that thing. You have to be so conditioned to maintain that pounding. I think it's great for body balance, stamina, aggressiveness, and quick hands. I'm always preaching the importance of active hands, so I'm going to figure out a way to have the tambourine held slightly above the players so they can punch at it. I'm sure they'll be thrilled.

I've already called my strength coach at Utah, and he called the Australian Rules Football people. We're going to get one of those tambourine things. I don't care if I have to pay for it out of my own pocket, we're going to get it. I have no idea what it's called, but it works. All I know is that those Australian Rules Football guys are in magnificent shape.

I also spent some time with the team psychologist of the Hawthorn Club, which is one of the teams in the league and is located in a suburb of Melbourne. He was a fascinating psychologist. His team played in a beautiful old stadium, sort of like the Wrigley Field of Aussie Rules Football. They were one of the most established franchises in the league and they had a player who was considered the Michael Jordan of Australian Rules Football. I can't remember his name, but he was about thirty-six years old. He was revered. He had broken all sorts of records and was loved for his classiness and longevity, as much as he was for his scoring ability.

So the team psychologist and I were standing out on the practice field one day. You have to understand that the fields can be of varying lengths. There's a mininum length, but there's no sameness to the fields. It's kind of like different-sized hockey rinks.

Let's say the field was 140 yards long. The players were out there on a drizzly day and on the horizon you could see this perfect rainbow. The players lined up in three different lines, with about ten yards between each line. They started moving downfield, all the time keeping the football alive with their fists or with their feet. The field was slippery, the ball was oblong, but they didn't have a single turnover in the entire drill. I was flabbergasted. It was like watching my team run a fastbreak drill, except that we always turn the ball over. And we do it indoors, with a smaller, easier-to-handle ball, on a smaller court, in dry conditions.

When the drill was finished, I told the team psychologist, "I can't believe it. These guys haven't turned the ball over yet."

He looked at me with equal amazement. "Of course not," he said, with a certain professional aplomb, "they're not supposed to."

You've really got to admire the simplicity and positiveness of that statement. "They're not supposed to."

I was disappointed we didn't do better in the World Championships, but I understood our limitations. And as always, it was an honor to represent my country. The whole USA Basketball experience has been great for me. I've traveled all over the world, met a lot of wonderful people, and learned more about myself as a coach. I fell in love with a giant tambourine and, as an added bonus, got to go snorkeling on the edge of the Great Barrier Reef.

Later in the summer, I took six of my Utah players—Andre, Doleac, Drew, Jordie, Dave, and Hanno—on a basketball exhibition trip to Europe. Remember my promise to Hanno about playing in his home country? The schedule called for us to play two games in Sweden, two in Finland, and two in Ireland.

The trip was a good prelude to the season. It got the guys some playing time, it exposed them to different parts of the world, and it allowed Hanno to show his teammates his home country. He was so proud to show the guys where he lived.

I had to do a charity fund-raiser in Chicago, so they started the trip without me. The team went to Sweden and Brock Brunkhorst coached the first game. Rich Panella was on the trip and he helped, but I wanted Brock to gain that kind of experience. I know it was only an exhibition game, but it was good for Brock to run the team. They were down at halftime, but came back to win. Now Brock can tell everyone he's undefeated as a Utah interim head coach.

. We only had six players, so practice wasn't a priority. I wanted them semifresh for the games. I also wanted them to have time for sightseeing.

We were scheduled to take a boat to Finland a couple of days after our second game in Sweden. On the night before the boat trip, I gave the team a one o'clock curfew. I usually don't set curfews, mostly because I've never needed to. We had never had anybody late for anything in five years.

But because we were leaving the next day, I decided on one o'clock. I thought that was reasonable enough.

Says Mike Doleac: *"Earlier that day we were at lunch with Coach and the Reebok rep from Sweden. The rep was telling us that the nightclubs didn't get packed until two A.M. at the earliest. We knew about the one o'clock curfew, but the thing was, we didn't have anything to do the next day. We didn't even have a practice scheduled. We were just going to hang out and catch a boat over to Finland.*

"So we were at the hotel, and we were in Andre's room watching TV. It got to be about one o'clock, and I said, 'You guys tired? You want to go to bed?' I mean, this was our last night in Sweden and we kind of wanted to see what the clubs were like. And anyway, what were the chances we'd ever run into Coach?

"Five of us went to the club—Drew didn't go—and as we were walking up, David Jackson said, 'Oh my God, there's Coach!' We thought he was joking. But then we looked up and it was like, 'Holy shit.' It was him.

"We were dead. We walked up to him, but he wouldn't say a word to us. I talked to him the next day, and that wasn't much fun. Our next free day we had the practice from hell.

"Drew wasn't very happy with us, but this was a team concept, so he had to practice. If it's one of us, it's all of us."

As soon as they saw me at the club, they knew they were in trouble. They didn't know if they should come and say hello or turn and run the other way.

The next day Doleac tried to explain to me what had happened and tried to rationalize the whole thing. But I told him, "Mike, this isn't what a captain does. I would have let you guys go out until two o'clock if you had asked. I'm the king of you guys determining that. The only reason I didn't want you out that late is because we have to play a game soon and there's only six of us. I don't want to embarrass you guys or the university or put you in jeopardy of getting injured because you're fatigued. You know yourself, Mike, that when we don't practice or play games, I'll let you stay out as long as you like. But last night wasn't one of those nights."

That curfew incident was a watershed moment for that team, and I'll tell you why. I got them up the next day at 7:00 A.M. and I practiced them from eight until noon. They almost died. I had told them that I wasn't going to have a practice in Europe, and I never had in any of the previous times I've taken teams overseas. But I also never had a team break curfew. To their credit, they expected the practice to be hard. They knew they were wrong, and in a very tangible way, I think the experience brought them closer together.

Drew had told them not to go to the club. He told them they'd never get back in time. But to Drew's credit, he didn't complain about having to go through the four-hour practice, even though he hadn't really done anything wrong. He was a captain, and a captain has to set an example.

Says Drew Hansen: *"During a short break in the practice, Coach came up to me and said, 'I'm really sorry you have to be here. But as a captain, you have to stop these things.'*

"And he was right. It taught me a good lesson. There are points in your life where you have to stand up and choose. That night in Stockholm, I walked the in-between line. They were the ones breaking the rules, but I didn't really do enough to stop them."

I think the team knew how disappointed I was with it. But you know what? The world turns every twenty-four hours. That practice was very tough, and I ran them up and down pretty hard. But they responded well. I was especially proud of Mike and Drew for the way they handled the whole situation.

Mike and Drew had to learn how to be captains and how to take a leadership role. Mike and Drew had had the luxury of having Keith as a captain for three years. Ben Caton was also a sensational captain. Ben and Keith were the two best captains, as a group, I've ever had. That's partly why I think Mike and Drew had a tough time crossing over that line from being one of the guys to being the ones who set the tone and yelled at other players. They had a tough time with that concept. That's something you have to learn, and eventually they did.

The highlight of the trip might have been the visit to Finland. Hanno was so proud. He showed them his house, the countryside, even a Finnish sauna.

We didn't play in front of a very large crowd, relative to what we'd get in the States. But in Finland, on a summer night when it stays light for a long time, it was a very big crowd for basketball—about 1,500 people. We won, and it was a great experience for Hanno, his brothers and sisters, and his girlfriend. Later, we played a game against one of the club teams Hanno used to play for.

We stopped in Copenhagen and then made our way to Ireland. I had originally wanted to go to Finland, the French Riviera, and Italy for the trip. But there was a problem with travel arrangements, so we ended up with a Sweden-Finland-Ireland combination. I had been told the basketball was terrible in Ireland, and they were right. At one game we only had nineteen people in the stands. There were almost more coaches and players than there were fans.

We played a game in rural northwest Dublin, a working man's town. The game was sponsored by the Holy Name parish and afterward something very touching happened. We were invited to a local beer hall, where they served little herring snacks. As everyone knows, Ireland is not the gastronomical capital of Europe. This isn't meant as a criticism, but their idea of a seven-course meal is a six-pack and a potato. I don't know what would have been better: famine or eating those herring snacks.

It was very smoky in the beer hall. Everybody was drinking and smoking, and if they weren't drinking and smoking, they were offering my kids some Irish cremes or pints of beer. Of course, the Mormon kids don't drink, and my other guys knew better. And they didn't know what to do with me. I don't really drink beer, but they kept offering the stuff. They couldn't believe I wouldn't quaff a pint.

Not long after we got there, the Holy Name Society director presented us with a plaque of appreciation. It was so touching. These people had spent their money and time to put together this beautiful plaque. It read, "To the Utes, our friends from faraway. Thank you for honoring our parish and thank you for coming to play us." The coach was so appreciative and so were the townspeople. What they did was such a wonderful gesture.

There was a jukebox blaring some sort of music. A TV was on in the corner. There were smoke clouds from the cigarettes. But that plaque presentation was a moment I'll never forget. It was such a poor parish in such a poor area. And basketball in Ireland means nothing. It's the equivalent of elephant polo in the States. In Ireland, the sports are horse racing, soccer, and a game that resembles field hockey.

We played twice in Ireland—the second night on the west side of Dublin, and in front of about twenty people—and each time, the towns-people took us back to a bar and gave us the best they had. They were wonderful people. Generous to a fault. But I don't think they were ready for the size of our players. One time this little man brought out a small bowl of peanuts. The bowl was about the size of a cup of soup. Doleac reached his hand in the bowl and it was like Godzilla . . . the peanuts were just gone. They brought out some small salmon chunks on little toast wafers. Our guys would stack them up like Dagwood sandwiches and inhale them. The townspeople weren't used to players who were that big and had those types of appetites.

I loved Ireland. The ball's bad, but it was a great experience for me and for my players. I loved the history of the country. And the people were as genuine and as giving as you'll ever find.

It had been an eventful summer, a memorable summer. But now it was time to concentrate on the upcoming season.

I wasn't greedy. All I really wanted in 1997 was a run at the WAC title and, if everything fell into place just right, an NCAA tournament berth. I would have been ecstatic if someone would have promised me those two things. I would have given up custard cones for that deal.

Every once in a while, I drop a little Shakespeare on my team. Some of them probably don't even know it's Shakespeare. They probably think I'm the guy who coined the phrase, "To be, or not to be." Anyway, when we had our first team meeting I told them, "Heavy is the head that wears the crown." I wanted them to understand exactly what was going to happen that season. The new guys didn't have a clue, so I made it perfectly clear.

"For the whole decade, we've been kicking ass in this league," I told them. "We are the biggest game on everyone's schedule every night throughout the mountain west. So you'd better be ready to play every night because you're going to get a different, higher level of effort from these teams. There's going to be a difference in attendance, a more vocal crowd. We're going to be on TV fifteen times this season, but the team we're playing might only be on twice. This is going to be their big mo-ment. But that's fun. That's the fun of playing at Utah. You're going out every night and you're going to get everybody's best shot. And let me tell you, that's a great feeling, when you beat a team that has given its very best against you. That will make you a better player and a better team."

Let's face it, when you think about the best programs in the '90s, you don't automatically think Utah. You think Kentucky, North Carolina, Duke, Arizona . . . those kind of teams. The marquee teams. But entering the 1997–98 season, we had five WAC titles and five NCAA tournament appearances, including one Elite Eight and two Sweet Sixteens.

As expected, the WAC coaches voted New Mexico the preseason favorite. I did the same thing. It was a no-brainer.

There was a lot of talk about the effects of losing Van Horn, sort of a post-Keith syndrome. This was a kid who was an All-American, the three-time WAC Player of the Year, the centerpiece of our offense, a clutch shooter, basketball obsessed, the leading scorer in the history of the WAC and Utah, the No. 2 pick in the NBA draft. During his sophomore, junior, and senior years, we finished 84–17 overall, 45–7 in the WAC, and won three consecutive league titles. Keith helped set the table for this program. He had an amazing work ethic. He was coachable. He had a wonderful practice demeanor. He was committed to academics. You don't replace somebody like Keith with another player. You don't even try.

Despite Keith's impressive resumé, I never felt we wouldn't survive without him. I think initially there were guys looking for Keith, guys who were used to giving him the ball and watching him make the big basket or the big play. But those guys learned to adjust. Drew was one of them. I told him, "Drew, take the shots that come to you. If a shot's there, I want you to take it. I've got no problem with that."

I also told him we'd never run a play for him, never set a shot for him. His job was to get other people their shots. I wanted him to work the ball inside to Mike. That was Drew's mantra: inside, inside, inside.

I've always tried to funnel the ball to the post. Keith was great at establishing position and posting low. Now I wanted Mike to do the same sort of thing. He had the size and the power to do it, plus he had the ability to keep defenses honest with a good perimeter shooting game.

People occasionally compare Mike to Bill Laimbeer, but it's not a good comparison. Mike's feet aren't as quick and he's not as athletic as Laimbeer. Laimbeer was a great shooter, maybe in the top 2 percent of shooters in the NBA. Mike's a very good shooter, but there's a difference.

We were ranked sixteenth in the Associated Press and fourteenth in the coaches' poll at season's beginning. I had no problem with that. I thought Arizona would be really good. I thought Kentucky would be great. I thought Kansas would be great and I thought Carolina would be really good. I also thought Duke would be very good. I just knew the personnel on those teams. Every radio or TV show I did, I always pointed to the Big Five: Kentucky, Arizona, Carolina, Duke, and Kansas. Those were the teams I expected to see fighting for those four spots in San Antonio.

As for us, we were without Keith, Ben Caton, Jeff Johnsen, and Ashante Johnson. Keith moved to the NBA. Caton earned his degree. Jeff went on a Mormon mission. Ashante transferred. We were a mid-to-low top-twenty-five team with three seniors, but ten freshmen and sophomores. We had a lot of questions to answer.

Who would be our new go-to guy?

Where would we get our three-point shooting?

How long would a nagging knee injury keep Britton from practice and games?

Could Al contribute after spending two years getting fat in London during his mission?

Would David Jackson progress or regress?

What would I do when Andre needed rest?

We had some experience, some depth, and I knew we would be a solid defensive team. But we certainly didn't have the look of a team that could dominate the WAC again.

Says Keith Van Horn: *"I didn't underestimate them as much as other people did. First of all, they only lost two guys. No matter what two guys they lost, they only lost two players. And I think an experienced team is always a better team. And a team that has played together is always a better team. Another reason I liked their chances was because they had three NBA players on that team. Anytime you have a college team with three NBA players, you're going to be successful. Mike became a first-round pick. Andre will be an NBA player, as well as Hanno. A lot was made out of me not being there, but I thought they'd be fine."*

What really worried me was Al's physical condition. Like every returning missionary, he was out of shape and had lost that edge you need to play successful Division I basketball. When Al was a freshman, he picked up our system as well as anyone I'd ever had. He was tough, he was lean, he was a greyhound who played disciplined defense and never lacked for hustle plays. He was the best freshman I've ever coached. He dove for balls, took charges, set screens, rebounded, looked for the open man, took the shot if he had it. When he left on his mission, I told a reporter that I genuinely felt sorrow. "We had all the pieces in place," I said. "I was sadder to see him walk out of my life than I was about any girl I have dated. Those weren't tears of joy."

When Al got off that plane in June, I almost wanted to cry. He said he weighed 250, but I say it was more like 270. He looked like the Michelin Man. He was wider than a doubledecker bus barreling down Kensington Road.

I can't say I was completely surprised. I had visited him in England and his living conditions weren't exactly plush. He was in London, but he was on the south side of London, on the other side of the Thames River. He was in a poor neighborhood, primarily Indian and West African. Everything is fried. Indians cook everything in some sort of fat that makes the food taste terrific. It's like cooking something in animal fat and lard, with emulsified butter. It tastes great, but it's the most nutritionally unfit food ever created. You might as well get an ice-cream scoop and just start eating straight butter.

None of this was Al's fault. When you're on a mission, you get your meals where you can. It's not like they had the world's finest salad bar on the corner. He lived in south London, so he ate what they ate. He didn't have much of a choice.

When he left on his mission, he weighed about 188. He was rock-hard, thanks to a lot of work with weights. I was actually on his case to gain weight. He gained it, all right. About eighty pounds, give or take a few. He had a big-time waist. He could have borrowed my belt. I told him, "Al, we'll be getting the same size clothing from Reebok."

As soon as he came back, I got him to the USA Basketball Under-22 trials. He needed to play—the more, the better. But the other coaches weren't impressed with Al. They hadn't seen him as a freshman in 1994, when he averaged 6.7 points, 6.1 rebounds, and 6.0 floor burns. They saw this overweight kid who was basically relearning the game. One of the coaches came up to him and said, "Al, I want you to shower with me tonight. That way I won't feel so bad about my own body."

Jim Crews from Evansville came up to me during the tryouts. I was sipping from a glass of water when he said, "Where'd you get that guy? You find him playing behind a senior citizens' home?"

I nearly spat out my water on that one.

Says Al Jensen: *"I didn't gain eighty pounds. It was more like sixty pounds. I ate fried foods and we lived off peanut butter.*

"Every week we'd get a day off to shop and do our laundry. If we could find another American, we'd try to go out and play basketball. But it wasn't like you could stay in real basketball shape.

"I know Coach thinks missionaries return home different from when they leave. That's something I've asked myself. You definitely grow up and you definitely mature. But from a basketball standpoint, I was so far removed from the game. You almost never saw it on TV. It wasn't part of your life.

"I knew it was going to take a while to get the fire back, the competitiveness. You're on a mission and you're nice for two years, and then you're back with Coach. And I was so out of shape. One of the hardest things I've ever done was get back into basketball shape."

Britton's situation wasn't very encouraging either. Shortly after the beginning of practice, his left knee began bothering him. He was diagnosed with patella tendinitis. The doctors thought rest might heal the injury, so we basically shut him down until mid-December. A redshirt year was a possibility.

Nobody really knew what to make of us. Andy Katz, one of my favorite basketball writers, proved to be something of a visionary. In his report for the Blue Ribbon College Basketball Yearbook, he said we were missing a proven shooter, but that "this squad might be more complete than a year ago, if the returning missionary (Al) and the newcomers (Britton and Carlisle) produce as expected." He also wrote that we had "a new hunger without Van Horn. . . . Now the passion is to prove that Miller and Doleac can be just as successful without Van Horn dominating the lineup." Then he picked us to reach the NCAA tournament and "be a team to watch come March."

That was easy for him to say. But as the season got underway, I started feeling better about my guys and about our chances. Hanno was developing much faster than expected. But the key guy was Caton. His maturity level was tremendous. Like I said, I've coached five sets of brothers in my career at Utah, but this was the first time the younger one had every character trait the older one did. Ben was seven years older than Trace, but they might as well have been twins. Trace shared his brother's work ethic, physical toughness, quiet determination, and courage. And already I could see that Trace was a better shooter than Ben, and a more physical player. When I yelled at him—and I yelled at everybody—he never sulked or needed therapy. He used it as motivation. He was becoming a very good role player for us.

Andre, too, was improving each day. His whole career came in such leaps and bounds. First, he sat out his freshman year as a Prop. 48. Then he didn't start until the second game of league play during his sophomore year. And we lose the game, but go on to have a hell of a record. He had a very good sophomore year, but was pudgy and fat and he had three chins. George Karl occasionally would stop by our practices and he'd grab Andre's chins and his stomach rolls.

By the time he was a senior, his body had undergone a tremendous amount of change. He still wasn't the most buff kid on the team, but at least he didn't have boobs and a saggy chest. When he first got here, he had the exact opposite of the classic basketball body. But he worked very hard to change that.

Says Drew Hansen: *"I knew with Alex coming back from his mission, that we were going to be an outstanding defensive team. I knew Andre was a great defender. I thought I was a pretty good defender. I knew Mike was a great defender. If you have four great defenders on the court, you have a chance to be really good. The question mark was whether we could score. But I kind of had an inkling that even without Keith, we could be so good defensively that it wouldn't matter if we couldn't score as much as the season before."*

Our exhibition season began November 6, with a four-point win against Hungary. Then we beat the California All-Stars by twenty-three points. We opened our regular season schedule with a victory against Cal State–Fullerton and finished the month 5–0.

December began with a trip to Chicago and the United Center for the Great Eight. The Great Eight is where they invite the final eight teams of the previous season's NCAA tournament. We practiced at the Berto Center, which is the Bulls' team facility in a north Chicago suburb. Bulls general manager Jerry Krause was there, so I asked him to talk to the team. He told the guys about the NBA, about what the Bulls look for in draftees, and about the draft in general. The players were spellbound. Plus, I think they loved being in a professional environment: the Bulls' logo on the court, red and white—Utah colors—everywhere. They were in the locker room . . . Jordan's locker room, and I think it was just a neat experience for them. For most of the kids on that roster, it was the closest they would ever come to pro ball. Maybe that's why so many of them wanted their pictures taken in front of Jordan's locker.

I also asked Dick Vitale to address the team. Vitale is so passionate about the game, and that was his message in his little speech. He was good about telling them that basketball was a small part of their total lives. He stressed the same things that we did as a staff: academics, decorum, responsibility, discipline. But it was good that they heard it from someone else.

The Great Eight isn't really a tournament, it's more of a basketball version of boxing night. There are two games one night, two games the next night. We were the undercard in the first night's doubleheader. It was us against Providence, followed by defending national champion Arizona against Kansas, which a lot of people, including myself, thought had enough talent to win the 1998 national title.

The next night it was North Carolina vs. Louisville, and then Purdue vs. Kentucky. Great matchups.

We beat Providence by six, but nobody is going to find a videotape of that game in any time capsule. We had twenty-one turnovers, but as I told everyone after the game, we played hard and beat a short, quick, and athletic team—a team that's everything we're not.

Dave Jackson got a lot of minutes in that game and he deserved them. It was the best he had played since coming to Utah. He had ten points, but what I really liked was his six rebounds, his four assists, and the defensive job he did on Jamel Thomas, an All–Big East Conference forward. Afterward, I guess he told some of the writers that I had challenged him early in the season, that I had been tough on him. And maybe I was tough on him, but no more so than any other player who doesn't give me 100 percent effort. I guess he also said that I'd been riding him, but that he didn't mind, that coaching brought out the best in him. I hoped so, because he was going to get coaching.

Our game finished about nine o'clock Central Time, and the next morning at 5:45, Drew was on a plane back to Salt Lake City for an afternoon interview with a Rhodes scholar committee. Only twelve candidates are interviewed nationwide.

I've always said Drew's mind is a gift from God. Until the end of his sophomore year, he had never earned a grade lower than an A. He got an A-minus in Judicial Process 512. The day after he got the final grade I told him, "You've got it made now. You're not going to graduate with straight As. So the easiest thing to do is get a couple of Bs and not worry about it."

He didn't listen. Telling Drew to settle for an occasional B is like telling me to eat TV dinners. It doesn't compute.

If ever there was a kid who fulfilled the qualifications needed to become a Rhodes scholar, it had to be Drew. I had coached Marc Marotta at Marquette and Rick Hall at Ball State when they were candidates, but of the three, I thought Drew had the most to offer.

No one can ever accuse me of emphasizing athletics more than academics, but with Drew I made even more allowances. Earlier in the off-season, my new strength and conditioning coach told me Drew was missing too many weight-lifting sessions. So the next time the whole team was together, I told the players Drew didn't have to go lift weights. He could skip the mandatory three-a-week workouts during the off-season and the twice-a-week lifting sessions once practice started. There were a few raised eyebrows.

"Look," I said, "if you guys are going for a four-point-oh GPA, summa cum laude status, and a spot in the Michigan Law School, then you don't have to go to weights either."

The way I look at it, it was a good trade-off. Drew's body paid the price, but his academics didn't suffer. I have no regrets about that. Of course, we now had Drew with a body showing wear and tear. We had Al with a fat body. And we had Hanno, and all his bad European basketball habits. But at least he wasn't throwing any more passes while he was in the air or throwing cross-court passes. In fact, I got a huge kick later that year when I heard Hanno doing analysis for a Finnish station during the NBA play-offs. When the Bulls were playing the Jazz in the NBA Finals, apparently Hanno became disgusted with Toni Kukoc's lack of fundamentals. "Look at Kukoc," he said. "Just like a European: jumps into the air and throws the ball."

As it turned out, Drew wasn't selected to advance to a second interview (a candidate from St. Olaf College in Northfield, Minnesota, was the only one asked to do so), but I'll always believe he would have been worthy of the honor. Oxford doesn't know what it missed.

While Drew was in Salt Lake City, we flew to North Carolina for our game against Wake Forest. They didn't have Tim Duncan anymore, but they were 6–0, ranked in the top twenty-five and playing on their home court, where they were 57–2 against nonconference opponents. We had lost to them each of the last two years, so I didn't have to worry about us being overconfident.

Andre was sensational in the 62–53 win. You could see him becoming an extension of the coaching staff. We would tell him something and it would appear in basketball form on the court. That game was the beginning of a new and improved Andre. It was a game where Andre began to establish himself as a consistent force.

We also got a nice effort out of Mike, whom I had really aired out after his effort against Providence, and also from Hanno and, in a reserve capacity, Nate. We held Wake Forest to 28 percent shooting from the field, and out-rebounded them, 43–33. That's what wins basketball games.

I know it wasn't the most artistic win, but I was feeling pretty good after the Wake Forest game. I did my postgame radio show with Bill Marcroft and afterward, several Demon Deacon fans wanted to take a couple of pictures. If people are nice about it, I'll almost always sign an autograph or sit still for a picture. It's not that hard to sign your name or smile for a few seconds. And these people were basketball fans. That's how it is in North Carolina. It's a basketball state, what with Wake, Duke, Carolina, and NC State. Those people down there can tell you who played for what coach in what year, if a kid has a decent drop step, if he can defend, if he has active hands. They're like pseudo coaches with season tickets.

When I was done with the photos, this local high school coach introduces himself to me and then introduces one of his players. I can't remember the kid's name, but I remember what the coach said: "This is the best junior in the state of North Carolina."

As soon as he said that, I knew there was no way he would ever be a Runnin' Ute. Utes don't come from North Carolina. Utes come from Tooele, not Tobacco Road. There is no way that kid was ever going to turn his back on Carolina, or any of those other ACC schools. There's just too much tradition, and probably too much pressure from the locals to stay home.

I asked the kid, "I'll bet you don't even know where Utah is on a map."

"Yeah, I do," he said.

"Okay, I'll bet you a barbecue dinner that you can't name two states that border Utah."

The kid said Nevada and then guessed Colorado. I owed him a dinner. Before he left I told him what I usually tell kids getting ready to make a decision about college. I told him to get a good education. There is nothing more important than a good education. I really believe that.

So there we were, 7–0, ranked in the top ten, and doing it without Keith and without Britton, who didn't begin practicing on a regular basis until December 10. But we were winning, and it wasn't hard to figure out why. We were getting the ball inside to Doleac. Andre was really pushing the ball. And our defense was good. That's the key. From day one, Drew was good defensively. Caton was good defensively. Doleac was good defensively. Al was really good defensively.

I know some coaches who love scoring lots of points and who think offense wins games. But if I had to choose between the two types of teams—a defensive or offensive-oriented one—I'd take the defensively skilled team every time. Then again, that's probably why I'll never win a national championship. You do need an offensive gun to win one of those things. But you coach like your personality, which is why I sit on the bench and coach like Mr. Defense. That's because I was such a crappy offensive player. When you need a radar screen to find the backboard with your J, then you'd better learn how to stay low and wide with your stance. And that's the truth. McGuire was the same way.

But at least I was smart enough to know to let a guy like Andre go offensively.

Because he was so far behind, and because I wanted my assistants to have a day off once in a while, I started working with Britton during Sunday practices. I wanted to encourage Britton and push him.

I usually try not to practice on Sundays. But in Britton's case there were extenuating circumstances and, anyway, he wanted and needed to work out.

With a significant portion of my team being LDS members, the issue of practicing on Sunday is a sensitive one. BYU, as well as several other schools in the country, won't play games on Sunday and, if invited to the NCAA tournament, are automatically placed in Thursday-Saturday brackets, rather than Friday-Sunday brackets. Larry Miller, the owner of the Utah Jazz, won't attend his own team's game if it's played on a Sunday, all because of his Mormon faith.

I respect and applaud those beliefs. But I'm also pragmatic and realistic. In today's world of college basketball, it isn't always possible to keep Sundays free from game schedules or practice schedules. I do what I can. I'm honest with the LDS kids when I recruit them. I tell them there will be occasions when we'll practice on Sundays. And if we do practice on Sunday, I tell the team to pick the time that best suits their church-going needs. If they want to attend church in the morning, then we'll practice in the afternoon. I'm flexible.

I also tell them that I have a lot of good Mormon friends, and I notice their stores are open on Sundays, that they cut a deal on a Sunday, that they make a buck on Sunday. Everybody would prefer not to work on Sunday, but the reality of life is you can't always do what you want to do. And if a recruit feels that strongly about practicing on Sundays, I tell them they shouldn't come to Utah. I tell them I can't promise that we won't practice on Sunday. So far, we've never played a Sunday game, except during the NCAA tournament and once during the 1998 regular season. I've always said I would never agree to a Sunday regular-season game unless it was absolutely warranted, and in the case of the New Mexico game, there were circumstances that had to be taken into account. The game was supposed to be played at the Huntsman Center, but then ABC asked if we would consider a Sunday tip-off. I knew that probably wasn't going to work because of our fans, so we traded dates with New Mexico. We'd play there Sunday on national TV, and they'd come to our place in late February.

At that point, Britton would have played in any game on any day. Sundays . . . Mondays at 6:00 A.M. . . . Tuesdays at midnight . . . it didn't matter. He was frustrated by his knee injury and he was frustrated by me. He was making slow progress, but not enough to satisfy either of us. He was a freshman. Worse yet, he was a freshman trying to overcome a knee injury. That isn't a good combination.

Says Britton Johnsen: *"I'm not going to lie. There were points where I wasn't sure I'd make it. I sat out the first two months of the season. Then I slowly started coming back. But there were points when I was so depressed that I didn't even want to look at the man."*

I wasn't about to risk Britton's health for basketball. He had a knee injury. The time off helped, but his knee was almost always sore. The kid lived on ibuprofen the whole season. After every game and after every practice he iced his knee. The doctors said the injury, patella tendinitis, wasn't serious enough to keep him from playing, but you could tell there was discomfort. Britton was smart about it. He said he would never risk playing with serious pain, and I would have supported him 100 percent. I will never compromise a player's health for a victory.

With any new player, there is an adjustment period. Britton had to get used to my standards, my system, my emphasis on academics, my yelling, and my decisions. He wanted to play. I wanted him to play, but only if he was ready. And he wasn't really ready.

It wasn't until midway through December that Britton made his Utah debut. He played eleven minutes against Azusa Pacific, scored seven points, had seven rebounds, three turnovers, two fouls, and generally looked like someone who hadn't been in live action for months.

I didn't play him on the road against Oregon State, barely played him when the WAC regular-season schedule began, and kept him on the bench the first time we played UNLV, UTEP, and New Mexico.

The Oregon State game was not Britton's finest moment as a Ute. This was a game I scheduled so Doleac and Jackson could play in Portland, in front of the same people who had seen them play in high school. We played it at the Rose Garden, which is where the Trail Blazers play, and it was a hell of a game.

We fell behind, 18–4, and committed fifteen turnovers in the first half. They trapped us, pressed us, forced us into a playing tempo that didn't suit our style. We eventually made some adjustments and kept our undefeated season alive. I was so happy for us, and even happier for Mike, who played so well in the game. He had twenty-one points, nine rebounds, hit a three-pointer, and converted seven of eight foul shots.

I remember when he signed his letter of intent in November of his senior year in high school. I was ridiculed by writers in Portland. They couldn't believe it. But Mike is what I call a manufactured player. He doesn't have an array of athletic skills, but he plays with such an intelligence and he compensates with heart, a big body, and a soft shooting touch.

After the game, I came into the locker room just in time to see Britton throwing soda cans against the wall in anger. He was mad that he hadn't played. Never mind that we had overcome a fourteen-point deficit, or that one of his teammates had had a special night, or that we were 10–0 and off to one of the best starts in Utah basketball history. I went right after him.

"Look," I said, "you just grow the hell up here, sit your butt down or else you're never going to play. We just had a wonderful win, we came back against a good team, and if I thought you could have helped us, I would have played you. But there was nothing I could do. You weren't ready for this yet. Your time is going to come. You're a hell of a player, but you've got to be happy for the success of this team. This team is built on guys supporting each other, and I'm not going to tolerate your behavior. If you want to act this way, then go back to your junior high friends, because this is what thirteen- and fourteen-year-old kids do. You'll play when I play you and when I feel you're ready. I'll play you when you have an opportunity to be successful and help the team."

And from that point on, I never had another problem with Britton. That was a watershed moment in his career.

Says Britton Johnsen: *"I could see why he was a little overprotective. I hadn't done anything the first two months of the season. I was a step behind and I wasn't picking up things very well. It was frustrating and I was always upset because I wanted to play. He was always asking me how I was doing. I understood why he was bringing me along slowly. But that didn't make it any easier to take. The only thing you could do was to try harder in practice and convince him you deserved the playing time."*

By the end of December, we were 11–0. By the end of January, we were 18–0 and hadn't had a game closer than six points. We were ranked third in the country, had set a school record for consecutive victories, and yet, as I would later find out, there was something wrong with our team.

We didn't suffer from a lack of effort. The guys played hard and, considering we had ten underclassmen on a thirteen-man scholarship roster, they played with a lot of chemistry and continuity. We knew how to play defense, how to rebound, and how to listen and learn. I knew we were living in a fantasy world—there was no way we were going to do an Indiana and finish undefeated—but I wanted the guys to enjoy the wave.

And that turned out to be the problem. Nobody was enjoying the experience.

When we beat BYU January 10 at their place, it was our sixth consecutive win against our biggest rival. But that was a game where we didn't play smart. Al fouled out with almost thirteen minutes left to play. We had a nice run in the first half and then let it get away from us. That's when I had a "discussion" with the team at halftime. One of the lone bright spots was Caton, who was fast becoming one of my favorites.

Playing at BYU is no easy thing. A year earlier Trace was riding a bus to and from games in Alamosa, Colorado. Try finding Alamosa on a map. I think somebody said there were three times the amount of people in BYU's Marriott Center as there are in all of Alamosa. But Trace played with so much poise. He was a difference maker. That was also the game when I was introduced to our new school president, Dr. J. Bernard Machen. I knew he had come from the University of Michigan, so one of the first things I said to him was, "You've got to help me get Drew Hansen into Michigan's law school." I guess you can call that power networking. Plus, I wanted the very best for Drew. I knew he had always dreamed of going to law school at Michigan or Stanford.

It was also during this win streak that I noticed Andre becoming more of a factor. There was no question he was the best point guard I had ever coached. But what really impressed me was his ability to stay calm under difficult circumstances. We played at Air Force in late January and something happened during the game where I started yelling at one of our guys. Instead of focusing on the game, I lost my concentration. Air Force switched defenses, but I didn't know it until Andre came over to the bench and said we needed to switch to another offensive set. I usually make those calls, but this time Andre was alert enough to make the call for me—and he was absolutely right.

There were a couple of other things that happened in that Air Force game. For the first time that season, Al bore a resemblance to the pre-LDS mission Al. He put a big-time glove on this kid from Air Force, Jarmica Reese. Reese was the seventh-leading scorer in the country at the time, but Al, as well as some of our other guys, did a great job shutting him down. Reese had averaged twenty-two shots in his three previous games. He got off nine against us and finished with thirteen points. Al had seventeen points, six rebounds, and some key steals down the stretch. And you could tell he was slowly working himself into shape. He still didn't have the spring and lift in his legs he had before he left, and his body wasn't what it used to be, but he was trying hard. He would stay after practice and ride the stationary bike for an hour. His body fat went down. His commitment was everything I had expected.

One other thing. A lot of people in our conference think Air Force is a gimme win. I know their record in WAC play isn't very good, but I always admire how hard they play. They play with so much tenacity and pride. I said it that night, and I'll say it again: Those are the kind of guys who should be flying the *Enola Gay*. If there's ever another *Enola Gay*, those Air Force guys will be the ones flying it. They're fearless.

As it turned out, February might have been the most pivotal month of the season for us. So much happened—not all of it pleasant—but no month helped shape us as a team more than those twenty-eight days.

Remember the schedule switch with New Mexico? Well, we went to Albuquerque and lost the game on national television, 77–74. It was a controversial finish. Some people say we got cheated in that game. All I know is that we had a nine-point lead with three minutes to go and we let it slip away.

Then we came home and beat BYU in a game where Al took an elbow on the chin and had to get twelve stiches to close it up. It was also a game where there were fifty-four fouls called. I told reporters that I had been to beerfests, bratfests, and now, a foulfest.

We beat Rice on the road, came home, and got ready for another road trip, this time to Wyoming and then Colorado State. That is a bastard of a trip, and the first mistake I made was flying the team into Laramie the day of the game. I've made that trip every way I can, but this time we took Huntsman's plane over there—it's only a forty-two-minute flight from Salt Lake City—and the plan backfired. I don't think I'll ever do that again.

Wyoming beat us by six in a game we let get away from us. First, we didn't play tough or hard, and we weren't ready to play. Second, Wyoming played with a great passion, especially after we had beaten them by seventeen points at our place. Third, Doleac didn't get down in the low post and establish a low post presence.

We flew to Colorado State and the staff and I watched tape of the Wyoming game until 4:00 A.M., and then again from seven o'clock to ten. The players watched it from ten to three. I wanted Doleac to understand how important it was that he get inside and stay inside. I told him I didn't care if he missed every shot from that point on, but that I wanted him to get wide, get those size seventeens close to the hole, and establish a post position. If he wanted to take an occasional three-pointer, fine . . . that's a bonus. But we were going to win with him in the post. That's where he had to do it for us.

Says Jeff Strohm: *"There was a play in the Wyoming game where Al Jensen didn't hustle and run. Coach ran that one play back and forth, back and forth, back and forth. He played it fifteen times. I counted. But Coach never brought the losing up."*

After the film session, we practiced. And after the practice, Mike and Drew approached me. They wanted to talk about some things.

Says Mike Doleac: *"Coming into the season, we had the same goal as usual: to take the season a step further. We were on our way to doing that, but something was different.*

"I can remember sitting on the bus after beating BYU in January, and we were all so pissed. We were undefeated and had just beaten our big rival, but there weren't many smiles. We were all looking at each other and it was like, 'What the hell?' We were a Division I team, we were undefeated, but we were all pissed and wondering why we weren't doing well. It was like, 'How is this happening?'

"Then later we lost at New Mexico and then at Wyoming. Even with those losses, we had a hell of a record and we were doing a great job, but nobody was having any fun."

Says Drew Hansen: *"We went up there on behalf of the whole team. We all took losing hard. But when we lost a game, Coach relived every play. Then he would relive every play with each player. He was yelling at every player. We had lost two games, but we felt like we had lost 100. We just wanted to loosen him up. So we decided it was time to talk to him. We spent maybe twenty minutes talking basketball and about ninety minutes talking about the function of a team. This was a big deal to us. It was a critical part of our season.*

"After that meeting, he went out of his way to build up our morale. He'd always ask, 'You having fun?' "

Drew and Mike took me upstairs at the hotel in Fort Collins and they didn't pull any punches. They said I had been really hard on the players, that I had been uptight, that I had been especially hard on Dave and Jordie. They also wanted me to bring Donny and Jud off the road recruiting. Donny and Jud are much more easygoing, and they thought those two guys would be a good counterbalance.

It took some guts to do what Mike and Drew did, but that's why they were captains. That's part of their responsibility, to step forward and be team spokesmen. They were respectful, but they also got their points across. It was a good meeting and I listened. I took what they said to heart.

It was also after the Wyoming game that I made the decision to start playing Britton. He had gotten minimal minutes and hadn't even played in the game in Laramie. I just didn't think he was ready. But now it was time.

"Britton, you've been practicing your ass off. I love the way you're working. You deserve to play. I still have a little bit of consternation, but I probably went too far with that. I don't want you to lose your confidence. Your practice habits have been outstanding. Now you go out there and I don't care how many mistakes you make, as long as you play hard. I don't care if we lose every game, you're not going to sit again."

We played Colorado State two days after the Wyoming loss and anyone tuning into ESPN that night saw one of the great defensive efforts in WAC history. We held them to fourteen first-half points, they held us to eighteen. We made seven of twenty-eight shots in the period, they made six of twenty-four. You could almost hear the television sets being clicked off around the country.

But I love defense. And even though Britton didn't know all of his assignments and made some mistakes, I loved his enthusiasm on the court. He had practiced so hard and he deserved the playing time. He ended up with six points and one rebound in twelve minutes, and we ended up with a 60–48 win.

It was a special victory for a lot of different reasons. It had been such an emotional trip, what with the loss to Wyoming, and then the meeting with Drew and Mike, and then the situation with Britton. But I was so happy with the way everybody played against Colorado State. It was also my three-hundredth career win and afterward, Strohm got the game ball and all the guys presented it to me. So the whole trip was a watershed experience. For me and for the team.

Says Jeff Strohm: *"I think about his three-hundredth victory and it still brings chills. The kids gave him a five-minute standing ovation in the locker room after the game. He kept telling them to be quiet, to stop the cheering, but they wouldn't do it. They gave him the game ball, and I can remember Doleac saying, 'Coach, whatever it took, we were going to win that game.' And I heard Andre tell Brock, 'I'm so tired, but I knew I wasn't coming out of that game. I wasn't going to let Coach take me out. I wanted to do whatever it took to win for him.' "*

We had a nice little run for the remainder of the month. We beat Air Force and UNLV, dodged snowstorms long enough to get into El Paso and beat UTEP, and then returned home for Senior Night and our game against New Mexico.

This time there wasn't an agonizing ending. We won by ten, claimed a fourth consecutive WAC regular season championship, and earned a No. 1 seed in the WAC tournament. This was a night for my players, especially Drew and Mike, who were playing in their final game at the Huntsman Center. I just wanted to sneak into the tunnel and enjoy their moment as the players took turns climbing up the ladder and cutting the net.

Drew and Mike had smiles as wide as basketballs. It was their fourth WAC title in four years and they had helped produce a 109–19 record during that time. Incredible. I doubt if two players will ever experience those kind of numbers and that many consecutive championships.

Drew and Mike each took turns on the public address system after the game. I got a kick out of Drew's comments when he said, "I know change is inevitable, but for four years we've owned this league." I liked that. I wanted the players to feel a sense of accomplishment. Of course, I could have done without Drew asking the crowd to chant, "Rick! Rick! Rick!" I know why he was doing it—there were all sorts of rumors concerning the Arizona State job—but I wanted this night to be centered on the players, not me.

Next up was the WAC tournament. To this day, I'll never understand why the league wanted to play the tournament in Las Vegas. First of all, I'm old enough to remember the City College of New York betting scandal in 1951, after they won both the NIT and NCAA in 1950, which ended basketball at CCNY. And you don't have to be so old to remember the Tulane scandal, or the Boston College scandal or the Northwestern scandal. To think there isn't a danger of gambling in college sports is beyond naivete.

I know the Vegas casinos don't take bets on the WAC tournament when it's in town. So what? It still isn't a healthy environment for a college athlete. We're supposed to show them a tape on gambling. Do I show it to the boys when they're checking their Keno cards? You want a kid to wake up in the morning, roll out of bed, brush his teeth, and then go downstairs to the lobby and roll the bones? Or see if he can double down on a pair of tens? Or maybe play a parlay? When we played UNLV earlier in the season, we stayed at the Crown Plaza Hotel. Why? No casino.

Don't get me wrong. I love Las Vegas. I love the restaurants, the shows, the casinos, the music, the hotels. You think the restaurants don't like seeing me walk in the door? And you should see the casinos. They love a sucker like me who thinks he's Mr. Vegas. Believe me, the chips don't spend much time in my hand.

Vegas is a great town. I just don't think the WAC tournament should be there. We constantly tell these kids not to gamble and to beware of gamblers. At Northwestern, they put in a new One-Strike-You're-Out policy. If you're caught gambling illegally—and that means Internet gambling, Final Four pools, fantasy leagues—you lose your scholarship. And if you're a member of the athletic department, you lose your job.

But at the WAC, we not only played our tournament at the gambling capital of the world, but we had our players stay in casino hotels. What sort of message is that? It can only lead to trouble.

We didn't stay long in Vegas. That's because UNLV upset us in the tournament quarterfinals, 54–51. I have to take a lot of the blame for the loss. Not only did we get out-played, out-rebounded and out-hustled, but we got out-coached. I didn't have the team ready for UNLV's zone defense and I made a mistake by looking ahead.

And once again I didn't trust myself with Britton. I only played him six minutes. I promised myself I wouldn't make the same mistake again.

Says Britton Johnsen: *"He called me in and actually apologized for not playing me more. How many coaches would do something like that? It happened right after our game against Las Vegas. I had had a pretty good first half against them: no big mistakes, hit a three, worked hard, blocked a shot. But then he didn't play me whatsoever in the second half. I couldn't understand why. He said he just didn't feel comfortable putting me in.*

"But at our next practice, in front of all the guys, he apologized and told me, 'For the rest of the season, we're going to win with you or lose with you. No matter what, you're going to play.'

"From that point on, I felt like I had his complete confidence. I think he realized maybe I could help out a little bit."

Says Mike Doleac: *"That loss to UNLV was the best thing that could have happened to us because we kind of looked at each other and said, 'We're not playing as best as we can. We're not being aggressive enough.' "*

Never did I think we'd finish the regular season with a 25–3 record, or another WAC championship, or a guaranteed at-large bid to the NCAA tournament. We had answered most of those questions asked at season's beginning.

Who would be our new go-to guy? Well, there were three guys: Mike, Andre, and Hanno.

Where would we get our three-point shooting? We picked our spots with threes, but Mike, Drew, Caton, and Dave all shot 40 percent or better from the arc, and Andre was close.

How long would a nagging knee injury keep Britton from practice and games? Britton was never 100 percent during the season, and he wouldn't be 100 percent during the postseason. He became close, personal friends with icepacks and ibuprofen. But as long as he felt comfortable playing with the nagging pain, I was going to play him.

Could Al contribute after spending two years getting fat in London during his mission? He still wasn't the old Al, but he was getting there. He had started all thirty games, been our second-leading rebounder and our second-leading assists man. And he was a joy to watch on the defensive end. But I still couldn't get him to shoot.

Would David Jackson progress or regress? He gave me glimpses of progress, but only glimpses.

What would I do when Andre needed rest? This was my number one concern entering the NCAA tournament.

One other question still remained: Would I make good on an earlier promise to give up custard cones if we made a run at the WAC title and were invited to the NCAA tournament?

Give up custard cones? Never.

7
Sheer Madness

F or whatever reason, we couldn't get a plane out of town after the WAC tournament, and we didn't have Huntsman's private plane this time. So I put the guys on a bus back to Salt Lake City and I rented a car for the six-hour drive. About thirty miles out of Vegas I said, "What the hell am I doing this for?" and I turned around and eventually got on a flight back to Utah.

When I got back to the hotel, I looked at tape from our Thursday night loss to UNLV. The team had off on Friday and we practiced Saturday. The NCAA tournament bids came out on Sunday.

We knew we were in the tournament, but where? And against whom? I wasn't so concerned about seeds, because if you don't win your first game, who cares what your seeding is? I mean, sure, a higher seed is better, but I'd never taken a first-round game for granted, and I wasn't about to start now.

When the bids came out, I was sitting with my friend Bob Henderson and Kerry Rupp, a really good coach at East High in Salt Lake City. We were talking and Bob said, "Well, there's one good thing about this bracket."

"What's that?" I said.

And Bob said, "Well, we'll have to beat the likes of Arizona or Maryland or West Virginia or Cincinnati. So if you beat them, you won't have to worry about Kentucky until the championship game."

I said, "Christ, that's the last thing we got to worry about. If we face Kentucky in the championship game, I'll lie down and let them run over me again."

When the tournament began, I didn't even know where Kentucky was seeded. All I knew was that they weren't around us. I hadn't even thought about any other brackets. I didn't even start analyzing the brackets until I got a call to go on the *Up Close* show and talk about the tournament. When I went on, I said, "If I had to pick somebody, I'd pick Kentucky. They were the national championship runner-up. They've got a lot of those kids back from that team. They've been there before. And anytime you can take a guy like Jeff Sheppard and say to him, 'You're redshirting, we don't need you to make another title run'— and he's in a title run subsequent to his redshirt year, then you've got a hell of a program."

I was really just focused on our first game: San Francisco. I respect those kinds of teams. I've never lost a first-round game in the NCAA tournament and I think part of the reason is that I don't overlook low-seeded opponents. In fact, I told our guys, "Look, I just want to win one more game. I just want to beat San Francisco. Pack for one night. If we win, I don't even care if you wear dirty clothes the next day. All we're worried about here, fellas, is San Francisco."

That's what I was telling the team, and I believed every word of it. But I did let my mind wander just a little bit. In the office pool, I picked us to win the whole thing. I always do. Hey, if you don't believe in yourself, no one else will.

The first and second rounds were played in Boise, Idaho. That was a plus for us. It was a relatively easy trip for our fans. It was in the same time zone, and we had played there before. Doleac and Drew had played at Boise State as freshmen, so that was somewhat of an advantage. I had some contacts up there as far as practice facilities. I also knew a restaurant I could send the kids to, and I knew a good restaurant I wanted to go to.

We were seeded No. 3 in the regional. Arizona was No. 2. San Francisco was No. 14.

San Francisco was a very athletic team. Phil Mathews was the coach. He had coached Brandon Jessie earlier in his career, and had been the best man at Donny's wedding, and vice versa. I liked the guy. When he came to Salt Lake City to see Donny, I would always let him watch our practices or sit in on our film sessions. Had I known we were going to end up playing them in the first round, I don't know if I would have

◄ My sisters called me "Ricky." *Rick Majerus Collection.*

▼ Me in 1962. *Rick Majerus Collection.*

▶ My high school graduation photo.
Rick Majerus Collection.

▼ Like father, like son: my dad, Raymond Majerus.
Rick Majerus Collection.

▲ Nellie (*center, kneeling*) didn't have to tell Dream Team II much about basketball. That's Joe Dumars, one of the classiest guys in the game, on the far left, sitting.
Courtesy University of Utah Sports Information Department.

▼ The blue blazer and Windsor knot years at Marquette. That's my assistant, Bob Voight, on the right. *Marquette University.*

The bench of the fashion-challenged: me, Don Nelson (*middle*), and Don Chaney (*far right*) with Dream Team II. *Courtesy University of Utah Sports Information Department.*

▲ Trying to get a point across to my Ball State team. Note the Avia shoes. Nike wasn't exactly knocking down our door in Muncie.
John Huffer, Ball State Photo Services.

▶ Coaching the Ball State team during the NCAA tournament.
John Huffer, Ball State Photo Services.

▲ Listening to one of my favorite players, MOKay McGrath, a captain on our 1992 team. *Courtesy University of Utah Sports Information Department.*

▼ Concentrating on the sideline during the 1996-97 season. *Courtesy University of Utah Sports Information Department.*

▲ Mike Doleac (*back row, second player from the left*) and Andre Miller (*front row, far right*) were members of my 1997 USA Men's 22-and-Under World Championship entry. *Courtesy University of Utah Sports Information Department.*

▼ Two of the best feelings a coach can have: climbing the ladder, cutting down the net after another WAC championship. *Courtesy University of Utah Sports Information Department.*

◄ Acknowledging one of my friends in the crowd after a big win.
Courtesy University of Utah Sports Information Department.

▼ A coach's nightmare: an indifferent referee.
Courtesy University of Utah Sports Information Department.

▲ The President of Armenia, me, and friend Jon Huntsman. *Rick Majerus Collection.*

▼ Giving instruction to Mark Rydalch (*left*) and Keith Van Horn.
Courtesy University of Utah Sports Information Department.

▶ Once the game begins, I don't spend much time sitting on the bench. Longtime Utah assistant Donny Daniels is on the left. *Courtesy University of Utah Sports Information Department.*

▼ Andre goes hard to the hoop against North Carolina in the national semifinal game. Andre finished with 16 points, 14 rebounds, and seven assists. *Courtesy University of Utah Sports Information Department.*

Taking the court minutes before our national championship game against Kentucky at the Alamodome. That's me, followed by our assistants Donny Daniels, Jeff Judkins, and Brock Brunkhorst.
Courtesy University of Utah Sports Information Department.

Kentucky's Jeff Sheppard and Andre embrace moments after the national championship game. Kentucky deserved its share of handshakes.
Courtesy University of Utah Sports Information Department.

A sight I'll never forget: Utah in the title game. *Courtesy University of Utah Sports Information Department.*

been so generous. But that's how it worked out and anyway, we had to beat them on the floor, not with VCR remotes.

This was San Francisco's first NCAA tournament appearance in sixteen years. Once upon a time, the program was a national power-house. They won the championship in 1955 and 1956, the first two of many titles—college and pro—that Bill Russell would win.

As athletic as San Francisco was, they couldn't match our size or strength. Doleac went to the foul line seventeen times. Hanno got a lot of good looks, but didn't play particularly well. Drew hit five of six shots. We shot 62.5 percent; they shot 41.5 percent.

It was a close game for a while, but by halftime we had a thirteen-point lead. With our style of play, that's a lot of points for our opponent to have to overcome. We're not going to shoot quick and let you get control of the tempo of the game.

I'll tell you something else that I'll remember from that game. It was Drew. There was about 1:28 left to play, we had the game in hand, and Drew went hard after a loose ball. He didn't have to do that. We had the game won. But that's why I love that kid. He wasn't playing San Francisco. He was playing against the proverbial toughest opponent: himself.

Afterward, Phil asked me to come on his radio show and I did it. But it was a little bit awkward. Still, I've never forgotten how nice Phil was to me when I was recruiting Brandon Jessie. It was the least I could do in return.

We had done exactly what I wanted to do: win the first game. So what if the guys had to wear the same clothes again? That's why God invented the laundromat and dry cleaning.

Says Jeff Strohm: *"People don't know this, but before the San Francisco game, Coach sat Andre down in the hotel restaurant in Boise. He said, 'If we're going to win, you have to have more freedom. Andre, I'll live with your decisions. You have 100 percent green light.'*

"That's really hard for Coach to do. But he did it, and I think that had a lot to do with Andre having such a great run in the tournament."

Arkansas was next. Nolan Richardson's team was seeded sixth and they had beaten Nebraska, 74–65, in its first-round game. This would be a tough matchup for us. Look, I've heard coaches say it doesn't make a difference who they play next in a tournament. Hell, I've probably said it myself. But let me tell you who you say that to: you say it to the press.

In your heart, if you say it doesn't make any difference who you play, that means you either have a hell of a team, or you're an idiot. With all due respect to Nebraska, I would have rather played them, not Arkansas.

At the subregional, you could watch all the teams practice. Anybody could. People off the streets, coaches, anybody. It was like open-gym night at the CYO. A lot of coaches don't like to watch an opposing team practice, but I think it's worth the time. It gives you a chance to see players in person, rather than just on film. You get a better sense of their size and athleticism. With Arkansas, Nolan has this style of play where his philosophy is a lot like McGuire's or John Chaney's at Temple. He just says: "This is how we're playing. Take a look at it. Beat it if you can. We're coming at you and we don't care how you play. We're playing our way, win or lose."

Arkansas was tenacious. That Forty Minutes of Hell slogan that Nolan has? He isn't kidding. That press of Arkansas' was just so tenacious. They led the Southeastern Conference in steals, turnover margin, and scoring. Now I know why.

Their backflow was sensational. What I mean by backflow is that as you beat their press, they would come from behind and strip the ball or steal the pass. You might beat the first line of their press, but they would do such a good job of establishing another line. And they really tried to get in the passing lanes, trying to pick off passes and deny us. But we did a good job of setting back picks and relieving pressure.

Drew was invaluable in a game like that. He knows how to move to get the ball and get it changed or get someone in position to get the ball and get it changed.

We knew who we wanted to stop. It was this kid Pat Bradley. He had led the SEC in three-pointers, so we made that a defensive priority. I told our guys, "This kid is not going to beat us." He's the guy we tried to shut down.

Arkansas was quick, but we handled what I thought would be the toughest press in the tournament. We had twenty turnovers, but we shot nearly 57 percent from the field and held them to about 42 percent. And Bradley? He got five shots, three of them from the arc. He made one. We won the game, 75–69.

We were going to the Sweet Sixteen.

After the game, Nolan came up and said, "Good luck," and he meant it. Some guys say it and don't mean it. He did. He said we did a good job. He's a classy guy.

There's another reason why I never look ahead in the tournament:

you can't predict what will happen. We thought we'd beat UNLV in the WAC quarterfinals, but we lost. Cincinnati probably thought it would beat West Virginia in the second round of the West, but it lost on a last-second shot by a kid named Jarrod West. No. 1 seeded Kansas thought it would beat Jim Harrick's Rhode Island team in the second round of the Midwest Regional, but it lost.

On the other side of the West bracket, things were going more according to seeds. Arizona was going to be in Anaheim, and so was No. 4 seeded Maryland.

As for my preseason Big Five, everybody was still alive, with the exception of Kansas. You know, say what you will about Harrick, but that guy never got the credit he deserved when he coached UCLA to a national championship. The guy knows what he's doing out there.

When we got back to Salt Lake City, I had the staff come over to the hotel and we had a Sunday afternoon meeting in the hot tub near the pool. That's probably not the way Phog Allen did it, but it was a good way to relax and get some work done at the same time.

Don Meyer, a highly successful NAIA (National Association of Intercollegiate Athletics) coach at Lipscomb University in Nashville, and Kerry Rupp came by later and we sat in the lobby with our yellow legal pads and talked about West Virginia. I've known both of these guys for years. Don has a lot of interesting ideas, and he and his assistants have spent lots of time at my practices and meetings. Kerry not only coaches, but he moonlights as the executive director for the Karl Malone Foundation for Kids. I asked him to break down some tapes of West Virginia while we were in Boise.

I don't have any problem with going outside my own staff for expertise and help. Ideas are ideas. It doesn't matter if they come from a local high school coach or someone from an NAIA program. I don't look at the source of the idea, I look at the merit of it. Anyway, who's to say I have all the answers? I like input. I like constructive criticism and suggestions. All those things can only make you a better coach.

I hadn't seen Betsy for a while, so I had dinner at her house, stopped on the way back at the 7-Eleven for some bottled water, Häagen-Dazs, and Tootsie Rolls, and then went up to my room to watch tape from West Virginia's games against Temple, Miami, and Cincinnati. A radio station called a little before eleven, so I did the interview while I was watching the tape.

West Virginia liked to apply pressure defensively, but as Don and I reviewed the tapes, I knew they were going to do more than press and trap. "They're going to zone the hell out of us," I told Don. "They'll see the Vegas tape from the WAC tournament. If I saw that tape, I'd zone the hell out of us too."

I don't take notes when I watch tape. I'm also not big on names. I remember jersey numbers and tendencies. Like, when I was watching West Virginia that night, I could see that number 24 was a hell of a wing player. I didn't know his name was Damian Owens, and that he was second in the nation in steals until he hurt his back against Seton Hall late in the season. Or that he averaged 16.7 points and 6.3 rebounds, and was probably the Big East Conference player of the year. I found that stuff out later, but when you're watching tape, you look at what kind of player he is. This guy was good.

"Don, when he gets on the wing, you better be ready to play," I said. "I can't put Drew on number 24. This number 24 is dangerous. He's a senior and he's confident."

The message light on my room phone was blinking like crazy, but I didn't have time for that. And it wasn't until later that I realized I had left the pint of ice cream, slowly melting in a plastic bag, on my bed. I wanted to see more of West Virginia. So Don and I went through the edited-down tapes of their key players.

There used to be a time when I was the king of the VCR remote control. Not anymore. I kept rewinding too much or fast forwarding too little. It was a mess. I tossed the thing to Don and said, "Here, run this thing. It's out of control."

I'm not good with high-tech stuff. I don't own a computer, nor do I know how to use one. I don't know how to turn one on, and that's the truth. It's easier to use a lawnmower.

Jon Huntsman and I talked about this once. Neither one of us is computer literate. I actually used to be proficient with electronic gadgetry. There was a time when I could stop a frame of film on a dime or go through fast forward and come within a couple of frames of where I wanted to be.

Not anymore. I can still use a VCR, but only if it involves a basketball tape and the most basic of skills. I have no idea how to set a timer or set VCR Plus or work the remote control with the required expertise to watch film.

We just bought a new video system at Utah. It cost $100,000. It's called AVID. A lot of pro teams have it. It will be good for Strohm and Brock. You can punch in exactly what video clips you want to see. It saves a lot of time.

Of course, my other two assistants, Donny and Jud, will be mystified by it. They'll have a better chance of figuring out the mystery of the Trinity. And I'm right with them. The three of us would be more inclined to discover the Father, the Son, and the Holy Ghost than to figure out how to use that machine. You almost have to be young, smart, and plugged into it. I'll never learn how to use it. I don't want to know.

I'm not the only one intimidated by the electronics and computer age. Krzyzewski still uses the old reel-to-reel projector. You get a comfort zone, and that's what you do. I'm the same way. To me, computers are like Far Eastern mysticism turned technical. Plus, my fingers are so damn big and gnarly. I can't type. I couldn't even turn the gas grill on the other night for a barbecue. How embarrassing is that? I knew the gas part was working because I could smell it. Then someone came out, flicked the switch, and that was that.

Some staffs are great at using computers and the latest video equipment. We're not. We're in the Stone Age. But you know what? That's okay. It's like I told this kid I was recruiting in Louisiana last fall. I said, "I'm going to come in and I'm not going to have any films. I'm not going to have a thing to hand you. I'm not going to have a card. And I'm not going to run a video or any presentation of any kind. I don't know what I'm going to say. But that's why I want Donny to come in later and show you those sort of things. He'll hand you some literature that your parents might find interesting. But look, I'm going to bet you anything that other college coaches are saying the same things I'm saying, either before I come in, or after. And if they're not, then I've lied to you and don't come."

I think sometimes you can get too fancy. Some schools have these wonderfully prepared videos promoting their programs. It's as if Francis Ford Coppola directed them. They're beautiful. You want to order popcorn and a soda, applaud and nominate it for the Short Films category of the Academy Awards. We don't have anything like that.

By the end of the film session, I knew 24 loved to go to his left. So did 23, the guy who beat Cincinnati with a last-second twenty-two-foot bank shot. The other guard, 5 (Adrian Pledger), liked to go to his right. I'd figure out the rest later.

It was 12:02 when we clicked off the TV. Don left, and all I wanted was a hot shower and then some sleep. I got one out of two.

Monday, March 16

I got up about 7:30 and watched film in bed for three hours. It's really the only quiet time I have each day.

My room was something of a mess. Boxes of size-twelve Reeboks stacked on the floor. Unopened three-packs of Nordstrom underwear. New T-shirts. Polo shirts and sweaters were everywhere. I had a half-packed red Reebok bag sitting near the bed. I had to get organized. I didn't even know the date. I had to ask Kelly Miller, our basketball secretary, what day it was.

Kelly had stopped by the hotel to go over all my day-to-day stuff. She spread thirteen manila folders on my king-size bed, each one containing a separate piece of required business; recruiting, speaking engagements, basketball camp planning, personal schedule. You name it, it was in those folders. When we were done, I told Kelly, "I'm going downstairs to try to get thirty minutes of exercise for this body. Tell Strohm to meet me down there."

I had to work out. When I get nervous, I eat. When I eat, I'd better exercise. So I went to the hotel workout room, which is this area, glass-enclosed on three sides, with a perfect view of the snow-capped Wasatch Mountains. It was a beautiful day . . . and I couldn't have cared less. I was preoccupied with 24, 5, and 23.

By the time Strohm got there, my USA Basketball shorts and Wisconsin T-shirt were soaked. I know I don't look like it, but I'm in pretty good aerobic shape. I pound the hell out of those Stairmasters.

As I did the Stairmaster, I started dictating thoughts to Strohm. Efficient as usual, he had his yellow legal pad and silver pen ready. He probably had a couple of extra pens in his pocket and a spare notepad tucked in the back of his pants. Very organized, this guy.

"Number 10 is a shooter," I said, referring to West Virginia guard Greg Jones. Jones averaged 12.2 points and had the most range from the perimeter. "Number 24 likes to run out."

I told Strohm that we might slip in a triangle-and-two defense or maybe a box-and-one. I didn't want to spend time on those during practice, but I wanted the kids thinking about them. "Now tell me about Solheim."

Brent Solheim, 45. Big kid, about six foot eight, solid and a clever player. A good shooter who wasn't afraid to play physical. He averaged 8.3 points and 4.5 rebounds and could run the floor.

"Britton or Hanno on him," I said. "And what about the big?"

Strohm read from the scouting report. Brian Lewin, a six-foot-eleven senior. Athletic. Averaged 7.9 rebounds and 7.4 points. Foul prone.

"Okay, I'm going to give Nate a chance," I said. "He knows how to run the floor."

Nate hadn't played since the February 26 win against UTEP, and even then it was only three minutes' worth of time. But Nate was six foot eleven, 245 pounds, and a tough kid who had practiced his butt off. West Virginia was a physical team, and I thought Nate could give Doleac some rest.

"I want you to put Jon on the Grey Team," I said. "I think Dave will do better against number 5 (Pledger) than 10 (Jones). Number 5's a lefty. Al's our best defender, so he'll be on number 24 (Owens). I want to finger touch and start the fight early on 24."

I took a break from the Stairmaster and started stretching against the wall. I knew Solheim might be a difficult matchup for Hanno, so I told Strohm to make a tape of eight clips of Solheim kicking somebody's butt. I also wanted a clip tape of Hanno playing well—his ten-of-ten game against Loyola Marymount would do—and one of him playing poorly—something from the Vegas game in the WAC tournament, when he was five-of-fifteen and didn't get to the foul line once, would be fine. "Maybe that will get his attention," I said. "I'm going to bring him in, just like I did with Andre recently. Show him the good tapes in Anaheim, and the bad tapes today."

Strohm thought the Hanno-Solheim matchup would be the key to the game. "He can't run with Hanno," Strohm said.

There were some other concerns. Caton's leg had been bothering him, so I told Strohm to make a note about resting the kid again for practice. I was also worried about Lewin getting Doleac in foul trouble. And it was final exams week for our students.

"How's your finger?" Strohm asked.

Oh, yeah, my finger. A few days earlier a friend accidentally (at least, I hope it was) rolled his car window up on my finger. It broke a bone and my fingernail. We went to the hospital to get it taken care of, but the emergency room people were busy taking care of a woman who fell off her horse. So we just left. The finger was eleven shades of purple.

After the meeting with Strohm, I had a luncheon date with Huntsman to discuss a charity golf tournament for his cancer institute. Anything for Jon. That got done about 2:15. Then I had to find enough tickets for my friends and family. I love doing nice things for them, but there is nothing worse than being a ticket broker. I had fifty, but I needed 112. Our school got an allotment of 1,300. The tickets sold out in two hours.

I wanted Betsy to come to the game in Anaheim, but I also wanted her to know how hectic it was going to be for me.

"I'm under so much pressure," I told her. "I just don't want you to get mad at me if I don't see you while you're there. I don't see my own mom during these things. That's why she isn't coming."

I had called my mom and told her I'd fly her to Anaheim for the game. But she didn't want to make the trip.

> **Says Alyce Majerus:** *"Yes, he called. But I get very nervous at these games. I have to get up and leave. I can't watch. When he called, I said, 'Rick, I'll tell you what. I'm not coming this time. But when you get to the Final Four, I'm coming.'*
>
> *"He chuckled."*

I thought about a lot of little things driving to practice that day. I thought West Virginia was a good team, but a team we could beat. They hadn't lost a nonconference game the whole season, so that was something of a concern for me. Coming into the tournament, West Virginia had lost three consecutive games, but you would have never known it the way they beat Temple by thirty in the first round, and then stunned Cincinnati in the second round.

Looking at them on film, I thought they were somewhat underrated, maybe seeded a little lower than they should have been. But now they had to play in a time zone three hours different than their own, while we were only one time zone removed. I really believe that makes a difference. Plus, I liked the idea of playing in Anaheim, because I knew we'd have a pro-Utah crowd. It's a relatively easy flight from Salt Lake City to Orange County, and southern California has its fair share of Mormons. Another helping factor was that we got to go home between rounds.

Still, I was concerned about West Virginia because of its press and its pressure. Their press was more organized than the one Arkansas played. The worst thing you could do against Arkansas was calculate, over-coach things and be overly methodical. With West Virginia, you needed to have deployment. You didn't need deployment—positioning of your players—against Arkansas. Arkansas' players didn't know themselves what they were going to do during the press. That's the nature of their press. But West Virginia's press had different levels and configurations. They gave you different looks and you had to be ready for each of them.

I thought about our players. Like Andre, what a great kid. Andre gave a ride to one of the walk-ons all the time. He probably doesn't know that I knew that. Andre treats everybody the same. It doesn't matter if you're a starter or a Grey Team kid. He is so humble and shy and sincere.

By the time I got on the court that day, Donny and Jud had already started some of the drills. My practices are closed to the media, but there were a couple high school coaches and friends in the stands.

I had the players put some folding chairs near the baseline and we had a little team meeting. I didn't waste any time.

"Hanno," I said, "if you play well, we can win this whole thing. And Nate, you're going to play. But I want you to play with balls, gusto, and aggressiveness. I don't want any fadeaway shots from you."

We practiced from three o'clock to 5:46. I talked to Nate about working hard and then called the team together. "I want to congratulate all of you," I said. "You've worked your butts off. This is a great time of the season. This is so special. So special. Years from now, you'll realize that."

Says Mike Doleac: *"I remember him saying that. I couldn't believe it was already my senior year and this could be my last game. It seemed like I had just gotten to Utah.*

"I don't think many other coaches could have taken our team, with the players we had, and been as successful. His style of coaching was perfect for a team like us. And his knowledge was amazing. We watched films that day. I'll watch, and I'll be able to see one guy do something. He'll be able to see five."

We had another staff meeting after practice. I sat in my beat-up reclining chair in our less-than-luxurious meeting room. We have four grease boards and one blackboard in the meeting room. That's where the assistants write down all the information about our opponents: position, jersey number, name, height, weight, tendencies, how to defend them, defense and offense.

We talked a little bit more about West Virginia. I also wanted to make sure we had a practice facility available when we got to California. There was a high school right near our team hotel in Newport Beach. "Tell them we'll pay rent for the gym, money for the janitors . . . whatever they need," I told Jud.

There was one other topic: Arizona.

Before we played San Francisco, I had my assistants put some tapes together of West Virginia and Cincinnati. And now that we were playing West Virginia, I had to know about the next possible opponent, either Arizona or Maryland. I thought it would be Lute's team.

Jud had done most of the scouting on Arizona. Mike Bibby, their sophomore point guard and first team consensus All-America, was the guy we worried about most.

"I think they'll put Bibby on Drew, Miles Simon or Michael Dickerson on Andre," Jud said. "But we're going to get good shots on Arizona."

Andre was going to need help, but that's where I had a problem. Jordie simply couldn't defend as well as Andre. If I took Andre out, I had Jordie trying to cover someone like Simon. If I kept Andre in, that meant playing him a lot of minutes.

"Let me see the USC tape," I said.

Just before the end of the regular season, Arizona played USC in L.A. They had won nineteen consecutive games, beaten some good teams on the road, and looked to be putting it all together for the NCAA tournament. But then USC beat them in overtime, 91–90. Now everybody—Maryland, especially—had a copy of that tape and was looking for chinks in Arizona's armor.

We ran the tape, made a few notes, and then called it a day. It was 6:48 and I had to go back, pack, get some dinner, and spend some more time in front of the VCR.

It didn't work out that way. Late that night, I learned that Jerry Hegarty's daughter had died. Jerry is my accountant and a good friend. His daughter had been ill, but I was so saddened when I got the news. I called Jerry and tried to console him as best as I could. What a terrible thing to lose a child.

Tuesday, March 17

I got up at 5:00 A.M. and called Jerry again. I wanted to make sure he was okay and see if there was anything I could do for him. Since I was up, I started watching more film of number 24, the Owens kid. The more I watched, the better I felt about our game plan.

I had an early morning flight on Delta. I try to time it so I can get out of the car and get to the gate just before the plane takes off. Strohm was on the same flight and he took care of all the equipment and baggage we had.

Since I knew almost all the people working the Delta counters, and because I had a ton of mileage points, they put me in first class. Seat 2D. I fell asleep with a *New York Times* on my chest and West Virginia on my mind.

We got to the Orange County–John Wayne–Santa Ana . . . whatever-they-call-it airport a couple of hours later. I rented the car and Strohm took care of the baggage, which was considerable.

It must have been sort of ironic for Strohm that we were playing in Anaheim. It was in Anaheim the previous summer—at an Angels game, to be exact—that I first met Strohm.

I was in town with the USA Basketball Under-22 team and I had invited a few friends to go see the Angels play the Seattle Mariners. I wanted to see Ken Griffey Jr. I love watching great players play. The friends wanted to know if they could invite Strohm and I said sure, no problem. We were introduced at the ballpark. I knew he had been an assistant coach at Northern Illinois for six years and I knew he was looking for a job. I told him I was sorry to hear about him leaving and asked him what his plans were. He said something about traveling and maybe working some basketball camps.

Says Jeff Strohm: *"About the sixth inning, I get up to go to the restroom. I'm in the bathroom and my friends come running up and say, 'I think he's going to offer you a job. Would you want to work for him?'*

"When I got back to my seat, Coach and I talked and he said he might have a job opening, and would I have any interest in it. I said, 'Coach, whatever it it, I'll take it right now. I don't care what it is. I don't care if I work for a penny. To work for you, I'd do anything.'

"He said to come talk to him the next day at his hotel. I did, he offered me the administrative assistant/video coordinator job, and about nine months later I was in the NCAA Sweet Sixteen.

"That night turned out to be a night of destiny. Ken Griffey hit a home run, his longest of the season. I saw a triple play. And I got a job working for the best coach in the business. I'm telling you, he's got a heart as big as his stomach.

"It turned out to be the greatest year of my life."

We bring a lot of equipment on the road: six VCRs, a projection camera, a tool box, laser pointers, markers, wires.

We waited forever for all the luggage and equipment. There were a lot of basketball fans flying in for the games and some of them would come by, say hello, want to shake hands. I felt like a casino greeter.

We stayed at the Newport Beach Marriott, the same hotel I had the Under-22 team stay at. Good hotel, and I love the location. By the time I got down to the meeting room, Jud already had the Grey Team running West Virginia plays on the lawn near the main pool area. That must have been an interesting sight for vacationeers: our walk-ons and some of our scholarship guys, in red practice uniforms, doing a walk-through of Mountaineer plays.

We had our team meeting at three o'clock. Strohm and the other assistants already had the scouting boards up and all twenty-three of West Virginia's plays on poster paper and taped to the walls. Two VCRs were set up, as were two TV monitors.

"Fellas, West Virginia is an interesting team," I said. "We have to make a five-man commitment to blocking out. We also have to make a commitment to spacing and awareness."

I pointed at the tendency board with the West Virginia roster on it. "This Jones kid is the guy," I said. "Number 10. He's a backup shooting guard, and we need to stop him."

Then I pointed at Hanno. "Hanno, you've had two bad games. Now I need you to play your nuts off. I don't care how many shots you miss, but I want big effort, big movement, big awareness, big rebounding, big defense.

"And the rest of you guys, you need to know that all five of these West Virginia guys can score and rebound. Remember, awareness. Okay, who has exams later today?"

Dave, Hanno, and Jordie raised their hands. Doleac said he had a final later in the week. Jordie had two more.

We ended the film session at 4:40 and minutes later, we had our first mini-problem of the trip—and it had nothing to do with basketball. It had to do with my student managers, who forgot to tip the bellhop. This poor bellhop probably lugged a million pounds of our stuff around the hotel, but my managers didn't give him any money. I took care of the bellhop, and then lectured the managers on the subject of tipping.

Practice was at nearby Corona del Mar High School, and I was really pleased with the team's effort. Dave and Jordie had a good practice, so did Britton, who was really beginning to get it. Hanno had an excellent practice, too, but I had to remind him about a bad habit he had developed: he only played hard if he hit his shots. I wanted him to know that you don't always have to score points to help the team win.

I went out to dinner that night, but when I got back, there was no way I could sleep. I channel surfed until my fingertips had calluses.

Wednesday, March 18

I got up at seven, watched more tape, made some calls, and checked on a recruit who was deciding between us and Stanford. I didn't like our chances. In fact, I didn't like a lot of things. I tend to be too negative, always thinking of ways we can lose a game. I told myself I needed to start thinking positive.

The Marriott has a great workout room, so I hit the Stairmaster for about an hour. It gave me a chance to focus completely on the game. I try to do that every day: spend an hour or so just thinking about things. Al taught me that.

I don't drink coffee, but I do love dipping chocolate chip cookies in the stuff. But on this trip, I was really trying to watch my diet. So I passed on breakfast and passed on cookie dunking.

It was a good news, bad news day. Doleac was named a first-team Academic All-American, and Drew was named a third-team Academic All-American. I was so proud of them.

On the flip side, I was beginning to worry about Britton going on a Mormon mission. I knew he was thinking hard about it. What scared me about missions is that players never came back the same way they left—at least, not as basketball players, they didn't. Al changed after his mission. So did BYU's Shawn Bradley. I didn't want the same thing to happen to Britton, mostly because I thought he had a real chance to play in the NBA.

Our meeting started right after my workout ended. The guys were already in the room when I walked in.

"Okay, Nate," I said, "you can miss fifty shots in this game and I don't care. I don't care, just as long as you play your ass off when you're in there.

"We're going to play eleven, maybe twelve guys against them, so I want everybody to be ready. The hardest thing to do is to play in this tournament. But if five guys play as one, and if we attack their pressure, then we're the better team.

"Look, we beat Arkansas. Arkansas had the best press I've ever seen, and I've been doing this for twenty-five years. West Virginia's is good, but it's no Arkansas."

Off went the lights and we started watching the film. I wanted them to see how West Virginia jumped the passing lanes. That's how they tried to force turnovers. As I waited for the next clip, I couldn't help but notice Nate. He had his notebook open and he was writing down everything.

We were scheduled to go over to the Arrowhead Pond that afternoon, but first I wanted another practice at Corona del Mar. I had one of the team managers get my rental car. He got it so fast that I was beginning to worry the managers were tipping the hotel help *too* much. I could see them handing out $20 bills like they were after-dinner mints.

There wasn't any parking near the high school gym, so I pulled the car into the handicap space. Hey, I had septuple-bypass heart surgery. That has to count for something.

We didn't go real hard, but I really liked Nate's effort, and I told him so in front of the team. Andre had a great practice and Caton looked like his leg was feeling better. I also told them West Virginia would go right at Britton and try to work themselves low and take advantage of their weight advantage.

Once again, I spelled it out for Hanno.

"Hanno, we've won two without you," I said. "Now we need you."

The team took a charter bus over to the Pond, and Jeff drove me over in the car. I spent most of the ride on my cell phone trying to get more tickets. You almost needed a ticket if you wanted to see this game. CBS was showing it to only 8 percent of the country.

Wednesday was the day of the mandatory press conferences. I didn't mind. Press conferences are easy; winning is hard.

As it turned out, the interviews only took about an hour or so, and I liked talking ball. I had already done a CBS interview and then sneaked out to watch Maryland put on a dunking exhibition during its one-hour practice.

I showed up at the main news conference with a little nick on my chin that was still bleeding. For some reason, that was of some interest to a reporter.

"I take aspirin for my heart," I said. "I bleed extra. I'd like to say I'm bleeding from body surfing or something like that, but I cut myself shaving."

Then came the revelation of the day. West Virginia Coach Gale Catlett had preceded me in the afternoon media session and someone apparently asked him about his team's role as the underdog. His answer was, well, unconventional.

"I wish that Rick and I could tee it up at 4:15 at midcourt and play one-on-one," he was quoted as saying. "Whoever wins advances. Because I would whip his butt. I wasn't a very good player, but I can whip him."

When I was asked for a comment, I was near speechless.

"He was a player of some repute, wasn't he?" I asked.

A reporter said Catlett had played on two NCAA teams at West Virginia in the early 1960s.

"I was a walk-on," I said. "They used to call me Rick the Pick. Now, if we can play two-on-two. . . I'd kick his ass. I could free up anyone in America."

I couldn't believe we were talking about this. I was fifty. He was fifty-seven. Our teams were a day away from playing the biggest game of their respective seasons.

"What precipitated that?" I said.

Another reporter said Catlett brought it up on his own.

"I've never heard anything like that before in my life," I said. "He wants to play me one-on-one? Oh, my God," I said. "He's been in West Virginia for too long. Maybe that's what you do there."

I was also asked about the post–Van Horn season and I was honest. I said that if I had my druthers, I'd rather have last year's team, the one with Keith on it. "You know, I just watched Maryland in that dunkfest out there," I said. "At our Runnin' Ute Night, Mike Doleac was our three-point champ, and he's our center. And I can't even remember who won the dunking contest. We had two guys standing, and one of them was a walk-on. So what does that tell you?"

There were questions from a Phoenix station about the Arizona State job, but I didn't have much to say. And I certainly wasn't going to volunteer any information about another school that had contacted me: Texas.

We got back to the hotel about five-thirty, and I did some radio shows and then had dinner at a good little Italian restaurant in Mission Viejo called Roma D'Italia. (Ask for Tiffany if you go.)

The watching-the-diet theme didn't do real well that night: mussels, clams, pizza bread, sausage bread, calamari, a couple of main courses, dessert. I didn't eat it all by myself. There was me, Hoops Weiss from the *New York Daily News*, Doug Trautman from Reebok, and Jim Edwards, a stand-up comedian I met through Jim Crews. But put it this way: I was full when we walked out of there.

By eleven-thirty, I was exhausted. I was in Doug's room trying to learn about the Internet and I actually fell asleep while standing up. I was either really tired or AOL has some work to do.

Thursday, March 19

I worked out and then made it short and sweet at the 10:15 team meeting. "Britton, you can't score enough points to make up for bad defense," I said. "You're on number 45 (Solheim). He outweighs you by forty pounds, I know that. But Britton, tonight it's on you."

We got to the Arrowhead Pond just in time to see West Virginia's players come off the court. There were a few nods, but nothing else. Al and Owens had played on a touring team in Japan, but I didn't see any handshakes.

I said hello to a couple of the NCAA basketball committee members—Rudy Davalos, the athletic director at New Mexico, and C. M. Newton, the athletic director at Kentucky. Then we had a quick shoot-around and headed back to the hotel. As we were leaving the court, Arizona's players were coming in. You could see the confidence in their eyes. I told someone, "Those Arizona guys are so loose."

There wasn't much left to do, but wait for tip-off. I wasn't going to allow myself to look ahead. I wasn't going to allow my players to look ahead. I told them, just like I told them in the regionals at Boise, to pack for one day. That's it. One day. Don't worry about anything else but the next game. That was because I felt like I hurt us in the WAC tournament by preparing for two or three games. I took the practices to that extent. I told the team that it was my fault.

But in the NCAA tournament, I wasn't going to let it be my fault when it came to preparing for teams. All I wanted to worry about was West Virginia. I knew Arizona was in our bracket. I knew our team knew Arizona was in our bracket. So I told them, "Look, if you want to day-dream, that's fine, but Maryland is fully capable of beating Arizona. I can't pick that game. I wouldn't want to put a bet on it—and I mean that in a hypothetical sense."

There are two pools at the Marriott, and I always like going to the smaller, less crowded one. You know why? Because of this body. I just sit in the water and I look like a walrus who has food coming. I just bob in and out of the water.

I had lunch and then a massage, but not before there was a minor incident with hotel security. It wasn't my fault. The massage room was located right off the pool area, but I first needed a place to change clothes. The masseuse suggested I use the men's restroom located on the other side of the pool. Fine, except that the door was locked. I was running late, so I tried the door to the women's restroom. It was unlocked, so I slowly opened the door, yelled to make sure no one was inside, and then went in to change. Before I did, I told a friend to keep an eye on the door.

I had just wrapped a towel around my waist when the door opened and in walked a middle-aged woman. She looked at me, I looked at her, and before I could explain, she let out a little yelp and ran from the room.

What had happened is this: my friend near the pool was too busy reading the sports section to notice the woman going into the restroom. By the time he saw her, it was too late.

Someone called security and they came just as I was explaining to the woman that I wasn't some sort of pervert, that I had a massage scheduled for one o'clock.

"Well, you did startle me a little bit," she said.

Startle her? How about me? I was the one in the towel.

Of course, that isn't the worst massage experience I've had. A few years ago, Rich Panella arranged for me to come to Cardinal Stritch University and get my back worked on. What he didn't tell me is that a nun would be doing the work.

She said she was studying physical therapy. She used to hang from a horizontal bar to stretch her chronically sore back. Rich called her "the Hanging Nun," or "Sister Mary Massage."

Without a doubt, it was the most painful massage in my life. She pummeled me. It was like she was working a woodshaver on me.

I called Jerry later in the afternoon to see how he was doing. You think a basketball game is the most important thing in your life, and then you remember a friend, and his daughter, and his family's grief. We talked about the possibility of a scholarship fund. Then I told him whatever he needed to start it, to count me in.

I got to the Pond at about four o'clock and didn't go out to the floor until the last moment. I'd rather stay in the locker room area and collect my thoughts, talk to the players after their warmup, and then go out.

Donny, though, likes to sit on the bench before the game and watch the warmups. Apparently a reporter stopped to say hello and then asked what would be the keys to the game.

"It will come down to foul shooting," he said.

He was right. West Virginia took eleven more shots than us, made five more, out-rebounded us by four, but we beat them at the foul line. And that would be the difference. We won, 65–62, thanks in large part to a twenty-two of twenty-seven effort from the foul line.

The Jones kid finished oh for four from the field, but number 45, Solheim, was very good. I liked the way he played.

But I also liked the way we played. Doleac was huge. He made shots, he made thirteen of fourteen free throws, he had nine rebounds, and he got their guys in foul trouble. Andre was our other guy in double figures. But what I liked best about Andre's game is the way he played defense. The same with Drew. He only had five points, and he missed some key foul shots with fifty-seven seconds left, but his defense meant so much more than points scored.

It was a close game, one that wasn't decided until the final thirty seconds. But I thought we were the better team. In the locker room, I told the guys, "That was a nice, gutsy effort. Playing hard is the determining factor. Now I think you should be with your parents tonight. And if you're not with a parent or relative, then I think you should be with the team. Make sure you enjoy this tonight. But you need to wake up tomorrow and realize we've got another game.

"Savor this. It's such a special thing. Saturday's game is going to be about mental toughness. But for now, realize that you gave a really gritty, gutsy effort. I was so proud of how hard you played. Rebounding, defense, and hustle were the determining factors. There are only eight teams left now, so enjoy this. A ten-forty-five curfew is fine tonight."

Nate, Drew, Al, and Britton had been selected for random postgame drug testing by the NCAA medical staff, so they had to leave. I told the assistants to make sure we could practice at Corona del Mar High on Friday, and to get us a bigger meeting room at the hotel. Then I had to sit down. My lucky short-sleeve plaid Polo shirt was soaked. I think my sweater was on inside-out. I was tired, thirsty, and hungry. I grabbed a Diet Pepsi from a counter in the middle of the room.

"This is a tough way to make a buck," I said to Mike Schneider. "Now I can see why Al walked away at forty-eight."

Hanno hadn't played well again—two of four from the field, no foul shots, no rebounds. That's why he only played twenty minutes. When the players went to slap his hand, he wasn't very enthusiastic. I made a mental note to talk to him one-on-one the next day.

There was the obligatory postgame press conference. Drew, back from his drug test (now there was a waste of modern medical know-how), sheepishly told the reporters, "You don't have to write about those two missed free throws, do you?" Later, Dave Jackson went up to Drew and said, "Quick, somebody resuscitate Drew. He's choking to death." And Doleac had a good observation about talent. "You look at our team and we're shooting our layups below the rim," he said. "It was not a game for the ages, but we won."

I was emotionally drained. "It was an ugly win, no doubt about it," I said. "And I know the specter of this dunk-a-rama looms over us."

The dunk-a-rama was Arizona vs. Maryland. They were the second game of Thursday night's West Regional.

Betsy, Del Harris, and Bill Dwyre were waiting at the locker room door when I got back from the press conference. George Karl, whose Seattle team was in town to play, also came to the game.

I owe a lot to Del Harris. We had talked during the week about ways of attacking the press. He gave me some great ideas, but I'm not sure I did them justice. "All that good stuff you showed me?" I said to Del. "I was an embarrassment to you." Del laughed, but to this day I know he is right about attacking the press. You can't slow down against those kind of teams.

As I was getting ready to leave the locker room to go watch the Maryland-Arizona game, some of the West Virginia players stopped by and wished us well. Solheim was in the group. "Hey, you played a hell of a game," I told him.

I sat in an empty seat on press row, right next to Hoops Weiss, and watched a track meet. Everybody talked about Arizona, but Maryland could play too. Both teams had amazing quickness and athletic ability. As the first half went on, I grabbed a piece of paper and wrote, "If we can beat their pressure—a big *if*—we can win." That's also when I started to tinker with the idea of using a triangle-and-two if Arizona won.

Says Jeff Strohm: *"He and I talked about it when we were watching the Maryland game. I said, 'Coach, I love it. I love it because we can't guard them.'*

"I guarantee you he was thinking about how to beat Arizona even before our game. He had probably been working on it for a month in his mind. I'd bet my life on it."

Arizona won, 87–79. To tell you the truth, I was actually relieved Arizona beat Maryland. I just felt we were better prepared for Arizona and more familiar with their style and personnel. I knew them. I didn't really know Maryland.

I went back to our locker room, showered, and apologized to the attendant for the condition our players had left the area. That would be addressed the next day. As I walked to the parking lot, Lute Olson was being interviewed by an Arizona TV station. We waved.

It was late—about ten-thirty—but I met George Karl, his wife, and his staff at a restaurant near the Pond. Jud had kiddingly asked if we could borrow Gary Payton from the Sonics for our next game.

I tried to be sociable, but what I really wanted to do was talk ball with George. George is a real innovator when it comes to running traps and applying pressure. He also wasn't spellbound by the college game. He had seen us play and he told me how slow and boring the college game was. All the pro coaches say that. They're used to twenty-four-second shot clocks, no zones, and a faster-paced game.

He started talking about their personnel, about Bibby and the playing tendencies he had. He said we should try to make Bibby score, rather than have him draw the defense in and then kick it out to somebody for a shot. We talked about matchups, assignments, Arizona's press, coming at Bibby late with the bigs.

So a few minutes after I sat down, I got right to it.

"What do you think about Arizona?" I said.

I borrowed a notepad from someone in the dinner party and we sat at the end of the table and drew up some things. He kicked his loafers off, and we scribbled some ways of attacking their press. Arkansas did a nice job with their press—they hustled and they had nice backflow. But their press wasn't anything like the one Arkansas had.

No one seemed to mind that George and I spent much of dinner jotting down ideas. I really respect his opinion. He gave me some things to think about, and confirmed some other ideas that I had.

Right before the end of the night, I told George that I was thinking about running the triangle-and-two. He seemed to like it.

On the way back to the hotel, I stopped at a convenience store near the Orange County airport and bought a pint of Häagen-Dazs and all the local newspapers I could find. There was a story about Andre in the paper that day, so I wanted to get copies for his mother.

By the time I handed the keys to the Marriott parking valet, it was past midnight. I went directly to our new meeting room, Salon 4. It was a ballroom, all right, complete with a huge chandelier that looked like something from the DuPont mansion.

Strohm had five VCRs, two twenty-five-inch monitors, the projector, and a ten-by-ten foot screen in place. He also had taped eleven sets of plays on the ballroom walls. Donny, Jud, and Brock were already there, as well as R. C. Buford, a scout with the San Antonio Spurs, and Northern Arizona coach Ben Howland. R.C. was an assistant coach at Kansas when the Jayhawks won the national championship in 1988.

I sat down with my pint of ice cream. "Run it," I said. "Run the Southern Cal tape."

I wanted to see that March 5 overtime game again. I also wanted to see the February 19 game against Oregon State, a game Arizona won on the road, 71–70. It didn't take very long to see who we had to stop.

"Bibby is the guy," I said.

Brock must have had some mixed feelings about this matchup. He was born and raised in Milwaukee, went to Marquette High, but later moved to Phoenix and was a four-year starting point guard for Lute at Arizona. He was a captain on Lute's first Arizona NCAA tournament team. In fact, he later played with Steve Kerr for two years. So this must have been a little difficult.

Says Brock Brunkhorst: *"I think Lute knew we could probably meet up. When I played for him, we played a lot like Rick's teams. But there wasn't any doubt where my allegiances were. For the first time in a long time, I wanted Arizona to lose."*

Friday, March 20

I watched tape until 2:45. Strohm said I fell asleep in midsentence. I went up to my room and tried keeping my eyes open for fifteen more minutes of tape time. Brock stayed down in the meeting room until four and Strohm stayed until five putting together seventy-seven separate clip tapes of offense, defense, and personnel. Strohm was back up at seven, and Brock at eight. When you only have a day to prepare for the defending national champions, you don't have time for much sleep.

I put a Do Not Disturb request on my room phone, but it still rang beginning at seven o'clock. I needed to watch more tape anyway.

I met with the staff and then took Hanno out into ballroom hallway for an individual meeting. He was still upset about his play during the last three games.

"I think I'm trying too hard," he said.

"I think you are too," I said. "Just let the game come to you. We wouldn't be here without you."

I didn't like his body language. You could tell he was feeling the pressure. And it didn't help that he was on the cover of *Sports Illustrated*. I had to figure out something to get Hanno back on track. You know, sometimes people forget that Hanno has had to make great personal adjustments to playing over here. He's like ET—he's 7,500 miles away from home.

Once the team meeting started, I congratulated Mike and Drew again for their academic All-American status. Then we got down to business.

"This is the second-best point guard I know," I said as I pointed at Andre. "You are a better player, but he is a better shooter, no question about it. I don't want to make Bibby bigger than life. He's not phenomenal. But he's bigger than life to Arizona because everything is around him, through him, and because of him.

"The number one thing? We've got to get back on defense. We want Bibby to score two-point layups. We don't want Bibby to sniff a three-pointer. We want him to score on layups or dish to someone else to shoot threes. We will never leave Bibby."

And that's when I told them about the triangle-and-two. We had used it twice all season, and only for a few minutes at a time. It's a gimmick defense, but I was seriously thinking of using it against Arizona after they made baskets. We called it "66," in honor of the 1966 Utah team, the last one to reach the Final Four.

Says Donny Daniels: *"We were talking about it as a staff and I said, 'Coach, the triangle-and-two? Who you going to leave open?' He said, 'Dickerson.' You see, he didn't want Bibby and Simon to go rampant. But I'm thinking, Dickerson is an AP third team All-American, Arizona's leading scorer, and I think the leading scorer in the Pac-Ten. We were taking a big chance. If Dickerson goes out and hits three of four, we're out of the triangle-and-two."*

We headed back to the Pond for a practice and media session. We were so close to the Final Four I could taste it.

Al had an exam, so he couldn't attend the press conference. Someone asked me about it and I said, "He's playing Catlett one-on-one."

Another reporter wanted to know about comparisons between myself and Lute. I guess Lute had said something about me eating a lot more pizza than he did. So I said, "I don't know about personality, but I do know I don't have a lot of combs."

I think the smart guys in Vegas had us as 10.5-point underdogs against Arizona. But I wanted our players and everyone else to know we weren't an afterthought. I reminded the writers that Kansas was a No. 1 seed, but they were gone from the tournament. Drew picked up on the theme right away.

"I think there's a reason you play the game," he said.

He wasn't smiling when he said it.

I didn't come right out and tell everybody what our defensive game plan was, but I did say we had a "little wrinkle" we were working on, that we were "going to visit an old friend that we haven't visited for a long time."

And if it failed? someone asked. "If it doesn't work, I'm going to say we didn't do it so that there's no accountability."

I talked about a lot of things at that press conference. I said Bibby was better than Jason Kidd. I said it would be nice to get to a Final Four, but there had been coaches better than me who had never made it. Guys such as Ralph Miller and Jack Hartman. A lot of it, I said, depended on luck.

I said I didn't fully appreciate the Final Four experiences I had with Marquette in 1974 and 1977.

I said I would happily coach the last ten years of my career at St. Mary's College in Moraga, California. Location. Location. Location.

I told them about the nicest phone message I received after the win against West Virginia. It was from Van Horn's mom. She said we were going to beat Arizona.

I said players should think long and hard about leaving college early for the pros, that you should live your own age.

The rumors about Arizona State continued to swirl. I said I hadn't pursued anything, but I would always keep my options open. I learned that a long time ago when Xavier offered me the head coaching job, but Marquette wouldn't let me out of my contract. I said I wasn't interested in heading to the East Coast for a job.

Someone mentioned that Michael Dickerson, Arizona's leading scorer, said he would have liked to have played for me. Jeez, I said, I wish he would have felt that way when he was in high school.

Salt Lake City, Mormons, and recruiting were the next topics. I tried to be honest about it. The Mormon religion does not have a good reputation with the black community. There are more blacks in Compton than all of Utah. I'm not even sure you can find a store that sells products geared to blacks in Salt Lake City.

Salt Lake City is what it is: it's Green Bay, Wisconsin, in the Rocky Mountains, that's what it is. But people talk about it as if it is a Stepford Wives community. It's a big city with a parochial, small-town environment. There are twelve good restaurants. I have a twelve-restaurant rotation there. If you go to Park City, it's sixteen. There are no foreign films to speak of. It's a nice place, but it's a small town, and like a lot of small towns, it closes in on you. Now if we were recruiting thirty year olds with families, we'd have it made.

On the way back to the Marriott I called Betsy, who was staying at a nearby hotel with family. "You know," I said, "the Final Four is one of the few things you can't buy. This might be the last chance to go for this old coach. You only get so many chances."

Ben Howland suggested I try to relax, maybe take a walk on the beach, meet Betsy for dinner, and get a good night's sleep. At first I said I would, but the more I thought about it, the more I remembered our game against Arizona in 1996. We were 4–0 at the time, but got beat because I didn't have them ready to play. Keith played badly, and we weren't ready for their traps, their press, and their pressure. That was my fault. I lost the team that game. So while a walk on the beach sounded tempting, I would feel terrible if that's why we lost the game, because we weren't prepared. Instead, I called Betsy, canceled our night out, and watched tape of our 1996 loss to Arizona until about dawn.

As I was watching tape, Doleac was doing exactly what a captain should do: he was looking out for his teammates. He, Jordie, and David took Hanno out to dinner and also arranged a little ceremony involving that *Sports Illustrated* cover. He handed Hanno a book of matches and then told him to set it on fire. And that's what Hanno did. Ashes to ashes, jinx to jinx.

You know, Mike was always the Dutch uncle of the team. He was the one who always had the cookout at his place, always had the barbecue, always took the recruits under his wing. Like when Andre was a freshman, Mike came in and told me that Andre didn't know how to study and that we should try to help him with that. Andre didn't really know how to take notes. That was his freshman year. Then, in his senior year, Mike came in and said we had to help Britton get organized. Britton needed to start taking responsibility for himself. Mike recognized that.

Mike always had very insightful comments. He cared about the other guys on the team. He was a really good guy, too, when I'd go off on someone. He'd put his arm around them, try to make them understand and explain what had happened. He'd tell them it wasn't a personal attack, but that I was upset with guys who didn't play hard. If you played hard, there was no problem. Mike understood that, and he made sure the younger players understood it too. He had a great way about him.

Says Jeff Strohm: *"It was a late night for everyone. I was in my room about ten, but before I went downstairs to do some more tape work, I said I'd just close my eyes for a minute or two. I woke up at two-thirty, fully clothed, and on top of the covers. I was mad at myself, but I also had had the strangest* *dream. I had dreams of cutting down the nets . . . of Rick cutting them down. And the fans were yelling, 'Rick! Rick! Rick!' "*

Saturday, March 21

Brock Brunkhorst: *"One of the UA [University of Arizona] radio guys came up to me the day before. He said, 'Lute is scared. He's scared he can't match up with your team's size.'*

"I said, 'Don't kid yourself.' "

The players had a team breakfast at eight-thirty and then started making their way to our ballroom. I liked what I saw. When Strohm reminded Andre about one of Bibby's dribbling tendencies, Andre just shook his head and smiled.

"I'm not worried about all that," Andre said. "Street ball. It's Street Ball Day. We're gonna play street ball." Then he started humming as he studied the play sheets on the wall.

Hanno came in next. For the first time in days, he looked relaxed. He was clapping his hands, being the old Hanno. Drew and Al came in a few minutes later.

Says Drew Hansen: *"Alex and I were sitting there, waiting for the meeting to start. Alex leaned over and said, 'Coach is going to walk in and say the triangle-and-two is off and send me in to rebound.'*

"I said, 'I hope so.' "

The meeting was relatively short. We looked at film from that 1996 game and we talked a little more about the triangle-and-two. We had never opened up a game in the triangle-and-two. In our case, that meant playing their guards—Bibby and Miles Simon—man-to-man and playing zone on everyone else. I told them we were going to use it.

The scouting report said Dickerson was a pure shooter, but a streaky shooter. He only made two of eighteen shots in the 1997 Final Four, but Arizona still won. He came into the 1998 tournament with more confidence and more to prove. He went eleven of eleven in the second half against Washington earlier in the season. He had twenty-one in the second half against Cal in February. He scored in double figures in fifteen of Arizona's first sixteen conference games. He was a senior, he had played on a national championship team, and he wasn't afraid to take a shot. He was so good that Arizona retired his jersey. But I had to take my chances with somebody. Dickerson was the guy.

I worked out in the morning, watched a Division II tournament

game, and then got a call from Keith. It was such a nice call. He really
wanted us to win. He's such an unselfish, thoughtful guy. And that's
the other thing: he called, and my mom didn't.

I'm superstitious. I wore the same plaid short-sleeve shirt I had
worn during the entire tournament. I wore the same pants, same
sweater, and same boots. I did change my socks.

On the way to the Pond, I started having second thoughts about
the triangle-and-two. Strohm drove, I ate Famous Amos chocolate chip
cookies and sipped water. "I'll think about it five minutes alone in a
room before the game," I told him.

I took my five minutes and decided we were sticking with it. If it
didn't work, we could always switch to something else.

Says Brock Brunkhorst: *"He came in and said, 'We're going to 66 right
off the bat.'*

"We all looked at him and said, 'What?' "

It worked. We won, 76–51, and that little gimmick defense worked
better than anyone, including myself and the team, could have imag-
ined. Dickerson didn't make his first field goal until there was only 1:21
left in the first half. He finished the game two of twelve from the field,
zero for three from the three-point line, and airballed three of his first
five shots.

Simon made one of nine shots and missed all three three-pointers
he tried. Bibby was three of fifteen from the field, and zero for seven
from the arc. Arizona shot 28.3 percent from the field, 18.2 percent
from the three-point line. Bibby, Simon, and Dickerson were a com-
bined six of thirty-six for nineteen points.

That silly little triangle-and-two. Our old friend, Mr. 66.

Says Keith Van Horn: *"I remember one time during my sophomore year,
we were playing UTEP, and Coach had us run the triangle-and-two for a
few minutes. They had no idea what to do against it. They were clueless. So
when I saw it against Arizona—and I knew Coach had barely used it all
year—I knew Arizona was in trouble. I knew Arizona hadn't been working
on the triangle-and-two."*

None of us knew it would happen like that. But the difference this
time was that they were prepared and they understood how to break the
presses, how to get the middle filled. They recognized that there were
going to be easy baskets against that press.

Drew said the last eight minutes of that game were the longest of his life. The players were so scared we would somehow blow the game. In fact, with two minutes left, David at the foul line, and the score, 74–46, Al told Drew, "Hey, this game isn't over yet." Then Doleac said, "If we blow a twenty-eight-point lead, I'll shoot myself."

During one of Arizona's late timeouts, I called Andre over to talk.

"I'm going to take you guys out," I said.

"No," he said, "we want to stay in."

My players know I don't like to run up the score. I would rather sub too early or too often than run up the score on someone. But in this case, Andre was so adamant about not wanting to come out of the game.

So I let them stay in. I certainly hope it wasn't interpreted by Arizona as anything disrespectful or a "We'll-show-them," thing. Our kids, truth be told, were a little nervous about sending in the second team. But most of all, I think it was one of those things where you wanted time in a bottle. You didn't want the moment to go away.

With a minute to go, I started shaking everybody's hand on the bench. Donny hugged Britton. Britton hugged somebody else. It was a hugfest.

Then came the final horn and we had won. We were going to the Final Four.

In 1966, I was a senior at Marquette High. It was open gym night and somebody had the Final Four championship game on a little black-and-white TV. The TV was sitting on a folding chair and I couldn't help but watch. Utah had lost to Duke in the consolation game. I was spellbound by Texas Western's mastery over Kentucky. David Lattin, Bobby Joe Hill, Willie Worsley, Orsten Artis, Harry Flournoy—those were the starters for Texas Western. Don Haskins was the coach. Nevil Shed and Willie Cager came off the bench. That team changed basketball for good. And it changed basketball for me too. That was the first NCAA title game I ever watched. I saw that game and I saw defense as something I could do, and gravitated toward that. I remember thinking, "I wish I could play in a game like that."

I never got that chance. But now I had the next best thing: a trip to San Antonio and an opportunity to win one as a head coach.

Says Jeff Strohm: *"We cut the nets down and when it was Coach's turn, the crowd started yelling, 'Rick! Rick!' and then, 'Stay! Stay!'*

"Remember that dream? How weird is that?"

When we got back to the locker room, Dave was sitting in a chair, one of the nets around his neck, and he was sobbing. I don't know if they were tears of relief or joy. He had played twenty-five minutes, scored ten points, grabbed two rebounds, and done a wonderful job in the triangle-and-two.

Drew presented me with the game ball, but then said, "Coach, can you put in your will that I get the ball if you die?"

He was completely serious.

I gave him the ball.

Everybody was yelling, "66! 66! 66!" The managers had already passed out T-shirts and baseball caps that read, West Regional Champions . . . Utah. It was such a sweet moment.

"You guys came through," I said. "What an honor and a privilege it is to coach you guys. You know, we should celebrate. We don't have any champagne, so everybody in the showers. Let's just go jump in the showers."

So we all raced to the showers, except Jud, who didn't want to get his expensive black wingtip shoes wet. We formed a circle—me, the assistants, the managers, the players, the trainer—and let the water soak us to the skin. We chanted, "Final Four! Final Four!" We sprayed cans of Slice and Pepsi at each other. Donny came staggering out and said, "This feels pretty damn good." Britton, who would never touch a drop of alcohol, kiddingly said, "Mormons are getting drunk—who's with me?"

Before I went back to the front of the locker room, I saw Dave and I hugged him. He had worked so hard in that game.

Then I saw Andre and he had this wonderful grin on his face. He played so well, finishing with eighteen points, fourteen rebounds, and thirteen assists—the first triple-double in an NCAA tournament game since Magic Johnson did it in 1979. A lot of people didn't know about Andre before the tournament started. He didn't make the first, second, or third AP All-America team. He didn't make the first, second, or third National Association of Basketball Coaches All-America team. *Sporting News* didn't have him on either of their first or second teams. He was an "others-receiving-votes" kind of player. Only the U.S. Basketball Writers Association selected him as an All-America—third team.

I grabbed a towel, tried to dry my face off, and then told the team, "You are what this game is all about." Then my voice started to crack.

"I can't thank you enough. It's a dream of a lifetime for me. It's like an opportunity of a lifetime."

Not long after that, I did what any good son would do: I called my mom.

Says Alyce Majerus: *"I had two TVs on in the house. Rick's game was on the TV in the bedroom, and another show was on the TV in the living room. I kept pacing, pacing, pacing . . . from one room to the other. I wouldn't let anybody in the house. Absolutely not. They'd think I was crazy.*

"When they won, I just can't tell you how wonderful I felt for him. His dad would have been so proud of him. I'm proud of him each season.

"And he was just so thrilled. And this is a mother talking, but he looked so cute walking off the floor. He had that little crooked smile. That's when I wished I would have been there.

"When he called, he was just so thrilled. I said, 'Rick, I knew you could do it. Now I'm coming to San Antonio. I'm coming to the Final Four.' "

That night, I didn't worry about a thing. I sipped on some Fuzzy Navels—McGuire calls them hooker drinks—and smoked a cigar at the hotel hottub with friends, Betsy, and her kids.

"I still can't believe it," I said.

We stayed there until about eleven and then went dancing at the hotel nightclub.

Sleep? Who needed sleep?

8
North Carolina

Sunday, March 22

Richie let us borrow his private jet for the flight back to Salt Lake City. It was great. You park your rental car right at the executive terminal and someone takes it back to the garage. You drop your bags off right outside the plane. You get on and there's plenty of room to spread out. I read the papers, had a little breakfast, and then fell asleep.

When we got back to Utah, I drove Betsy and her kids back home and we sang Elvis Presley songs. I love the King. I'm the king of the King. Then I dropped my stuff off at the hotel and went to work. I had some ideas for a new press alignment, and I wanted to work on our Monday practice schedule. I also knew I had to keep Dave Jackson on a roll.

Back at the basketball offices, Strohm was putting together tapes of Carolina losses that season—all three of them (an overtime loss to Maryland, a fourteen-point loss to North Carolina State, a two-point loss to Duke). I also wanted a clip tape of us beating the press, and all updated Carolina team and player statistics.

I also had to deal with a budding catasrophe: one of the managers apparently had lost my lucky plaid shirt and black pants. That shirt, those pants, and my sweater, belt, and boots were like a school uniform with me. I didn't have to make a clothing decision that way. All I did was change the socks and underwear.

There would be hell to pay if I didn't get those clothes back.

Says Tim LaComb: *"During the 1994–95 season, Coach didn't wear the Reebok sweater. He had two Banana Republic sweaters, one blue, one brown, and he would stick with what was hot. He's superstitious that way.*

"We had just beaten Colorado State on a Tuesday night at Fort Collins, and it was the best motion game I'd seen in the two years I was there. We won by thirty-five.

"After the game he gave us the sweaters to get cleaned, take them home to Salt Lake, and then have them delivered to his hotel because we played a Thursday game. Sometimes we used to put the sweaters on, shove pillows up in them, and then go knock on the players' doors. I'd say [in a perfect Majerus voice]: 'Uh, you know, it would be nice if you guys would get off your ass and do a little studying. It is college, you know. You're here to get a degree.'

"For some reason, our wake-up call never came the next morning. Everybody was already down on the bus waiting for the two managers—the same two managers who are supposed to pack the bus in the first place. We got a call from one of the assistants, jumped out of bed, grabbed our things, and rushed down there. I didn't even put my contacts in. We had a half hour to get to the airport.

"We got on the plane, sat down, and I looked at Mike Curtis, the other manager.

" 'Do you have Coach's sweaters?" I said. I was terrified.

" 'No, I don't have them.'

" 'Dude, I don't, either. We left them in the room.'

"We got back to Salt Lake, called the hotel, and luckily the sweaters were still there. The hotel overnighted them to us and we had them in time for the Thursday game. But I was so scared. I didn't want to face what would come if I lost them."

As usual, I spent about ninety minutes by myself, just thinking about the team. Nothing else, just the team. I learned that from Al. Al wasn't much for watching film of games or practices, but he knew his team. He was a master of understanding what made his team work.

I knew the Carolina staff pretty well. Phil Ford was a member of a clinic staff that I took to Japan several years ago. Dave Hanners, another Carolina assistant, is a good friend. He once took me to a great restaurant in New Orleans. He also was nice enough to explain, for example, Carolina's secondary offense off the break.

I didn't know Bill Guthridge as well as I knew Dave. But his reputation in the business is very good. Dean Smith knew what he was doing when he all but named Guthridge as his successor.

I was in Chapel Hill the day Dean resigned. But it was by accident, not because I was a job candidate.

ESPN had invited me to be in a commercial promoting their college basketball TV package, so I flew from Salt Lake City, connected in Atlanta, and then took a flight to Raleigh. Then I got the rental car and drove to Chapel Hill. I got to the hotel at about midnight. As I was checking in, the clerk said, "Are you here for an interview?"

I didn't know what the guy was talking about.

"Interview?" I said. "No, I'm not here for an interview."

"I was just wondering," said the clerk, "because Dean Smith is resigning tomorrow. I thought maybe you were interviewing for the job."

There had been rumors that Dean might quit, but I didn't know how serious they were.

"Sir," I said, "I couldn't get that job in a million years."

I watched the resignation speech the next day. Every station in North Carolina cut into their regularly scheduled programming to carry the speech live. I think there were more TV cameras there than when Nixon resigned.

I've always had a soft spot for Carolina. The night before we played Wake Forest in December 1997, I made a special trip to Chapel Hill with Brock's dad, Buck. Buck was a former NBA referee, but he had never been to Tobacco Road. So I drove him over to Duke and he met Krzyzewski.

"If only I could see Carolina," Buck said.

So I drove him over to Chapel Hill and we went to the Dean Smith Center, which is where Carolina plays its games. That's how big Dean Smith is in Carolina. I'd be lucky to get a concession stand named after me.

Buck and I were standing outside the arena, trying to peer in through the window when this kid came up to us.

"You've got a good team," he said. "I'm a big fan."

They love basketball in the ACC. The arena doors were locked, but the kid told us to go over to the aquatic center, then take the stairs down to a tunnel, and then cross over to the arena concourse. It worked.

When we got to the court, all the lights were off and it was hard to see anything, including all the jerseys hanging on the walls and rafters. That's when a janitor sort of appeared from nowhere. I told him I was the coach at Utah, that I had a friend who had always wanted to see Carolina, and would he mind if we just walked around for a few minutes.

"Let me turn on the lights for you," he said.

The janitor gave us a guided tour of the place. He was so nice. When he was done, we shook hands and he said, "Good luck against Wake."

I don't think I had told him we were playing Wake Forest. He just knew. And sure enough, we beat Wake the next day.

We played Wake in the afternoon, and then Buck and I drove to Charlotte to watch Carolina play Virginia Tech that night at the Harris Teeter Pepsi Challenge. We didn't have tickets, but the people there were so nice. They treated us like kings. They found us a spot on press row, gave us parking passes. We went there with nothing. I'm telling you, I'm not sure there's a better basketball state than North Carolina.

After the game, I went down to say hello to the Carolina coaches. Guthridge came out and I said, "I'm so happy for you. You're doing a hell of a job."

Carolina had beaten Virginia Tech by twenty-one points, but Guthridge made it sound as if he had barely had anything to do with the win.

"I wish I could be more like you," I said. "You're happy and loose. I get a knot in my stomach when I coach."

"I'm just trying to enjoy this," he said.

"You should," I said.

Now we were in the same Final Four.

This was old hat for Carolina. It was their twenty-fourth consecutive NCAA tournament appearance, their fourteenth Final Four appearance, their fifth Final Four in the last eight years. No other program except UCLA had been in as many Final Fours as North Carolina. And this was Guthridge's thirteenth Final Four as a player, assistant coach, or head coach.

We didn't quite have the same history, which is why I would have liked to have practiced my team five straight days. But I didn't want our kids to get off their normal routine. So I compromised and added just one more workout to our schedule.

That afternoon I went out to lunch. Some lady walked up to me, offered her congratulations, and said in honor of our win against Arizona, she was giving her cat a new name: Mrs. Majerus.

Monday, March 24

For days, probably even weeks, I had been worried about an intestinal problem I had been having. I kept hoping it would go away, that it was stress or diet related, but it persisted. There was bleeding and pain, and I thought the worst: cancer.

I went to go see my doctor, who was concerned enough to schedule more tests for the next day. I knew something wasn't right.

Tuesday, March 25

A procedure was performed and the doctors discovered two polyps on my colon. The polyps were removed, but the doctors said it wouldn't be until late in the day before they had the results of the biopsy. I don't think I've ever been more scared than I was waiting for those results.

Finally, the news came: the polyps were benign. I guess I had a little angel on my shoulder.

Before we left for the Final Four, I had an open night where anybody could come and meet the players and coaches. Hoops Weiss came out from the *Daily News* and said it was one of the most touching things he'd seen in college basketball, and this boy has seen a lot. It was for people who didn't have season tickets, who couldn't afford to see a game. About 6,000 or 7,000 people came to it. It was a great success. Utah basketball is important to these people. It's important to me. That's why we had the open house.

And by the way, I got my lucky game clothes back. The managers lived to see another day.

Wednesday, March 26

We flew into San Antonio Wednesday night. But it didn't really hit me that we were at the Final Four until we saw the Alamodome on our drive in from the airport. What an exciting moment that was.

Now I'll tell you how nice our kids are. They love to play cards. It's an obsession of theirs. So after we got situated at the hoel, we all went out to dinner. It was me, R. C. Buford, Bob Henderson, our assigned host from San Antonio, and the players. The dinner party was so big we needed two tables.

The team got served first, and the kids finished before our table was done. They didn't know our table hadn't been served dessert. So they started to get up to leave when the host said, "Coach hasn't had his dessert yet."

Andre didn't miss a beat. He just looked at the other players and said, "Deal 'em up. Guess we're going to play some cards."

He didn't throw a fit. A lot of players might have said, "C'mon, let's go. What does that fat ass need another dessert for? We want to go to the Riverwalk, or back to the hotel."

But those kids were so nice. They didn't care if they had to wait. It was like, "Coach wants dessert, so we'll wait for our coach." They were so courteous. That made me proud.

Late that night I called Tom Izzo. Izzo's Michigan State team had lost to Carolina, 73–58, in the third round of the tournament. I was just looking for a little information and insight.

Thursday, March 26

We had an afternoon practice at Trinity University. It was a great practice, and I loved the energy our kids had. We talked about taking good shots from the corners, about going to the refs if Carolina's players used a certain move on rebounds, about defending Antawn Jamison, about stopping their transition game.

"I want each of you to study fifteen minutes of film on the guy you're guarding," I said.

Joey Meyer was at practice that day, so was Doc Rivers and his son. Doc had talked to the team in Salt Lake City. His advice: be aggressive and don't be a spectator. He said that players tend to freeze up in these kind of games. He warned against that.

I let some other friends and coaches stop by, but otherwise it was like the Iron Curtain.

The players had an eleven-thirty curfew and I had dinner reservations with friends. But I told the players I didn't want them to spend their night walking the Riverwalk. I wanted them to have fresh legs.

At the very end of practice I told them, "You guys are the better team—*if* you block out and get back on transition."

Our team understood the importance of those fundamentals. We were not a team that took a lot of bad shots. We were a team that stressed defense. I told them all the time, "To those who don't think defense is important, you'll get the best seat on the bench."

We were not a SportsCenter type of team. Production assistants back at Bristol didn't have a lot to choose from after Keith left. We didn't have any power dunkers. What were they going to use on the air, *"Here's a downscreen and here's a jump shot"*?

That was our team. But you know? Coaches liked us. They liked the way we played. They appreciated what we did.

Friday, March 27

We practiced at Trinity at eleven o'clock. By then I felt fairly comfortable with the matchups: Doleac on Jamison, Andre on Ed Cota,

Drew or Dave on Shammond Williams, Al on Vince Carter, and Hanno on Makhtar Ndiaye.

The preliminary game plan wasn't particularly complicated. With Jamison, their first-team consensus All-America, we wanted to make sure he didn't outrun us and that he didn't get any second shots. Our goals were: no second shots, no rebounds, don't let him outrun us, and stay down on his little jump hook.

Jamison was the quickest big guy in the tournament. His second-best shot was his miss. He had an uncanny knack for getting offensive rebounds and turning them into points.

On Carter, a second-team consensus All-America, I put in a new little defensive wrinkle that I hadn't used all year. I kept a quarter-man denial with a body on him. I wanted him to catch the ball out on the floor. I didn't want him backdooring us or coming off a back pick. I told my guys that if he came off a back pick, I didn't want him going baseline-side. I wanted him to go over the top to the middle. And I wanted to front him on the post. In other words, I didn't want to see Carter sneak behind us and get one of those SportsCenter highlight dunks on us.

With Williams, I knew he was going to score. He's a great shooter, but he had struggled in the previous year's semifinal game against Arizona (one of thirteen from the field). I wanted my guys to at least get a hand up against him, and not be too concerned about him taking the ball to the basket. He usually didn't take the ball all the way to the hoop. I just wanted our guys to be there, try to deny him the ball, get a hand up, and make him go backdoor. Don't let him catch the ball without challenging him.

With Cota, we wanted to keep him in front of the defender. And we didn't want to double on Cota. We wanted to make Cota beat us. We didn't want him to be able to get in the paint and dish. In that respect, he was like Bibby.

With Ndiaye, as well as Ademola Okulaja, we wanted to keep those guys off the boards.

There was an NCAA-mandated gambling seminar that day for the players. Then we had a forty-five-minute shootaround at the Alamodome. The place was filled with fans. And there sitting in the second row of the media seats were members of the Carolina coaching staff.

After the shootaround, I had to do an interview with CBS, and then report to the general press conference.

The legend of the triangle-and-two still lived. People wanted to know if it would be making a return against Carolina. I said I didn't think so.

"You know," I said, "the triangle-and-two should get a website, it's been so popular. It was some little junk thing we threw in and they struggled with it, and it went well for us."

The players were also on the dais. Had it been up to me, they could have answered all the questions. I just wanted to get out of there and watch more film. In fact, I spent some of the dead time during the press conference scribbling down diagrams.

One thing I didn't mind talking about was the small ribbon I wore on my shirt. It was an organ donor ribbon. I wore it in memory of Jerry Hegarty's daughter, Sarah, and to help promote the cause of organ donorship. I told the writers that I didn't have a great heart to donate, but that my kidneys were good for the taking.

My dad was an organ donor. It's like the epitaph on Ben Franklin's grave:

> Like the Cover of an old Book,
> Its contents torn out,
> And stript of its Lettering and Gilding,
> Lies here, Food for Worms,
> but the Work shall not be wholly lost:
> For it will, as he believ'd, appear once more,
> in a new & more perfect Edition,
> Corrected and amended
> By the Author.

Saturday, March 28

Kevin Costner was in town, which meant daily pickup games featuring Costner and his buddies. Costner is a huge sports guy, and he almost always comes to the Final Four and puts together a game.

I've played in them before. I got involved through Billy Campbell and kept getting invited back each year. It wasn't like I made a special trip just to play in Costner's game. Any coach who belongs in the National Association of Basketball Coaches gets a couple of tickets to the Final Four. I always came because I had to teach a clinic or give a speech or something like that.

The way it works is like this: there are games every day. There are no set times, just whenever Costner and everyone shows up. Kevin and I aren't close buddies. I've given him tickets before, and he's been nice enough to invite me to the games. A very nice guy.

One year we played in this beautiful old gym in Indianapolis. It would have been a perfect setting for a basketball commercial. Costner and his people arranged everything. There was a little buffet set up, and people would bring you water and towels when you were playing.

I've played in five or six of the games. Costner isn't a bad player. He's athletic and he plays hard. I don't know if he's a chucker, but he'll shoot the ball. Everybody in that game shoots it. Believe me, that game doesn't need a shot clock. Nobody in that game is ever going to be accused of help-side defense either. And there is no post play. The next pass into the post will be the first. You don't want to set up in the post because, let me tell you, that ball is not coming in there.

I'm not a big-time scorer in those games. I understand my limitations. First, I like my team to win. And second, I try to cover the backcourt, pass and move the ball. I'm not that good a shooter, but I'll do my Rick the Pick stuff. I don't coach while I'm out there. I want to play, not be Mr. Instruction.

But it's a lot of fun. Costner is very gracious. In Indianapolis, somebody was taking about fifty pictures. Dave Odom's kids were in the game. Krzyzewski's wife was there. One of Rick Pitino's assistants was there. Andy Katz, a newspaper guy from Fresno and a good friend of mine, played in the game. So did former Old Dominion star Nancy Lieberman-Cline. Krzyzewski played, but he played with a bad back. He also coached while he played. The other guys really liked that. It was like getting a golf lesson from Jack Nicklaus.

Somehow this Costner game has grown into a happening. People I knew were trying to get into the game so they could do something with me. Alex Wolff of *Sports Illustrated* wanted to get into the game, but it's not my game, it's Kevin's.

I didn't play in the game in San Antonio. Doc Rivers did. So did a player from Michigan State. A couple of other actors might play, that sort of thing.

I still try to play ball when I can. I always keep a ball in my car. I don't think I'm the best-playing Division I coach. Lorenzo Romar at Pepperdine is pretty good. Billy Donovan at Florida is in good shape, and he's young.

Our team war room was located on the hotel's third floor at the end of a hallway. There was a big sign at the entrance of the Rio Grande Room—Restricted Area. Authorized Access Only. Yeah, sure. A friend of mine went up there one time and the security guard, who was supposed to keep all strangers away, was sound asleep in his chair.

Brock and Donny were still looking at Rhode Island-Stanford tape, just in case we beat Carolina, and Stanford beat Kentucky in the other semifinal game. Jud, who watched film until 3:00 A.M., was back and busy looking at St. Louis-Kentucky tape. In all, we had twenty-five Stanford tapes, thirty-eight North Carolina tapes, and seventeen Kentucky tapes.

There was a breakfast buffet set up, as well as all our scouting and assignment boards. And just as we had done at our hotel in Newport Beach, we had taped poster sheets of North Carolina's sets on the meeting room walls.

The assignments had been altered slightly. Depending on need, injuries, or foul trouble, the best-case to worst-case matchups would go like this:

Cota—Andre, Jordie

Williams—Drew, Dave, Andre, Jordie

Carter—Al, Trace, Britton, Hanno, Drew, Dave

Jamison—Mike, Carlisle, Hanno, Britton, Al

Ndiaye—Hanno, Britton, Mike, Al, Carlisle

Okulaja—Al, Trace, Britton, Hanno

The main thing we stressed was keeping Carolina off the boards, especially Carter, Jamison, Okulaja, and Ndiaye. Plus, we never wanted to leave Williams alone, and we wanted to sit on Jamison's left shoulder, try to make him go a way he didn't want to.

Under Ndiaye's name, one of the assistants had written, "Very foul prone."

The players started coming in at nine-thirty. Drew started talking about something Vitale and Digger Phelps supposedly had said on the morning ESPN broadcast, that we were putting in a two-three zone for Carolina. If so, it was news to us.

Then Drew started imitating another announcer. "There is no way Utah will go to a triangle-and-two," said Drew in his best broadcast voice. "They can't match up man-to-man with North Carolina."

The players seemed loose enough. but my stomach was doing backflips. At about ten o'clock, I sent one of our managers down to the exercise room to save me a treadmill or a Stairmaster. I needed to exercise.

We had a quick shootaround at the Alamodome, but not before a small driving incident. The team went over on the charter bus, but I followed in the rental car. I think Rich drove, but somehow we got lost trying to follow the bus. I'm not the most patient passenger, so I told Rich to pull over and switch seats with me. I wasn't going to be late to my own shootaround, so I broke a few minor traffic laws to get there.

"I can run over a widow in this town and get away with it today," I told them.

The rest of the day was spent watching clips, reviewing notes, and worrying. Carolina was 34–3; we were 29–3. But they were Carolina. We were good, but we didn't have anybody with, say, Williams's Final Four experience. This was his third Final Four. And athlete for athlete, we didn't have anybody with the pure talent of Jamison or Carter.

Another concern was Final Four tickets. Thanks partly to my school president, and to a lot of phone calls on my part, I had 340 tickets for family and friends. What a pain. I don't recommend it to any coach trying to win a national championship.

A lot of people were nice enough to send telegrams or leave messages that day. A lot of people mentioned my dad. I usually don't get emotional about things, but I found myself tearing up and crying a lot.

Tom Schmit, a buddy of mine from Milwaukee, put his arm around me one day and said he wanted to talk to me. I thought he wanted another ticket or something.

"You know," he said, "your dad's watching and my dad's watching."

That was really special. It's hard to think about. It's even hard to talk about now. But I think my dad would have been proud of me.

Says Rich Panella: *"I've seen Rick speak at a number of camps. Every time he gets to the part where he tells the basketball campers to appreciate their parents, he gets choked up. He's not a touchy-feely kind of guy, but he gets emotional when it comes to his dad. Now me, I grew up in a neighborhood where men hugged and kissed. But Rick isn't like that."*

I thought about my dad all the time during the Final Four. You know, Don Donoher sent me one of the nicest gifts I've ever received. It's a wood clock and there's an inscription on a brass plate. It reads: Time Never Erases the Memory of One's Dad.

Don will never know how much that inscription means to me. It was such a touching and heartfelt gesture.

My dad was such a great dad. Like, when we needed $20 for a baseball league, he came up with the money. And this is when he didn't have an extra twenty bucks to give to some kids for Little League baseball.

Or he'd go find an alderman to help arrange for a backstop to be put up at a baseball field. Or when Mike Schneider wanted to go to West Point, my dad helped arrange the appointment. All my friends loved my dad.

That was the thing about the Final Four: my dad would have loved it. He would have loved seeing all those boyhood friends of mine, and he would have been happy for my success.

When I was growing up, most of my friends lived in very modest homes. Mike's dad was a cop and there were seven kids. You'd go to a house and you might get a glass of Kool-Aid. At my house, we never had Coke, we had American Soda. My parents would go out every week and buy cases of American Soda, which is as generic a soda as you can get. That's what my dad and mom would give my friends when they came over.

My dad shared everything. I wanted to share the Final Four with him. I love my mom. She's such a nice person, but what has happened in my career, well, it sometimes escapes her. A dad knows. For instance, when Doleac was drafted a few months after the tournament, his dad had that ear-to-ear smile. It was like Phil wanted to go around and be introduced as Mike Doleac's dad. That was like the pinnacle of being a dad for him. I would have liked my dad to have been able to do that at the Final Four.

That's why I was so happy to see Hanno's dad, Kari, at the Final Four. He flew in from Finland just to see his son play. I told the kids, "You don't know how special this is. Let me know what I can do to help."

The Kentucky-Stanford game was first. I didn't actually see it, but somebody told me the Stanford band, which has a reputation for irreverance, was tough on the Wildcats as they came on the court for warm-ups. The band members started shouting, "Alcohol! Tobacco! Firearms!" Of course, this is the same band that instead of yelling, "Defense!" like most bands, yells, "Pursue them, pursue them! Make them relinquish the ball!"

Stanford almost beat Kentucky. Kentucky was down by nine in the second half, and then went on a 16–4 run to move ahead. The game went into overtime, but Stanford couldn't hang on. Final score: Kentucky 86, Stanford 85.

Donny made another pregame prediction. He said we'd win because of our rebounding and free throw shooting. I felt good about our chances, but I was worried about Jamison and Carter. I didn't want Carter to rev up the crowd with one of his famous backdoor dunks.

We went on a six to nothing run to start the game, had a twelve-point lead with 9:13 left in the first half, and a sixteen-point lead with 8:29 to go. At halftime we were ahead, 35–22. By then, Ndiaye had already picked up his third foul.

As for a certain announcer who said we couldn't use the triangle-and-two . . . we did. And it worked fairly well. Whenever Williams tried to drive the lane, we collapsed on him and tried to strip the ball. Carter had ten points, but no killer dunks. Jamison had eight points and eight rebounds, but everybody else on Carolina was struggling.

Meanwhile, eight of our nine guys had scored, led by Andre, who had eight points and nine rebounds.

Even though we had a double-digit lead, I knew Carolina would make a second-half run. After every timeout I told them to expect a trap or a double team. "I'm going to tell you something," I said. "I lost to Carolina years ago when I was at Marquette. We were ranked in the top twenty-five and we had beaten Dayton at Marquette. Then we played Carolina on national TV and we were up ten or twelve points, just kicking their butts. Then with about four minutes to go, they start coming with these traps. These guys are going to come with the traps against you. That's their M.O. They're going to body you low and I don't want you to be surprised by this."

Ndiaye got his fourth foul with 17:50 left in the game, and fouled out with zero points and only two rebounds about two minutes later. But Carolina slowly whittled away at our lead, cutting it to two points with 2:01 to go.

With forty-nine seconds left and us up, 59–54, Carter fouled Drew—the same Drew who had missed a pair of key foul shots with less than a minute remaining in our game against West Virginia.

Jud had given Drew some advice about free throws. He told him to move back a couple of inches. Drew had been missing some of his foul shots long.

Says Drew Hansen: *"As I was getting ready to go up to the line, Mike came up and said, 'Drew, we need to make these. C'mon.'*
"I said, 'I know, Mike.' "

Drew made both shots. About fifteen seconds later, when Cota fouled Mike, it was Doleac who only made one of two free throws.

Carolina kept fouling, and we kept making just enough free throws to stay ahead and slowly add to our slim lead. They tried a couple of desperation threes, but it didn't matter. We won, 65–59.

Somehow we had done the unthinkable. Again.

I shook Guthridge's hand and then, as I was walking off the court, I pointed to my mom in the stands. That was about as emotional as I had ever gotten. I saw Betsy too. She had tears in her eyes.

It was an amazing win for a lot of different reasons. We were in the Final Four championship game for the first time since 1944. Andre had been magnificent: sixteen points, fourteen rebounds, and seven assists. If he had another game like that Monday night against Kentucky, I was going to retire and become his agent.

Andre had come so far, so fast. Just about five weeks earlier, Nellie had seen him play and said he was a CBA guard, at best. "Nellie," I said, "I'm going to tell you something. He's damn good."

Carolina's Carter finished with twenty-one points (but no lob dunks). Credit Al for doing a nice job that probably went unnoticed by the guy watching the game at home. It also went unnoticed by whoever typed up the postgame player quotes for the media. They attributed his comments to *Andrew* Jensen.

Williams missed two of twelve shots, and Jamison's fourteen points was one of his three lowest scoring totals of the season. When it was finished, Jamison went to center court, kneeled down, and kissed the hardwood. I think that was his way of saying good-bye to the college game.

Our kids were jubilant. I told them to enjoy the victory, to go back to the hotel, order some pizza, play cards, have a good time. "Don't give a fleeting thought to Kentucky," I said. "We will get together tomorrow and have something ready for you."

Britton had done a nice defensive job and added seven points. Here he was a freshman, and he was going to play in a national title game.

"I don't even know how to celebrate," he said in the locker room. "I'm so much in awe. I think we just beat an NBA team. We're just teaching everybody that the game can still be won below the rim."

Britton was asked about his matchup with Ndiaye. There had been some jawing back and forth, but I wasn't aware of anything more than that.

Says Britton Johnsen: *"One of the reporters after the game said, 'What happened with you and Ndiaye?' I told him what happened, because I figured he had seen the whole thing. But it turns out nobody really saw it, except a couple of players.*

"We were talking trash on the floor. All I said was, 'I'm 100 pounds lighter than you, and I'm kicking your butt.'

"He kept telling me he was going to mess me up. He was running smack about me pretty much the whole game. He even spit on me."

I didn't know about any of this. I was at the main press conference telling reporters about our man-to-man defense. And when I got back to the locker room, I just wanted to savor the moment. Hunsaker was there. So was Mike Schneider. In the other corner of the locker room, a reporter from Helsinki was interviewing Hanno in Finnish.

"I could stay here all night," I told them. "It's just so special. I'm just so happy for the players."

I did a few more interviews, took a shower, changed, and then gave my clothes to Bruce Woodbury, our director of media relations. "I'm sorry they smell, Woody," I said. "But make sure the managers get them."

Doug Trautman came into the dressing room still carrying a cigar from the hot tub in Newport. I had told him that night in California that he should go ahead and smoke it, that all I wanted was to make it to the Final Four. But he wouldn't light up. "No," he said, "I'll wait until a Monday night game."

Ben Howland was in the dressing room too. "You're going to win, you know that," he said.

"I know," I said. "Right now, I am so happy."

Maybe it was the euphoria of the moment, but I really did think we could win the damn thing. Maybe Strohm was right about the Utes and destiny.

But before any of that, before another game, another VHS cassette of clips, another coaches meeting, we had a party to go to—my treat. A cop escorted us out of the Alamodome and we were on our way. Of course, we ran a few red lights on the way there. "Hey, we're the Utes," I said, as I gunned the car. I didn't figure any cop would give me a ticket that night.

It was an evening to remember. We had beaten Carolina and in less than forty-eight hours we would be playing for a national championship game against Kentucky, the same program that had eliminated us from the tournament in 1993, in 1996, and in 1997. Van Horn had good reason to call Kentucky "The Big Blue Nasty."

Still, I was on a victory high. I couldn't sleep when I got back to the hotel at 2:00 A.M., so I stayed up and watched film.

What I didn't know—at least, not until the next morning—was that a major controversy involving race had begun to unfold. At the center of it would be one of my players.

9
Two Days
Like No Others

Sunday, March 29

I don't know how they got my number, or why the hotel kept putting them through, but my phone was ringing off the hook that morning—radio shows, TV stations, sports writers, editorial boards of newspapers. They were all calling me about an article in the morning newspaper.

An excerpt from the *San Antonio Express-News:* *"[Britton] Johnsen accused [Makhtar] Ndiaye of spitting in his face during the first half of Utah's 65–59 victory over North Carolina on Saturday in the national semifinals at the Alamodome.*

"Ndiaye countered by saying he never spit on Johnsen and that Johnsen directed a racial slur at him throughout the game.

" 'I don't have anything to say about spitting on him,' said Ndiaye, a native of Dakar, Senegal. 'Why don't you ask him about what he said to me. He has no right to use the N-word at me. He used it more than once, and I'm not sure that's the first time he's done it. He said it to me the whole game, every time we got into contact.'

"Johnsen denied directing any racial slurs at Ndiaye. He said Ndiaye spit in his face while the two were running side by side down the court."

Another story, this one in the *Chicago Tribune*, quoted Ndiaye as admitting he had spat on Britton. "Yes, I did. He called me the N-word. You call me that, I'm going to do something about it."

That's how I started my Sunday. From the time I got up that morning, to the end of the shootaround that day, the incident was the focal point of my life.

The reverberations went through the press corps with lightning speed. And with our team being almost all white, and with many Mormons, that's a very easy song to play, supposedly. I may have, and we may have, been more sensitive to it because there's always an inference about Mormons relative to blacks, that supposedly Mormons aren't as tolerant or as accepting, or whatever. That isn't true, by the way.

The first thing I did was call Britton in. I said, "You've got to tell me exactly what happened. If you tell me, and you're wrong with what you did, I can live with that. But you've got to tell me what happened."

So he told me, and I knew he was telling the truth. I knew he wouldn't lie to me. He said he didn't say it, didn't call Ndiaye the N-word. He told me the kid threw a cheap shot and then spit on him. Britton said he told the kid, "I'm 100 pounds lighter than you, and I'm kicking your ass." So he was talking some trash. The kid was talking to him.

We talked about it a little more and then I said, "Since you were there, rather than have this cloud of mystery as to what happened, I want you to talk to the media." I knew this kid was telling the truth. I knew he hadn't done what Ndiaye said he did. So I decided to bring Britton to this press conference. He wasn't happy about it, but he trusted me.

Meanwhile, Carolina had left town, but there was something about them releasing a statement. Then Dean Smith went on TV and said what a wonderful kid Ndiaye was, and how all the secretaries in the Carolina basketball office loved him, and all that.

Here's Dean the Deity—and I love Dean, I respect Dean—but I wanted everyone to know that my kid didn't say what Ndiaye said he said. I don't blame Dean for sticking up for one of his players. But I said to myself, "Hey, I've got some credibility here too."

We had a press conference right before practice started. Now you have to understand that this is like the worst nightmare for a player and for a coach. Even worse, it's happening at the NCAA tournament, the day before the championship game, with a kid who did absolutely nothing wrong. And as we're getting ready to do the press conference, the rest of my team is down on the floor with no direction. The assistants are there, but it's not the same thing. I've got the game plan. And then you have the NCAA, and they're waiting to start the practice clock, and believe me, that clock starts the minute you set foot on the floor.

It was not a question-and-answer kind of press conference. We had to get to practice. Plus, I could tell Britton was upset by the whole situation. The whole thing took about five or ten minutes.

"I have simply asked Britton what happened and I want him to tell you," I said to the media. "Maybe the language is a little graphic, but I think I would like him to speak the exact truth from his heart."

Britton leaned toward the microphone and told his story.

"Well, just to start out with, before the game started, Coach told us to beat this team we had to play a physical game," he said. "I went out and was throwing my body around on Ndiaye and, you know, that's the game of basketball. We were getting really competitive and our bodies were clashing into each other. He slapped me across the face at first, and I kind of ran by. And he told me he was going to kick my f-ing A, and all this. And it kept happening and happening. And the only words that came out of my mouth, I said, 'Look, I'm a hundred pounds lighter than you and I'm kicking your butt.' And he spit at me.

"I never called anyone the N-word. I never did. It is a joke that this is happening. I'm a freshman and this is like, you know, blocking some of our success and happiness. It shouldn't even have been an issue. It did not happen, you know.

"That's it."

I told Britton to leave and then made one final comment.

"I'm only going to say this once. No one has more respect for Dean Smith, Guthridge, and the North Carolina program than me. And I went to visit them. I am friends with those people.

"I know what Dean Smith did at those lunch counters and buses. I tell you what, I've been in more civil rights marches than probably most of you, with my father. I stand by this boy's statement 100 percent. I know this boy's family. I know his character. I know his older brother who played for me. And I know this boy. And I think that it would detract from this great program that Carolina has, the class and dignity with which they conduct their program, the person and the man that is Guthridge and is Dean Smith.

"I think this is really an unfortunate incident. This boy is very upset about this. But rather than have to address this with 200 people, or some specter of racism be cast over him the rest of his life, he has spoken to you what he believes. I stand behind his statement. And I'm very sorry that it had to come into one of the nicest events that anyone could be a part of.

"So that's it. I don't have anything else to say about it. I think we have tried to be very fair and I hope that you would respect the fact that he's nineteen years old and believe me, I mean, I stand behind him 100 percent. If in fact that happened, I will resign."

And I would have resigned. I can't say that, and then not do it. But I knew the kid hadn't said it. I was so sure of it, I offered to have Britton take a lie detector test—and North Carolina could choose the tester. Still, I wanted to add a punctuation mark to the press conference. I said what I said about resigning because I thought it would give tremendous credence to Britton's situation. I thought that would allay any concerns that people had. But had it turned out to be true, I would have felt the responsibility to resign. I tell my team all the time, "We're not a black team. We're not a white team. We're not a Mormon team. We're not a Catholic team. We are the University of Utah."

Right after the press conference, they put Britton on a golf cart and drove him out to the court. Then I got on one and headed out to the floor. It was ridiculous.

I got out of practice that day knowing we hadn't practiced well. Britton was still upset, and the team was worried about the kid. So it wasn't like the normal preparation, where you're discussing tendencies and stuff. You know, "23 goes left," and "42 likes to drive to the middle."

I also met with the NCAA basketball committee about the entire incident. And then I had a meeting with the CBS guys—Jim Nantz and Billy Packer—and they were terrific about the whole thing. Obviously this thing had taken on a life of its own and was bigger than it should have been. I knew they were going to say something about it on TV. They had to say something about it.

Nantz and Packer weren't at the press conference, so I had Britton meet with them. Nantz said, "Look, we know you didn't say it," which I thought was a strong statement. He said, "We're going to have to address it Monday night, but it's not going to affect you in any way."

They were very good. They helped settle me and the kid. I mean, that's a serious accusation, what Ndiaye said.

That night Guthridge and I kept trading phone messages. We finally talked, and he apologized for what had happened.

* * *

Want to know what a good guy Karl Malone is? He called twice to wish us well against Kentucky. The first time he called, I was in the middle of watching film, so I couldn't get away to talk. Then he called again when I was talking to Britton about the Ndiaye incident. Britton was really upset about that whole Ndiaye thing, so I wanted to make sure he was okay. I felt bad that I couldn't take Malone's call, but I hope he knows how much I appreciated the gesture. That was really a classy thing for him to do.

At least the day wasn't completely devoid of humor. Earlier, a writer asked Doleac about playing for a coach who was "the king of one-liners." It happened at a team press conference held a few hours before the one with Britton.

"We don't hear the one-liners very often," Mike said. "We are not normally up here to listen to this. Our practice is a little different. There might be one-liners, but they're not quite as funny."

Monday, March 30

North Carolina released its statement. Ndiaye retracted his accusation that Britton had called him the N-word. He also denied having spit at Britton.

"I got upset in the locker room when some reporters were asking me about what we were saying to each other and I let my emotions get away from me," Ndiaye said in the written statement. "I have sent Britt a letter of apology and wish him and the Utah team well tonight in the championship game. I am sorry that this has caused any distraction for Britt and his teammates as they prepared for tonight's game."

There was also a very gracious statement from Guthridge. Among other things, Guthridge said, "[I] hope this matter is closed so that Utah can concentrate on its game tonight for the national championship."

But the truth was, we were into game day and I was still having to deal with this Ndiaye incident.

Weeks later, the NCAA reprimanded Ndiaye for his comments. I'm not sure what purpose it served, other than to further embarrass the kid and draw attention to what was now a moot point. What's the reprimand going to mean to him? He's out of the NCAA. I think it shows the political nature of the NCAA and the importance of good press that it tries to cultivate.

Later that summer, Ndiaye came up to me during a Lakers game and said he had told reporters in San Antonio that Britton hadn't called him the N-word. But I wasn't going to get into that. There were 15,000 people around. It was June. I was doing some TV stuff. What's the point of discussing it with him? He wasn't being conciliatory. I'm not going to argue that point there. So I said, "Okay."

I think this about the incident: it was terribly unfortunate. I don't think Ndiaye represents Carolina basketball. I think Michael Jordan, George Karl, Bobby Jones, Larry Brown . . . there's 200 guys who represent the best of Carolina basketball. You'd want them for sons, for husbands, for brothers-in-law.

It was time to focus completely on Kentucky. This was a program that was making its third consecutive championship game appearance. Knowing how hard it had been for us to reach the Final Four, I found that almost incomprehensible.

First of all, they have perhaps the best athletic director in the business. I couldn't imagine working for a better guy than C. M. Newton.

They also have the legacy of Rick Pitino. His drive and determination revitalized that program. The way Van Horn helped us establish something here, Pitino helped them.

And you have to give Tubby Smith a tremendous amount of credit. He had to combine new players with existing players, and he had to do it with a new staff and a system that somewhat resembled the one used by Pitino. And he had to do it at a program that is accustomed to success. It is one of the premier basketball programs in the country. Think about it: thirteen Final Four appearances. Only UCLA and North Carolina have reached the Final Four more often. So if you're Kentucky, you can go into a recruit's house and say, "Look, if you come here, on average you will play in the Final Four at least once during your career." Arithmetically, this is what has transpired. That's an amazing thing to be able to say to somebody.

Tubby's team didn't have the sheer talent that Carolina had, but it had enough. It also had depth, athleticism, and discipline.

Andre would guard Wayne Turner. Our scouting report on Turner:

Strong, aggressive penetrator. Prefers to get left. Looks to take the ball strong off pick and rolls. Likes to shot fake. Has a strong hesitation dribble in transition. Looks to stay in and rebound when he penetrates. Will use a right shoulder spin move in the post.

Keep him in front of you. Sit on his left toe. Force him into the picks on the ball. Deny two steps past three-point line. Get a strong driving line. Stay down on shot fakes and hesitation dribbles. Block out.

Two-guard Jeff Sheppard was next. Drew would take him, with Dave, Al, and Trace next in the rotation.

Tremendous shooter with tremendous NBA range. Shoots the ball quick off the single and double staggers. Likes to lower his head and force penetration left into the lane. He drives left to score, right to pass. Will dribble the ball up in transition when he gets the rebound.

No help. No cover. No catch. Deny two steps past three. Never leave him. Sit on his left toe. Get a strong driving line on him. Block out!

Al would guard Allen Edwards, Kentucky's small forward. When Al was out, Trace, Drew, or Dave would get Edwards.

Good three-point shooter. Runs left lane in transition. Drives right for layup, left to jump shot.

Deny two steps past three. Make him dribble to a shot. Block out!

Hanno had Padgett, their strong forward. Britton, Al, and Trace were also in the rotation.

By the way, Padgett and I saw each other a day or two before the game. I shook his hand and congratulated him. No hard feelings. He's a good player and not a bad guy.

Plays inside and outside. Takes the ball out in transition. Usually dribbles in the post. Likes a left shoulder. Jump hook in the post. Catch and shoot three-pointer on perimeter. Will drive both directions on perimeter. Good rebounder.

Three-quarters to position. Make him score through you. Be physical with him. Shade his left shoulder in the post. Deny two steps past three. Block out!

Mike would have Nazr Mohammed, with Carlisle and Hanno in backup roles.

Runs to ball side in transition. Likes to look for the lob from the wing. Good offensive rebounder, usually dribbles in the post. Likes a left shoulder spin move or jump hook in the post. If he catches it on the perimeter, he likes to shot fake and take one or two dribbles for shot.

Three-quarters to behind. Must be physical with him and do your work early. He must score over you. Deny to fifteen feet. Block out!

Those were the starters. But Kentucky's bench saw a lot of playing time.

On forward Heshimu Evans, a former star for Fran Fraschilla at Manhattan before transferring to Kentucky:

Could start. Plays perimeter and post. Very good rebounder. Standstill three-point shooter. Struggles dribbling with his right hand. Always dribbles in the post.
Must make him dribble to a shot. Sit on his left toe. Make him score over you in the post. Deny one step past three. Block out!

On center Jamaal Magloire:

Physical, strong player. Runs to ball-side block in transition. Left shoulder jump hook. Likes to spin drive to his right shoulder.
Make him score over you. Be physical with him. Deny to fifteen feet. Gap yo-yo. Block out!

On guard Cameron Mills:

Three-point shooter. Likes to shot fake one and two dribbles for a shot.
Deny two steps past three. Make dribble to a shot. No help. No cover. No catch.

On guard Saul Smith, Tubby's son:

Mostly plays backup point guard. Thinks pass first, shot second. Good quickness. Poor free throw shooter.
Deny first step past three. Keep him in front of you. Gap yo-yo his post feeds.

To beat Kentucky, we wanted to control tempo, rebound, pressure Sheppard and Mills, try to limit threes by Sheppard, Edwards, and Padgett, and not allow one steal to become two or three.

Once again, the players seemed loose, especially Doleac. Mike had grown a goatee earlier in the tournament and said he wouldn't shave it off unless we beat Kentucky.

The players had a late breakfast and then got their per diem money. We had a quick meeting and a twelve-thirty shootaround at the Alamodome.

It was quiet in our locker room before the game. Plus, I was struggling with a decision involving Drew. Our new president had sent me a telegram. It said that Drew had gotten into Michigan Law School. I still get emotional just thinking about it. Even as we were going to the game that day, I asked Dick Hunsaker, "Do you think I should tell him he got into Michigan?"

I decided not to. It wouldn't have mattered one way or the other. That was the great thing about Drew. You could have told him, "Drew, if you win this game, there's $50 million for you." Or you could have said, "Drew, if you win this game, there's five cents in this envelope for you." He wouldn't have played any harder for the $50 million or any less for the five cents. That's Drew.

I didn't head out to the court until about four minutes before tip-off. I walked down to the Kentucky bench and shook hands with Tubby.

"Congratulations on reaching the final and have a good game," I said.

I think he said the same thing back. I also shook hands with the Kentucky assistants, the game officials, and some of the NCAA tournament committee members. Then I got a drink of water and waited.

Kentucky pressured Andre early, and forced a couple of turnovers that turned into points, but then we settled down. Doleac was getting good post position and making them pay, and Hanno was also a presence inside.

We had a 41–31 lead at halftime, but I didn't feel we had momentum going into the second half. Hanno had two fouls. Andre had six turnovers and had played eighteen-plus minutes. Doleac had twelve points and six rebounds, but he also had played sixteen hard minutes against that tag team of Mohammed and Magloire. Caton's leg was bothering him. And Drew was hurting.

Says Drew Hansen: *"Nobody outside the team knew. I think I strained my back two days before the Carolina game. Halfway though the Carolina game it was just killing me. But then it loosened up at halftime and I was okay for the rest of the game. But during the postgame press conference, it started to tighten up again.*

"I got back to the hotel that night and I was in a lot of pain. I didn't leave my bed hardly at all during the next two days. It was pretty bad."

Drew played fifteen minutes of the first half, but his defense wasn't as crisp. The will was there, but not the body. He came into the locker room at halftime and you could tell he was in a lot of pain.

Drew wanted to go ahead and get a shot so he could play the second half. I called him over for a private meeting.

"Drew, don't try to be a hero here," I said.

"Coach, I want to play."

He said it through gritted teeth.

So they gave him the shot. I watched the doctor do it and I got really emotional. It bothered me. I've never advocated that. I've never wanted to do that.

I always tell my medical staff, "If you ever put a kid at risk, I will get you fired and then I'll resign." I never want to win in a way that would remotely hurt a kid or put a kid at risk. But in Drew's case, they said, "This shot is never going to hurt him. It's never going to cause any damage. We're just deadening the pain so he can play."

Our ten-point lead didn't last long. Kentucky cut it to seven points with 15:15 left to play. About a minute later, Hanno picked up his third foul. Our lead kept shrinking, Andre and Doleac kept getting more tired, and my substitution options kept decreasing.

With 4:54 to go, Kentucky took the lead for good, 65–64. By then, we were out of gas.

Says Keith Van Horn: *"I was watching the game. I thought we had it won until I saw Mike and Andre walk up the court. I noticed the same thing in the North Carolina game too. They were so tired."*

Says Mike Doleac: *"One time Andre brought the ball over and about fifteen seconds later, I crossed over the half-court line. So I guess I was tired."*

When the game was over, the first thing I did was walk up to Tubby and tell him congratulations.

"You were the better team tonight," I said. "You'll be a great champion and you deserve it."

He said, "Nice job," and after that I don't remember another word. He wanted to get with his players and start cutting down the nets. I wanted to get to my players and get in the locker room. It was a bitter defeat.

After the game, I tried to express to each of the players how much they had meant to me and the program. I went to the seniors first. In fact, it was after the game that I told Drew the news about Michigan Law School.

Says Jeff Strohm: *"Rick was crying. He was all misty eyed. Typical him, he set the tone for the postgame. He handed Drew the letter from Michigan. Drew got emotional. Everybody did. He said, 'Fellas, if this is the biggest loss you have in your life, then you're very lucky people. The success we had this year is going to be small compared to other things.'*

"He built everybody back up."

I told Mike that it was an honor and privilege to coach him, that he was a great captain and that he had had a great career at Utah. I told him he would go on to pro ball, and that was very special. And I made sure to tell him that I appreciated how hard he had worked and how well he had represented the university.

I pretty much told Drew the same thing. "You got a lot of blood out of that turnip," I said. "You came the furthest with the least ability of any guy I've coached." And I had had a lot of guys like Drew.

I'll also say this about Mike and Drew: never again in the history of the Final Four will a team have two academic All-Americans. It won't happen. We were the first, and we'll be the last.

I told Hanno, "I'm so proud of you coming from Finland and doing well in school. You were 7,500 miles from home and you conducted yourself with dignity and class. I know it wasn't always easy for you. There must have been times of great loneliness." I also told him that I appreciated and enjoyed his enthusiasm. He was always happy for everybody else's success. In the worst of times, when I would get into a heated tirade, he would always come out clapping and try to spur the other guys on.

I told Andre, "Andre, I'm so proud of what you've accomplished. There have been better players in this tournament, but there has been no better competitor. Your competitive nature and instinct drove us all. It was so much fun to coach you.

"You just got tired, Andre, that's all. But you should know that as proud as I am of what you accomplished here on the court, nothing even approximates how I feel about you relative to what you've accomplished in the classroom. Your achievement there is wonderful. You're going to go on, graduate, and one day you're going to have a basketball career ahead of you. We'll sit down and see where you're at."

I told Al, "You fought back so hard. The last ten games, you were the guy I was so enthralled with. You were the Al that left me as a freshman: a great competitor, a great spirit. You really got it back, you got in shape. Now you've got to use it as a great jumping-off point for next season. You're the best defender I've ever coached. You and Drew were the two best blockout guys I've coached. The ball would bounce before anybody from the other team had a chance to get it. You guys put a body on somebody every play.

"I know sometimes I look like I'm from Mars. I'm so competitive, and my hair is sticking out, and smoke is coming out of my nose, but I really enjoyed your unselfishness. You're unselfish to a fault."

This is no secret: Al is my favorite. The players know that. He's my favorite because he plays such great defense with a modicum of talent. He's such a great warrior, without a warrior's body. He's such a great competitor. But Al doesn't bring a lot to the table. He kind of has a blocky body. He doesn't have real long arms. In fact, he has kind of short arms. He's got those Tyrannosaurus Rex arms. But I love that kid. He truly understands the geometry of the game.

I went to David and said, "David, I know it's been tough for you. I've been hard on you. You're a great kid. You've really grown as a person here. You've really emerged as a student, and those things stand out more than the basketball.

"Basketball-wise, I realize it was hard for you not to be 'The Man,' hard for you to be the third or fourth scoring option. But you never pouted overtly and you never tried to take anybody down with you. You kept your head up and you kept fighting through it and persevered."

At the time, I didn't know if Dave was coming back or not. I had told him during the season, "If you don't want to play this way, then you should leave."

I told Jordie that I appreciated his efforts, that I thought he gave us what he could. "You were a guy on the team who tried hard, a guy with relatively limited ability and you played to the best of it," I said. "I know that you incurred my wrath—because I'm hard on point guards—and you did a good job of hanging in there. You made big shots for us during the year."

In fact, I told both he and Dave that we wouldn't have been there without them. We wouldn't have been there without any of those guys, but I think the other guys knew it. I don't think Dave and Jordie, in particular, knew it. And I meant it when I said it.

I told Caton, "You were the toughest freshman I've ever coached, including Alex."

There was a game early in our conference schedule—it was at BYU—and Caton hit some big shots. Afterward, some of the writers asked him about it and he said, "I just try to do what I can do, and not what I can't do."

More than any freshman I've ever coached, he let the game come to him, but was opportunistic about taking shots. He knew exactly what his limitations were. He knew exactly where his range ended. But he didn't err on the side of caution. If he was open, he would shoot it, and I wanted him to. He lacked fear in every aspect of the game. He'd take big free throws confidently. He'd take big open shots. He'd step in on anyone and take a charge.

Now, by nature, he's a very poor rebounder. I don't know why that is. He just does not have the knack for it. But he played through injuries like you wouldn't believe. He never once said one thing about them. He'd tell the trainer that he had a "dead leg." That's what he called it: "dead leg." He was hurt, but he never complained and he never wanted out of practice. I would get on him and say, "Look, I don't want to baby-sit you when you're hurt. You've got to play with pain, but not injury. You're injured, now sit down." But he just wanted to play basketball. He loved to compete. I told him he had a great, great year.

I told Britton, "This was a great year for you. You overcame a lot of adversity. I realize how difficult all this must have been given the notoriety, given all the attention you had as you were recruited. But you handled it beyond your years."

Carlisle was next. He had already decided to go on a Mormon mission, and in this case, I thought it would benefit him. I said, "You are a great guy who has to come out of your shell to play tough and play physical. You can't be Mr. Congeniality. You have to be mean on the court. Not dirty, not a cheap-shot guy, but tough. Then, off the court, if you want to save souls, then go do that.

"You have a lot of ability. You had a good year. I know, contrary to my personality, your personality is a lot different. I really appreciated how you stuck with it, how you started to become a good talker and be a good competitor. You really are a pure person, a great guy, and you don't realize how far you've come, and how much self-confidence and self-esteem and sense of self you have. A mission will be good for you. It will be a great experience and a great opportunity for personal growth. You're going to be a hell of a player when you get back."

I thanked Barratt and Sharp. I said, "Barratt, you did a good job. You and Sharp headed up that Grey squad. You guys went out every day and tried to replicate the other team's plays. And Adam, you really worked hard and got better as the season went on. Both of you were very positive on the bench, happy for your teammates. You knew you weren't going to get in, but you were consummate team members. You rose above a difficult situation. I appreciate that, and everyone in this room appreciates it."

I told Nate, "Let me tell you something, Nate. You could be a hell of a player. You really grew this year. Next year it's going to be on you. You're going to be a hell of a player in this program. You've come a long way. I used to critique you and you'd cry. Now you've really become a man here and done better in school. I'll tell you something: if you don't give us that lift off the bench against Wake Forest, we don't win that game. All year long I felt comfortable when I had to play you. I knew you'd play well. When I played you against West Virginia, your head was into the game. You bounded higher and nobody relished other people's successes more than you and Hanno."

And that's another thing I loved about that team. It would really be hard to pick the most animated guy on our bench. In every game during the tournament—and I took a lot of pride in my team when it happened—the refs would come over and say, "Get your bench down! Get your bench down!" And I'd say, "Who said something to you? You tell me who said something and I'll talk to them right now."

But they'd just say, "No, no, nobody said anything to us. Just tell them to sit down."

I'd say, "All they're doing is cheering. But I'll try to get them down."

But I never did a thing. I'd kind of smile benignly and then start focusing on the game again. I wanted my bench players up clapping. And Nate was always excited.

I told Brandon Sluga, a sophomore guard from West Jordan, Utah, that he was a great walk-on, one of the best I'd ever had and certainly the best on the team. I told him I appreciated his unselfishness.

I told Zac Dalton, a nonscholarship freshman guard from Boise, that I really appreciated his enthusiasm and how he handled never getting to play. "You got a lot of shots for the guys, and you were subservient to what we needed as a team."

I thanked our managers, Jake Noel, Brian Bolinder, and Ryan Hackett. I thanked our assistant coaches.

I was very proud of the whole team and I told them so.

"For you guys coming back, there is another day," I said. "For Doleac and Drew, this is it. You know, it would be easier for me to get up here tonight and say it was a great season—and it was a great season. Retrospectively, it's going to be chronicled as one of the great accomplishments in college ball in the annals of Utah basketball history. But the reason you got here is because you felt bad every time you lost. You always had that sting and that burn of defeat.

"Kentucky is a hell of a team. We got beat by a better team tonight. We gave a great effort and we can feel a great sense of accomplishment. But we didn't win and we should feel bad tonight.

"Next week when we have the banquet, or next year, and years from

now as your life goes on, there's going to be a thousand positive moments, and maybe hundreds of very nice moments for all of you. Like,
I'll always remember the night I took you to El Paso in the private plane,
and it was just you and me—no managers, assistants, trainers. Just us
in that plane telling jokes. I'll always remember how you reached out
and helped other people. And I'll always remember that you were students. You represent the best of what this tournament is about. For that,
I just thank you for allowing me to coach you."

I wanted them to go away feeling good, but I didn't want them to
forget how close they had come. The same applied to me. Maybe one
year—and I don't think it will ever happen—I'd like to walk out of the
locker room the last night of the season and say, "Jeez, there is nothing
more. We are the champs."

I think it's hard for people to understand what it takes to win one
of these things. I think sometimes it's hard for our players to understand
what it takes. That's because our fans, the parents of our players, our
administration, the whole state of Utah were thrilled with our season.
And on one level, they should be. I certainly was.

I really believe this of the fans in Utah: I think they'd rather not go
to the NCAA tournament than compromise the academics. If we lost
and the players were classy and the rules were adhered to, and the education remained a top priority, I believe I could go on there forever with
mediocrity, as long as the kids played hard. I couldn't have kids who
didn't play hard. But I could have kids who weren't good players.

I really believe the fans and people of Utah would accept that. They
are good people with high morals, and they value education and fair
play more than they do an NCAA championship. And that's the way it
should be. Now maybe some of this sounds naive, but I really believe
this to be true.

But that doesn't mean they weren't excited about our accomplishments. When UCLA wins a national championship, they've got 1,000
people waiting for them at the airport. We get to the Final Four, and
there's thousands of people at the airport. We get to the championship
game and lose, and there's still something like 50,000 people downtown
for the parade. And that's great, and a wonderful gesture by our fans
and supporters.

The thing is, they had people patting them on the back, and it
would have been easy for them not to realize they had lost that night.
They needed to know they had lost that night, and they needed to know
they should never accept that, that you always have to feel bad about it,

as much as you have to move on and try to get better from it. But you
don't want to accept it. You don't want all those family and friends to
say, "It's all right." No, it isn't all right. You lost. But what are you going
to do to make sure it doesn't happen again? That's why when I talked
to every returning player after the game, I tried to give them something
to think about and work on during the off-season.

I was so tired after that game. I hadn't had a day off in fourteen
months. I was basketballed out.

And I was so discouraged. It hurt so bad to lose. But despite the
loss, I didn't think there was anybody in the country who could say we
were anything less than the No. 2 team at tournament's end. And with
all due respect to every other team, I would say this: our kids were No.
1 in the country.

I sat in that locker room for a long time. It was just me and a couple
of buddies. I stared at the stat sheet, but then let it fall to the wet tile
floor.

"I don't think I want that," I said. "It's not going to be in our scrap-
book."

Someone mentioned that John Wooden had been pulling for us.

"Is that what Wooden said? That makes my night," I said.

Dean Smith and I talked for a few moments. He said, "You ran out
of moves." And he was right. But maybe I should have called that full
timeout to let the guys rest. Who knows?

I did make one decision after that game: to go to the Kentucky
Derby this year. I better win too. The Commonwealth owes me.

Loss or no loss, I wasn't going to miss my postgame party. And
once we got to the restaurant, people were very nice. I think I got my
first-ever standing ovation in a restaurant. Also, Vitale, Digger Phelps,
and Chris Fowler came over to the table and said congratulations. That
was nice of them.

By the time I got back to the hotel and shot the bull with my friends,
it was about one-thirty. Then I went to bed and I think I caught the
latest edition of SportsCenter and saw all the plays from the game. Then
I switched to CNN and saw some of them again. I had a morbid curios-
ity. I wanted to see it, and it was available. It was like watching your own
car crash.

I was broken-hearted and discouraged, but I wasn't upset. It's so
hard to get to the Final Four. Nobody can really appreciate that difficulty
except a coach.

I knew my team had done everything it could. How can you be

upset with a bunch of guys who have given you every last bit of them-selves in a game? Doleac, God bless him, was so tired he couldn't have jumped over a piece of typing paper. Andre was totally spent. Drew was playing with a bad back and had taken a shot at halftime. Caton's leg wasn't 100 percent. Britton was still bothered by the Ndiaye thing. These guys couldn't have done any more.

Looking back, we won the Carolina game against overwhelming odds. We led Kentucky by double digits at halftime. We had a four-point lead with less than six minutes to play, but I could tell we weren't going to be able to hang on.

I replay that Kentucky game in my mind all the time. The four big-gest moments of the game:

1. When Andre got tired.

In the second half, I took Andre off the ball and put him on the shooter, Mills. That way he didn't have to expend as much energy.

We were up by four with 5:32 left and Mills feeds the post out of the corner. Now Andre is supposed to be on the deny back, which means he's not supposed to let Mills get the ball from the post. And if Mills does get the ball, Andre is supposed to make sure the kid has to dribble to his shot, not just catch and shoot. But Andre was so fatigued. He looked like a punch-drunk fighter. You could see it on film: Andre turns on the post feed and he can't even bend his knees. He was ex-hausted. He was sitting there gasping for breath. Mills gets the ball, and hits the three to cut our lead to one.

And there was another time when we ran a play we call "22." We get Andre on the post and then duck him in. Andre got the ball, but he had no legs. He couldn't get the layup to go. Just plain missed it because of fatigue.

But what could I do? I wasn't going to pull the trigger on Jordie and bring him in. The year before, Turner went right at Jordie, got the turn-over and it was game, set, match. Jordie simply wasn't ready for this. Again, that's nothing against Jordie. It was a coaching decision, one I had to make and one I have to live with.

Now the question to this day in my mind is this—and I'll go to my grave wondering about it: Should I have let Drew play the one? Drew had gotten the pain-killing shot at halftime and he was beat. He was really hurting. But there was no one else to play at point guard. It was either keep Andre in there—even though he was exhausted—or put Drew on the point when we had the ball. I kept Andre at point when we were offense. Maybe I should have switched.

Of course, I could have called a timeout at the six-minute mark, but that would have taken away the TV timeout at the four-minute mark. I knew Kentucky was going to come back with a press, and I thought we were going to need the timeout for press reorganization. I got ahead of myself again. I have a tendency as a coach to do that. I should have maybe taken a timeout at six, taken my second full timeout at four, and then got us to where we could survive.

2. When Hanno missed all three open looks on shots.

Hanno had three wide-open shots: from the foul line, from the top of the key off the motion game, and from the right corner.

On the shot from the corner—it was off a play we call "34 Spread"—he hit the side of the backboard. On an open shot. And he airballed the shot from the circle off the T play I called. His composure and confidence were totally shot.

3. When Doleac ran out of gas.

He had a hook shot in front of our bench—to the middle, which is his shot—and he couldn't even bend his knees. His knees weren't bending at the reception, and they weren't bending when he went to take the shot.

There was another telling moment with Mike. We were trailing, 67–65, with 3:51 to go. It was still anyone's game, but he missed the first of two free throws. He just had nothing left.

Plus, Tubby is no dummy. He could see we were tired. By the end of the game, I was out of timeouts and Kentucky wasn't going to stop the clock so I could substitute. That's just smart basketball on their part. They were a deep team, and we weren't. You look at their roster and it's ridiculous. They have ten, eleven McDonald's All-Americans. Who on that team wasn't highly recruited? Who on that team wasn't a great athlete? That's the power of Kentucky, of its tradition. That didn't happen overnight. They've built that tradition and legacy over many, many years.

Magloire was recruited all over the country. Mills was a former walk-on, a fifth-year senior who understood the game, and understood pressure. Plus, being a basketball walk-on at Kentucky is like being a football walk-on at Nebraska: you have to be good to get a uniform. They don't just hand those out to anybody.

Then you have Sheppard. They take a guy who played three years, who averaged thirteen minutes on a national championship team in 1996, and they redshirt him.

They come in waves at Kentucky. They had two centers to play

Doleac. Carlisle wasn't ready to step in, nor was Nate. I like Nate, but he wasn't prepared for that moment. Just like Jordie wasn't prepared for it.

Had I had my choice, I would have wanted to play Stanford instead of Kentucky. We had similar styles of play and I liked our matchups better. But you don't get your pick, do you?

We had beaten two No. 1 seeds, Arizona and Carolina, and I think it was just a cumulative fatigue, both mentally and physically. And I'll tell you another thing that gets forgotten: Kentucky had won the national championship in 1996, lost in the championship game in 1997, and then won it again in 1998. There is absolutely, in every endeavor in life, but particularly in those situations, a lot to be said about having a familiarity with the whole process.

Kentucky was familiar with Final Fours. If we went back to the Final Four again, I know there would be a lot of things I would do differently. I would make sure I had an administrative assistant with me at all times to help with tickets, the press, the phone calls. Strohm told me I had at least 500 messages that week. I tried to return as many as possible.

My friends who were staying with me tried to help out, but every call-in show in America wants you on their program. You don't mind going on WFAN in New York and a couple of other ones, but when some 35-watt station in the middle of who-knows-where calls you in your hotel room at 11:35 at night, then it gets to be a distraction.

I would also hire a police escort to and from practices and games. I would stay, if I could, in a smaller hotel. We had every booster and reveler in our hotel. I would have liked something more self-contained, but that's not why we lost the game, believe me. I also would have stayed at a hotel with voice mail capabilities. We were at one of those hotels where the operator scribbled the message down on a little pink pad and you were lucky to get any of them.

There are some things I wouldn't change. I had Dick Hunsaker and his son stay with me. Mike Schneider stayed with me. So did Bob Henderson early on. Rich Panella came out a day early and stayed with me. I'm guessing Lute and Krzyzewski didn't have schoolboy buddies bunking in the same hotel room. But it was fun for me. I enjoyed those guys. It was very comforting to have them there. They were terrific, helping me with detail stuff.

I threw a party every night. Since I didn't know if I'd ever coach in a Final Four again, I decided to throw a party every night for my family and friends. I rented a restaurant, rented limos, paid for everything, and invited everybody I could think of.

I tried to make all the practices available to people who meant something to me. I tried to get tickets for as many people as I could. I tried to accommodate everyone in the media, especially CBS, for obvious reasons—they pretty much bankroll that tournament. But one morning I'm sitting in my room and people from CBS are having a fight with people from ESPN. Lesley Visser wanted to tape CBS taping me. And the CBS people got into a big fight with the ESPN people about it. And I was in the middle of it.

But when all is said and done, the bottom line is this: Kentucky was good, too good for us in that one game. Even if everything else was perfect for us, we still could have lost that game.

I was in Laguna Beach to give a speech during the off-season and I just walked down to the ocean, sat on the sand, watched the waves crash in, and thought about that game. It still hurts. There's a big difference between being No. 1 and being No. 2. It's the difference between being the Pope or a Cardinal, or being married or engaged. They're worlds apart.

I'm still haunted by it. It's self-flagellation to a certain degree. It's self-pity. It's anger. I'm still not over it. I don't know if I'll ever be totally over it. I should have a hot-line to Dr. Laura.

At the Nike camp at Indianapolis, Guthridge came up to me again and said, "I hope we didn't cause you a lot of problems. We're sorry for what happened there." He was talking about that whole Ndiaye thing. I thought that was very nice, very classy.

Says Drew Hansen: *"I don't think the incident affected our team much, but I do think it affected Britton. That's because even if you say you're sorry and apologize for making that kind of accusation, there's still one whole day where everybody thinks, 'Britton Johnsen—that's the white, Mormon guy who's a racist.' That's not fair. But I don't think it had an effect on the outcome on the Kentucky game."*

I saw highlights of the game, but as late as eight months after that loss, I'd never watched the tape from tip-off to final horn. And I don't know if I ever will. Drew said he watched it once, and will never do it again. He said if I watched it, I'd probably go insane.

The thing is, I really don't have to see it on tape. I can close my eyes and remember every play.

10
Looking Back, Looking Ahead

The players move on, I stay put.

A few days after the Final Four, I turned down the Arizona State job. The official statement that day: "I wish them all the luck in the world. I'm staying where I'm at. Arizona State is a wonderful situation, a tremendous school. Kevin White is a good friend. His kids are going to my camp. I think it was flattering. You should listen. You explore options. It doesn't hurt to talk. I'd rather not do it publicly."

A few weeks after that, I turned down the Texas job.

And a few months after that, I turned down the Milwaukee Bucks job.

I would really like to make this clear. There really are only three reasons why I don't leave Utah.

First, and this is the primary reason, is my allegiance to players. I really like the guys, and in many cases, I've told them and their families that I will be there.

In Nick Jacobson's case, the kid I signed from North Dakota, the dad said, "Look, you are not part of the deal, you are the deal. My son does not want to go to Utah, does not want to be at Utah unless you're there."

There's a kid in Europe, maybe the best young player in Europe, who might want to come to Utah. But the question over there is, "Are you still going to be there?" And I say, "Yes, I am," and then it becomes hard to leave.

The second part of it is that people here in Utah have been good to me. I come and go as I please. They're supportive. I think they genuinely care about me.

I have terrific boosters and friends. I know I have friends there who would do anything for me—Kent Jones, Jon Huntsman, Richie Smith. I've had university presidents that I really like: Chase Peterson, and the guy we have here now, Dr. J. Bernard Machen, who I really like.

I had a blood panel drawn one day. We had a big NCAA compliance athletic department meeting the same day. I told my athletic director, "I need to go to the doctor."

He says, "The president's going to be here."

I say, "I'll call the president."

I called the president and he said, "Don't worry about it. Go see the doctor. With your track record and the way this program has been conducted, we'll be fine. In fact, I'll tell you what we'll do. We're going to go out to dinner and have our own compliance meeting."

That's an understanding president.

In 1996, I called Jon up to get his plane. "Jon, we're in the NCAA tournament and we're in Tucson," I said. "We don't have flights to San Jose. Jon, they didn't think we'd win. Our school didn't think we'd win."

"When do you want the plane?" he said.

"Tomorrow?" I said.

"Nah," he said. "Let's get it down now and get the kids to San Jose early."

Everything's legal. Everything's checked out.

You can't put a premium on being left alone. Autonomy is a big part of it.

And you can't put a premium on fan support. There is this letter I got, a letter from a guy I don't even know. This guy wrote this tear-jerker letter that I found when I was going through my mail months after the NCAA tournament. I don't know this guy, but he wrote about how much Ute basketball meant to him. And he was so passionate about it. It was everything to him.

There's another guy, his name is Paul. He sends me these heartfelt poems about Utah basketball. I know he doesn't send these kind of poems to his own wife and kids. I know the guy, and I know how much our programs mean to him too.

There are other people who have become attached to our program. There's Fred Wydner, a sixty-six-year-old guy who comes to one of our early fall workouts.

I feel a special sort of indebtedness and bond with these people. I know they are not part of the grand scope of my life, but it is sort of heartwarming.

The third reason has to do with a personal realization that I'm probably best suited to be a college coach. I love coaching ball—and I'm not afraid to coach ball in the NBA—but I also love seeing guys develop off the court. We have this kid, Gary Colbert from Etiwanda, California. He came in this year and I am really proud of what he did academically. He's excited about learning. Those sort of things don't happen when you're an NBA coach.

Then there's May Van Horn. She wrote me the greatest letters I've ever gotten in my life. She made me feel ten feet tall by telling me what I had meant to her son. Same with Larry Cain.

Or there's Craig Rydalch, a former player of mine. He became a high school coach and they did a big article on him in the *Salt Lake City Tribune*. Reading Rydalch's comments . . . it was like I was talking. If you would have put his name for mine, and mine for his, we could have been each talking about our team.

I'm not sure you have the same kind of impact in the pros. If I had accepted the Warriors job, I don't think any of the Golden State guys would have taken high school jobs and appropriated my patterns of speech and recited my basketball philosophy verbatim. I don't think Latrell Sprewell would have come back and coached college ball and harped about getting low in your defensive stance like I do.

I don't think I can impact any of those pro players' lives. I think Nelson, when he was coaching the Warriors, did that with Tim Hardaway and Chris Mullin. But I think that time is gone. I remember looking at Nellie's office at Golden State, and behind his desk chair was an autographed jersey from Hardaway and Mullin thanking him for his help. Nellie did help them with their lives in a pro setting, particularly Mullin. But now it's so much agents, contractual concerns, the players union, and business that I'm not sure Nellie could impact him the way he did when he got him off of alcohol years ago.

I get my share of calls concerning other jobs. I've gotten calls from competing schools during the season, even as early as January. But I've always told them, "If you need me to talk to you now, or you need to name a coach a week before my season ends, then I'm not your guy and you should move on. I won't even entertain thoughts of it while my season is in progress." And the second part of the equation is that I'm not so sure, even a week after the tournament, if I can make any kind of evaluation.

Not long before I made my final decisions, I talked to one of the priests I know at Marquette. He asked if I was going to Arizona State or Texas. I told him I wasn't sure I was going to either one.

"Well, then, use your Ignatian Discernment Process," he said.

That's a core doctrine with the Jesuits. I'm taking liberties with it, but basically you take five issues and spend and hour or two on each. You take the pros and cons of each of those issues and write them down on a ledger of sorts. You study one, and then move on to the next, and the next one after that, and so on. By the time you're done, you should have a clearer idea of how to proceed. You put the issues in priority of importance and then make a decision. That's what I did, and in the end I knew the right choice was to stay at Utah.

I'm not married, but being wooed by other schools is sort of like if you were married to Mrs. Mixmaster or Betty Crocker, and all of a sudden Cindy Crawford and Kathy Ireland came calling. Arizona State and Texas were Cindy and Kathy. They were warm-weather areas, schools with beautiful physical plants. Here's Cindy and Kathy knocking on your door saying, "C'mon on over and let's keep house together."

It's hard to explain. It's like you're in West L.A. and somebody says, "Come on up to the Pacific Palisades."

They look good, these other schools. They always look good. But then you get there and you start to see the same nicks and cuts your school has.

And it also gets back to what I was saying about the Jacobsons. I sit in that kid's house and I tell him I'm going to be at Utah. So what do you do?

I've turned down other offers since I've been at Utah, but I've never come back and asked for more money. I've never leveraged Utah in any way when it comes to money. What I have done is tell Chris Hill, our athletic director, about the experiences I've been exposed to at other places. I'll tell him about the other film rooms I've seen or the weight rooms I've been in or the gym schedules that are favorable to the men's team or the meal plans for student-athletes.

Look, anyone in the world would look at ASU and Texas. All you've got to do is drive around those campuses. Both of those physical plants are imposing. The weather and the communities in which those schools are situated are unbelievable. Everyone in the world would say two of the best places to live are Austin, Texas, and Tempe, Arizona. And in some ways they're probably much better places to live than Salt Lake City.

But then I remember Jacobson. The kid only visited one school: Utah.

Texas and ASU didn't do anything wrong. In fact, quite the contrary. The ASU athletic director is a good friend of mine. And I really enjoyed the people at Texas. But the whole process is like having an affair. I can honestly say this: I've really only seriously dated four or five girls in my life, and I've gone with each of them for a long time. I would not take Cindy Crawford over any of them, but I would like to go out with Cindy Crawford once.

Texas is a gold mine. It sits in a state that has so many athletes and it is *the* university of Texas. We're *the* university of Utah, but we sit in a state with hopefully three Mormons who will want to come here every year. At Texas you sit with world-class jumpers, runners, shot blockers, defenders. I really felt that I could have put the best defensive team together of all time with the athletic talent that's available in Texas. You go to Bay City, Texas, or Houston, or anywhere there, and you're looking at guys like Rod Strickland, Dominique Wilkins, and Doc Rivers. That was the allure of Texas.

The allure of Arizona State begins as soon as your flight makes its approach into the Valley of the Sun. You're always flying into sunshine. You never have to worry—like we do here when recruits come in for visits—"Boy, I hope we have good weather this weekend."

It's such a happening campus and place. You've got a great atmosphere on a Friday and Saturday night there. It's always warm, and it's always pleasant. Here, we're walking out of the game at 10:00 P.M. and the players are going to the Pancake House and I'm going to Little America for a meal. That's the way it is.

The people at both Texas and ASU were very accommodating. But at the end of the day, it would have been tough to leave Andre and Hanno. After all, they could have gone to the pros, but they decided to stay at Utah. People say, "Well, then maybe you'll never leave." Maybe I never will.

I know this: when I left Ball State, I never realized how tough that was for the players there, and how tough it was for me. I still have mixed feelings about that.

I know I won't end my career here. I want to make one more move.

But you listen to these parents, to the kids, and you hear yourself saying, "I'm going to be here." It's a vicious cycle, and I don't know what the answer to it is. I guess the answer is procrastination. I don't want to deal with it, and I don't want to discuss it or talk about it.

I really do grow fond of players, as you can tell by Drew and Al and all those guys. I love talking at camp about Al. I love telling young kids about Al. I'd really miss a kid like that.

The Bucks job was intriguing, but I don't think it would have been a great fit. First, there's that pro mentality that I talked about. Plus, it's hard to coach in your hometown. I learned that at Marquette. I don't know if I would have wanted to do that to myself, or to my mom and friends. It's tough on everyone if you don't succeed. There's a lot of pressure.

When the Bucks fired Chris Ford, I told the kids, "I've turned down the Bucks job. My name might surface. I'm going to Milwaukee for a charity engagement. I'm not leaving you. I've turned it down."

They rarely get rattled about these job rumors. I always tell them, "You'll never hear it from anyone but me."

It all goes back to that Cindy Crawford thing. But when you get down to it, most places have the same guy in the business office, the same faculty rep, the same set of economic problems. There are a few Kentuckys, Dukes, and Carolinas out there. But they're literally a handful. The other gold mine is Illinois, because of the recruiting.

I tell the players, "I'm 90 percent sure I won't leave. Almost nobody can tell you 100 percent."

I also tell them there are only two kinds of coaches who can say they'll always be at the school: the ones that nobody wants—unsuccessful coaches, the 250 or so coaches who don't have any mobility—or coaches at the end of their careers.

Let's face it, the legendary coaches, the fixtures, aren't going anywhere. Bobby Knight is not going to leave Indiana. And he shouldn't. Lute Olson is not going to leave Arizona. Gene Keady isn't going to leave Purdue. Tark isn't going to leave Fresno.

Because my name comes up for jobs, other recruiters might tell a kid, "Don't go to Utah. Majerus isn't going to be there long."

They said that to Van Horn, and he's two years gone and I'm still here. Even during the Final Four, David Letterman was saying I would leave. Letterman, a Ball State alum, was saying things like, "Majerus is gone. He did it at Ball State, he'll do it now."

And maybe I will leave one of these days. But I'm here now and I've been here as long or longer than eleven other coaches in the late, great sixteen-team WAC.

Meanwhile, Drew is attending Stanford Law School. He was supposed to go to Michigan, but that was before a Stanford alum, who practices law in Salt Lake City, called him and asked if he had applied to Stanford. Drew said he had, but didn't think he had much of a chance to get in. Stanford was actually his first choice.

The Stanford alum called the admissions office, and later called seven or eight other alums who wrote letters of recommendation on Drew's behalf. Somebody must have been impressed because Drew was offered a place in the first year class. He left Utah last September and eventually wants to practice corporate law—antitrust, patents, that sort of thing. I know he doesn't want to be a divorce attorney or a tax attorney. Whoever hires him will get a hell of a player for the company basketball league. But compared to the Final Four, he'll never play another basketball game of any consequence.

As strange as it might sound, I think us being in the Final Four had something to do with Drew getting into Stanford. If nothing else, other Stanford people were aware of him and his academic and athletic achievements. And I think if you asked him, he would say the same thing, that it was to his advantage that we were in the same Final Four as Stanford.

Says Drew Hansen: *"It's different when you know you can't lace it up again and play. I'm going to miss it. I'm really going to miss it. I tell everybody that I played for the greatest coach in America. I think he respected our team. I think we were the team he wanted us to be."*

Doleac is going to the NBA with a lucrative deal worth about $5 million. I'll never forget that kid, or how far he's come since being a benchwarmer on his high school team.

I think that from the first time he played in Hawaii as a freshman, to his last game as a senior, I always felt good about Mike. I would have liked to have seen him be more aggressive for his size, but that's semi-nitpicking. He's always been very vocal. He's always tried to please me. His problem was—and I told him this—that during the first three years of his career he kind of slipped through the cracks. He was such a nice kid and such a good student, and I had to spend so much time on the point guard situation, and with Keith, and then on Hanno, that Mike kind of escaped some scathing criticism of the type that I think leads to growth. I cut him a lot of slack because he's such a nice guy. Sometimes it was hard to yell at him. But I almost wish he would have been more testy, more ornery.

Britton, Trace, and Carlisle went on missions. Britton went to Houston, Trace to Mexico City, and Carlisle to Ecuador.

I'm not going to lie to you: I wish Britton wouldn't have gone on a mission. We talked after we got back from San Antonio, but I think he had already made up his mind. But I respect his decision and I am very proud of him.

I went to Britton's going-away party. His twin brother Brandon also was getting ready to leave on a mission, to Calgary. When you go on a mission, you don't get to pick the location. One of Britton's other brothers went to Costa Rica. It's not an easy two years. It's hard, lonely work. And you can only call your parents a couple of times a year—Christmas and Mother's Day. But you can write as many times as you'd like.

You know, Britton has never had a room to himself. He's always shared it with Brandon. Now they were going to be separated for the first time in years. It'll be tough for both of them.

As a going-away present, I bought Britton a University of Utah tie. I had the girl at the Marriott gift shop wrap it, because if I tried wrapping the thing it would have looked like some ribbon-challenged person was involved. I also got him a card and stuck $250 in it. I gave Brandon some money as well. I don't know if that's against NCAA rules, but if it is, I'll fight it. I know what the headline will say: "Majerus Gives Player Cash." But I would have done the same if he were getting married. The kid is going on a two-year mission. It's not like my $250 is an extra benefit. I won't see him in a Utah uniform until the fall of 2000. So if the NCAA wants to make a big deal about it, then they can go ahead.

Shortly after the season ended, the doctors went in and found a tear in Britton's patella tendon. So they performed surgery and the prognosis is good for a full recovery.

Says Britton Johnsen: *"Coach Majerus just wants me to concentrate on being a good missionary. That's what he told me, and that's what I've decided to do, and to do a good job at it. He told me he'd give me a program to follow when there are about ninety-four days left in my mission.*

"Life isn't always perfect. It was really hard to play for him at first. He expects so much out of you. But he also taught me so much about things, and I love him for that."

Andre graduated last June, and it was such a nice day. Andre, Drew, and Kelly Miller, my administrative assistant, all sat together at graduation. Here were three of the unlikeliest people who would ever sit together, and it was kind of cute the way they did it.

Kelly was a Mormon girl who married one of my walk-ons. Drew was a kid from Tooele who was sort of introverted and without a lot of self-assurance, but always very, very bright. And here's Andre from Compton, the former Prop. 48 kid. All three of them go up and get their degress . . . boom, boom, boom.

What a special moment that must have been for Andre's mom. All her hard work had paid off.

And what a special moment for Andre. He had come so far. I remember when he was trying to qualify as a freshman, but got only a 690 on his third try at the SAT. I took him out to dinner that night and I said, "Andre, I know you think I'm a real old guy, and I never was a player, and I can't relate to a lot of things about you. But if this test score is the worst thing that happens in your life, then you will have a wonderful life. Something like one out of four Americans die of cancer. One day your mom will be gone. One day something will happen, something bad will happen in your life.

"I know this feels terrible right now. But problems create opportunities."

And that's what Andre did, he took advantage of an opportunity and ultimately succeeded. Was it fair? I don't think so. Andre is a very bright man and a hard worker, and he has demonstrated that by earning his college degree. To me, Andre is an academic giant.

I think the Prop. 48 status is the worst bias in America. I don't think it is a racial bias, but an economic bias. Who is victimized by underfunded school systems and neighborhood libraries? It's the people in those poor economic environments.

But in sitting out his freshman year, I think Andre discovered a sense of self. Something he loved was taken away from him, but in the end, he probably gained a greater appreciation of life without basketball.

He was in a reading program at school—for no credit, mind you— and did well in that. He was the poster boy for comeback kids.

Andre graduated last spring on a team with two academic All-Americans, nine honor roll members, and three others who were recognized for their academic achievements. But of all those kids, I'm proudest of his academic achievement. He is the nicest kid and he has come the farthest and tries the hardest. Honest to God, if we had given an academic award to a team member, I think the players would have unanimously voted for him. I say that from my heart.

He has developed so much as a person. When Andre first came here, he was introverted and shy. You'd shake his hand and he'd never look you in the eye. He had this dead-fish handshake. He couldn't put a noun and verb together. The writers who cover the team couldn't get him to say three words. This is the same kid who called his mom during his freshman year just to tell her about Doleac, who was his roommate at the time. "Mom," he said, "you're not going to believe how big this boy is."

Now he runs the team and is such a nice, sweet kid. He isn't afraid of speaking in public. He looks you in the eye. His self-esteem has improved greatly. You know what he is? He is a great kid off the court, but a killer on the court. He's Stockton-esque. He hates to lose, is a great competitor, and works hard in every practice drill. But once the game is over, he's gracious, affable, a sportsman.

You know, Andre could have skipped his fifth year and gone to the NBA. But in order to come back to Utah for a fifth season, he had to graduate. That's the NCAA rule relative to Prop. 48 kids: you get an extra year of eligibility if you complete your degree in four years. Andre sat out his freshman year, but because he graduated in four years, he could choose to come back. In fact, he became one of the first players in the country to take advantage of the rule.

The other thing with Andre is that nobody was exactly sure where he would go in the 1998 NBA draft. I knew he'd get picked, but I could never determine how high. There were some questions about his perimeter shot.

I sat down with Andre, like I did with Keith and Doleac, and I made it very clear to him. I said, "You have no allegiance to me or the guys. You have no allegiance to the program or the school. This is a very, very personal thing here."

In Keith's case, it was better that he stayed. And in Doleac's case, it was better that he stayed for his last year. They helped themselves and they helped this team by staying and improving their games.

Late last summer, after Andre had decided to return for his senior season, I told the players at the team meeting that we had an obligation to Andre. I told them I wanted to make sure the season was good for him. I didn't want him losing out because we weren't committed or because we were immature. I didn't want there to be any excuses. We owed Andre that much.

And if Andre ever wants to come back here after his playing days are finished, he has a standing offer to join my staff. He'll be a terrific coach.

Hanno could have turned pro too. He could have very easily signed a lucrative deal to play in Europe. Hanno really wants to play in the NBA, which had a lot to do with him coming back for his senior year. But Hanno also had an obligation to Andre.

The thing with Hanno is that he goes back home to Finland during the summer. And every strength coach I've ever had tells me not to let him go home. He doesn't lift. He doesn't get stronger. I know that. But that's not fair to Hanno. In a way, it's almost better that he goes home. We all need to be around the things and people who make us comfortable.

People forget that Hanno spends nine months of his year 7,500 miles away from home. It's a different culture, even within Europe. It's a different way of life and mind-set. And being Finnish is different from being European. His life is radically different from the life of other kids on the team. He gets the best of both worlds, but sometimes he gets the worst of both worlds. I think he's a happier person when he gets to go home. He's a better student, more productive. Plus, he doesn't lose his identity as a person.

He worked on his game during the off-season. In fact, he spent a little time with Keith in New Jersey, so I know he did something basketball-related. Keith can't go long without playing.

Dave transferred to Oregon. Jordie also left the program. He transferred to Idaho State.

I never really clicked with Dave and Jordie, and maybe some of that is my fault. Doleac had a big personal crisis that I had to help him with one time, and Drew needed my help with some specific academic issues, and Britton needed some special attention, and Andre was somebody I stayed involved with. Meanwhile, Jordie and Dave never had any off-the-court situations that required my assistance. So I think they never saw that side of me. They always saw only the coach part of me. That might be part of it.

Part of it, too, might be that they never understood that I wasn't there to be their best friend. No one has ever accused me of being too easy on them or too jovial or anything like that when it comes to basketball. That's never been a concern of mine. Players have come to me before and said that we were practicing too hard, too long, and too much. And I've listened to them. And I'll listen to them in the future.

One thing all my players, with the exceptions of Dave and Jordie, always understood was this: if practice ended at 6:31, then at 6:32 it was over for me. I wasn't going to dwell on anything bad that happened during practice. I wasn't going to hold a grudge. If I yelled at a player, I quit being upset the second they left the floor. Now the next day at 3:30 I might start yelling again, but that's just how it is in coaching.

I also think that Dave always fought the role bit. He believed he was much better than I believed he was. I wish him the very best at Oregon and, without him on the 1997–98 team, I'm not sure we would have beaten Arizona as decisively as we did. He played very well in that game. Afterward, he got very emotional and started crying.

I think that game was a vindication for him. Also, I think Arizona was one of the schools that initially recruited him, but pulled out at the end. Arizona is where his hero, Damon Stoudamire—a Portland kid like Dave—had gone to school. And it was vindication for him because he showed he could shoot and defend. And I was happy for Dave, I really was.

I spent more time with Dave individually last season than I had during his freshman year. I took him out to dinner a couple of times, and I also tried to make him understand what it took to be successful in our system. One day I stopped practice and brought him into the locker room, just him and me, and he started to cry. I put in the practice tape and I said, "Dave, look, this is what I'm trying to say to you: these films don't lie. Look at yourself. Here's Drew running and here's you running. Now you tell me who's running the hardest?"

He said, "I know, Coach. But I haven't been comfortable since I came here."

Then he started crying again. I told him, "Dave, I know I'm a hard coach to play for. I told you that when I recruited you. You should have known that. It wasn't like I lied to you. You run hard when the ball goes into the basket. You want the freedom that Van Horn had, but you don't have the ability that Keith had or the commitment that Keith had."

I saw some of the comments he made after he transferred. There were some pretty strong comments, I thought. He got me pretty good. I would have liked to have had Dave stay, *if* he had done what I wanted. But he didn't want to buy into what I wanted done, so I was okay with him leaving. But I like Dave.

But you know what happens? Up until sixth grade, people would ask me, like they ask all kids, "What are you going to be when you grow up?" And I would tell them, "A major league baseball player." And then in eighth grade, I started to see some really good eighth graders. And then by high school, I realized I wasn't going to be a major league base-ball player. I think Dave feels he's an NBA player, and he resents me telling him he's not. I hope he proves me wrong. I really do.

Says Britton Johnsen: *"Dave just never wanted to let Coach be his master. He just wouldn't buy into what Coach was saying. He always kind of wanted to have it his way.*

"I love Dave. I was really good friends with him. I felt bad for him, but Dave didn't want to do everything Coach said. He tried to do everything Coach said, but it was just difficult for him.

"I'm sorry he left, but in another way I'm happy for him. I'm happy because he's so happy. I love him. I think he's a totally good kid. And it was hard to see him go through that. But when Dave steps on the court he kind of gets this attitude and that's what kind of hurts him.

"The way Dave played just didn't fit our system. I hope Dave does awesome at Oregon. I think he will. He's going to redshirt, and that will give him a chance to work on his body, work on his shot. I hope more than anything he plays awesome."

Jordie was a different story. Jordie didn't hit the weights as hard as he should have. And Jordie was so wrapped up in shooting and scoring. I would tell him, "You're a midget." But you have to understand, I told players all sorts of things. I'd tell Doleac, "Never leave your feet. You're not a shot blocker. Never will be. You couldn't block a shot if you were in a six-foot-and-under league."

I told Jordie he was small, and because he was small he had to play tougher, like Stockton. Being small is not a reason for failure. But maybe I'm too honest with the players and not diplomatic enough.

I recruited Jordie and Dave. I recruited every guy on the team. I make the final decisions on whether to offer these guys scholarships. So if it doesn't work out, I'm the guy responsible.

When I was recruiting Jordie, I saw really good shooting skills and really good passing skills. But one thing Jordie never did—and I can't stress the importance of this enough—was hit the weights the summer before he came to Utah. He is one of the very few players who hasn't done that after signing with us. And when he did hit the weights, he never did so with the passion he should have, especially since he was small.

If you look at my team, one thing that would characterize it is the bodies and the strength, right? Even Britton made big gains from high school. He's six foot nine and growing into his body. Jordie is five foot ten, with his body basically developed.

Jordie could have stayed at Utah and kept his scholarship, but he would have rarely, if ever, played in another game. I told him I was putting him on our Grey squad. I told Barratt the same thing. I said, "You will be on the Grey squad your entire career. Now, if you're able to accept that and you play spirited basketball—and that's what you want—then we'll never have any problems."

I told Al Jensen's brother the same thing. Now everyone knows how much I love Al as a person and as a player. And his brother Andy is a great kid too. But I told him when he wanted to transfer from Southern Utah, "Andy, you're not good enough to play here. Go to Weber State." I told him before I took him on the team that we'd have a one-year deal. I'd take a chance; he'd take a chance. We'd see how it worked out. I was up front with him. He understood that.

At the end of the year, when it was apparent to me that Andy couldn't play here, we moved on. I told his dad, but his dad couldn't come to grips with that. His dad said, "Are you sure?" I said, "Yeah, I'm sure. This is my business." I don't know how I could have been more honest in that situation. Andy went to Weber State and has had a wonderful career, as opposed to doing nothing at Utah.

As a coach, I have to make hard, sometimes unpopular decisions. I have to do what's best for the team, just like a university president or an athletic director has to. I wanted Jordie and Dave to succeed. It doesn't do me or the team any good if they don't succeed.

Jordie's dad, Ian McTavish, a lawyer from Salmon Arm, British Columbia, was very upset. He was quoted in the newspapers as saying that Jordie was "devastated," and that my decision wasn't "fair and it's not right."

I finally had about a three-hour talk with Jordie's dad. He had written me letters about the situation and I decided to call him back and discuss it with him. I said, "Ian, everybody sees things different. I'm the coach. I'm a successful coach. I'm a committed coach. Your son is not good enough to play here. You think he's really good, so, A) you should coach him, or, B) find someone else who feels the way you do, or, C) step out of the way and let it take its course. If you want to coach him, then I'm all for it. But you won't step aside and let it take its course. So your other option is to go find somebody who feels Jordie is a hell of a player."

At the end of the conversation I think he understood what I was trying to tell him. I said, "Ian, I probably made a mistake. I was really sort of abrupt when I told him the news. But I wanted to tell Jordie right away, so he'd have a chance to go somewhere else. I was pressed for time that day when I talked to Jordie and I made a mistake in how I presented it. I realize that. Didn't you ever make a mistake, Ian?"

"I've made a lot of them," he said.

"Well, I made one too," I said. "I'm a human being."

Barratt transferred to Utah Valley State College. I talked to Yale about him and maybe he'll end up there. All I know is that he should go where he can play. The same for Jordie and Dave.

Barratt accepted my assessment. Dave could not accept the idea of not being a star. Jordie still thinks he should be playing for us, as does his dad. Sometimes it's like me thinking, Gosh, I want to go out with that beautiful woman, so why wouldn't she want to go out with me? And nothing is going to change just because I tell myself, She probably would have gone out with me if I had just nurtured the relationship.

Sometimes it just doesn't work out. I miscalculate. A player miscalculates. It doesn't mean I'm a bad guy or that the player is a bad guy. There's no right or wrong in that situation.

Everyone on the staff got bonuses. The assistant coaches got bonuses. I got a bonus from the school. The bonuses are nice, but what hits you in the aftermath of it all is that you might never get another chance at a Final Four. People talk about a window of opportunity and that might have been mine. It probably was my one chance. But you could wallpaper a restaurant with the photos of coaches who haven't gotten to a Final Four.

Not long after the tournament, I went down to Louisiana to recruit a kid. Bill Foster was with me, and he asked how I was doing. I said I was fine, but he wasn't buying it.

"You're going through a little depression, aren't you?" he said.

"Yeah, how'd you know?" I said.

"Because I went through it when I lost in the Final Four when I was at Duke."

My whole dream for the last sixteen years was to get to the Final Four. I told myself I didn't care if we lost, if we got blown out. I just wanted to get there. Just one time I wanted to say I coached a team and took it to the Final Four.

Then it happened, and there were so many poignant moments. But nothing beats what it was like coming in and seeing the Alamodome. I'll never forget it. It was just me, two of my best friends, and the scholarship players. To see the name, your school's name. To walk on that practice court with all the coaches from every level—from old NBA coaches to high school coaches—in the stands watching you and your team.

No victory was ever as much fun as beating Carolina. No one ever thought we'd beat Carolina. Be honest. Nobody did. And nobody thought we'd beat Arizona to get to the Final Four. There might have been a couple of the players' parents, family and friends, and Mormons who took us in the office pool, but that was it. So to play that string out was wonderful.

But when we lost that game, I kept thinking, Well, I'll probably never get back there. I mean, we could have won it.

The best part about the Final Four has to do with two levels of satsifaction: professional and personal. From a professional standpoint, it's the pinnacle. To do it with such great kids, with good students, and to go so far playing basketball the right way, meant a lot to me.

I also relished the underdog role. At one point in the season, especially in our league, we're almost expected to win every WAC game. But during another point in the season, when the NCAA tournament comes, we're almost expected to lose. What a contrast, and maybe that's what made it so rewarding and fulfilling as a coach. We did something we weren't supposed to do. And for a guy like myself, a guy who spent his whole life trying to get into games, to play games, and play on a team—and who couldn't—the Final Four was very special. That's because the next best thing to playing on a team is coaching a team.

There are a lot of great memories. Seeing a kid like Drew, who probably couldn't play on a team like Kentucky or Arizona or Carolina, be successful on the court was very satisfying. For him to get that chance, and deserve it and work to reach it, was a special thing.

From a personal standpoint, it was fun to have my mother, my sisters, my nieces, my cousins, and my friends involved in the experience. I think McGuire enjoyed it. So did the guys I grew up with, hung around with, and worked with. I got so many letters from guys I knew as a kid or teenager who just wanted to say congratulations. And I think a lot of ex-players got a kick out of saying, "I played for that guy."

Says Al McGuire: *"He's a special type—and he didn't get it from me, he took it from a higher level—who has a way of touching the people in the cracks of the world. There's something people can see about the guys who shower twice a day, who wear Brooks Brothers suits. Rick is genuine. That's something he got from his dad."*

There were some neat little perks coming out of the Final Four. I made an appearance on *The Tonight Show* with Jay Leno. That was a lot of fun. I mean, to see your name on the Green Room door, and to know you're going to be on with Leno. Me, this kid from Milwaukee. That's something you don't expect in life.

Leno came back to the dressing room before the show started and shook hands. He was very nice and very gracious. And Billy Crystal, who was also a guest on the show, had the dressing room next to me. He was talking ball with me. He's a big Clippers fan, a big basketball fan. He made a movie, *Forget Paris*, which was about an NBA referee.

I met a couple of writers on the show. And I brought a couple of friends—Richie, Billy Campbell, Jim Edwards—to the show, so that was fun. I've really enjoyed sharing whatever success I've had with the people who are close to me.

I had to do a pre-interview session for the show. Jim, who's a comedian and who's opened for Leno and appeared on his show, was helpful. He knew a lot of those guys. He was getting a big kick out of telling them what kind of ice cream I wanted and what to get me to eat.

I was nervous right before the show started. Until then, I was fine. I wasn't going on to upstage Billy Crystal. This is a guy who makes the world laugh on the Academy Awards. He's a comedian; I'm a coach from Utah.

Leno helped calm my nerves. He is such a nice man and is absolutely devoted to his work. He is so prepared. Plus, the organization and structure of that show is impressive. Anybody could learn from that type of organization.

I think I did okay. I was on for about seven minutes, and told the story about my brush with celebrity. It happened a few years ago when I was in Cincinnati. I stayed at the same hotel Paul McCartney and Wings were staying at, and when I came out that morning to go jogging, there was a huge throng of people being held back by police barriers. They were obviously big Paul McCartney fans.

Just as I was walking by, I heard someone say, "Who's that? Who's that? Is it somebody from the band?" Then I heard someone else say, "Nah. It's someone from the Three Stooges."

They thought I was Curly.

Everything was first class. After the show was over Leno stayed and posed for pictures with me and my buddies. He didn't have to do that.

Crystal said he had watched some of the NCAA tournament and the championship game. The guy knows his ball. Leno said he had watched some of it, too, but I don't think he's a big sports fan. He's more into cars and motorcycles.

What was really neat about the whole thing is when Leno signed off. He said, "I want to say good night to Alyce and Aunt Mary." I had told him that my mom and my aunt watched his show and really enjoyed it. So for him to remember them on national television was extremely nice.

After the show the staff gave me some T-shirts and hats. That's a wardrobe for me. Plus, they paid me scale for being on the show. I think it was about $294. I told Leno to keep the money and donate it to the charity of his choice. That's what I always do on shows where I get a check.

Says Jim Edwards: *"After they beat North Carolina in the Final Four, I knew* The Tonight Show *people would be after him. I had been telling them about Rick for three, four years. I knew he'd be perfect for them.*

"The Late Night with David Letterman *show also called, but not until Rick had already committed to* The Tonight Show. *He apologized, but said he had given his word to Leno's people.*

"I had told him, 'Rick, give me a call and we'll go over some bits.'

" 'No, I'll just wing it,' he said.

"You don't just wing it on The Tonight Show. *I don't think he had any idea what it was like to do your first* Tonight Show. *They booked him not only because he's a great basketball coach, but because of his great personality and his humor. He was under the gun to be funny, and I'm not sure he realized that.*

"He got to the show that day, and he didn't have any idea how nervous he would be. The tension builds, and you could see it. This strong rock of glib was clearly very, very nervous, as anybody would be in that situation. I can tell you from experience, there's nothing like it.

"He delivered. He had some big laughs, but he was out of his element. He confessed to me later, 'I understand what you're talking about now.'

"But I thought it was a great experience for him. I thought he did a great job."

I've done talk shows before, but not talk shows like Leno or Letterman. I've done *Up Close*, about a dozen times dating back to when Roy Firestone was the host. I've done the Sunday Conversation on Sports-Center. I've been a guest studio analyst for CBS and ABC during games. I've done that TNT NBA draft day stuff.

I was also on *Arli$$* last summer. Robert Wuhl is the star. He plays a sports agent. In a dramatic stretch, I played myself. I had about two lines—something about food. They paid me $600 for that.

Jim Edwards helped set that up. Jim opens for Leno on Sunday nights at a comedy club in Hermosa Beach. I went there with some friends to see Jim and then Leno. Wuhl made a guest appearance that night. After the comedy acts, we all met for a drink at the Ritz-Carlton, where I was doing a show for a local Salt Lake City station. This was during the NBA playoffs and I was the station's NBA/Utah Jazz expert analyst.

Says Jim Edwards: *"He was late for the show because, surprisingly enough, he hadn't finished eating dinner. I had a great set and he missed the whole thing."*

The next day someone from the *Arli$$* show called and asked if I'd like to be on an episode. So I went on the show. I even played ball with Jim Turner, the guy who plays Kirby in the show.

I was in L.A. anyway, going to Pritikin with Nellie. I just drove over to the studio during the day for taping. The plot was provocative: one of Arliss's clients, a pro hockey player, leaves his wife, and the wife hooks up with Arliss on the rebound. Arliss and the wife partake in some sexual escapades, which is why I think they cut out most of my lines. I think they wanted to see more skin and less of me.

I like doing different kinds of shows because it's fun and an adventure. Plus, not many teams in the West get much recognition. The time zones have something to do with it, and there's just not that many good college teams in the West. A lot of people think it's heresy to say that, but it's a fact. So when I get an opportunity to go on one of these shows, I like to do it. It's beneficial to the basketball program and to the university. It's beneficial for recruiting and for promotional reasons. It opens up some career opportunities.

Eventually I would like to do some TV. I don't aspire to be Vitale, but people see me on TV and tell me, "Hey, you're not bad." So I think about that. I met Sandy Montag, John Madden's agent, about six years ago, and he told me if I ever wanted to try TV, he'd like to be my representative. He thought I'd do a good job. I knew he was serious because he came over to see me at Christ the King Middle Village School in New York, where I was watching a recruit. The city was enveloped in a terrible heat wave, but he made the effort to come see me.

The heat was unbearable, especially in the gym, but we sat and talked as I watched some kid who ended up signing with Syracuse. Sandy was very nice. I told him I'd like to coach for about ten more years, but that I wouldn't forget what he said. And he said he wouldn't forget about me either. So we'll see.

I was invited to be part of TNT's 1998 NBA Draft coverage with Ernie Johnson, John Thompson, and Hubie Brown. I think the TNT people were a little worried about my wardrobe. Harvey Schiller, the president of TNT, told the producer or somebody to make sure I wore a coat and tie, and that if I didn't own a suitable one, that they should buy me one. So they did. Now I've got two sportcoats: a blue one and one in Utah crimson.

I had mixed emotions during that broadcast. I got real sad watching those high school kids who were back there in the waiting room and didn't get drafted. I knew they had gotten some bad advice. I don't even know those kids personally. I'm sure they would have never come to Utah. But I just felt bad to see them lose an opportunity. I'm hoping that kids who saw that will think twice about coming out. They saw what happened. It was very sad.

But on the other side of it, I was overcome with a sense of pride and happiness for Doleac. Here was a kid who did things the right way.

Another highlight of my post–Final Four summer was coaching in Michael Jordan's Senior Flight School. What an experience that was.

I'm not close, personal friends with Jordan, but we have the same agent, David Falk. In fact, the night the Bulls clinched the NBA championship in Salt Lake City, Falk invited me up to Jordan's hotel suite. I got there at the tail end of the party when everybody was bailing out. Dennis Rodman was still there and when I walked in, he said, "Hi, Coach." I was shocked. Maybe he said it because he recognized me, but couldn't remember my name. Or maybe I'm too much of a cynic. Maybe he was just being courteous to a coach.

By the time I got there, Jordan had quit playing the piano. And from what I heard about his piano playing, maybe that was a good thing.

Falk had also asked me to come into the Bulls' locker room after the game, but I didn't do that. I didn't feel it was my place to be there. Also, too, as happy as the Bulls were, I knew the Jazz players were that sad. I felt bad for the Jazz.

This was the second year of the Jordan camp, but the first time I had been invited to be a coach. Ed Janka, a Nike consultant, ran the camp and it was organized beyond belief.

There were eighty-six campers, from ages thirty-five to sixty-nine, each paying $15,000 apiece for the four-day Flight School at Bally's in Las Vegas. There were sixteen coaches, two for each of the eight teams in the camp. Jordan was there, of course, but he didn't coach any of the teams. He spoke at a question-and-answer session, did demonstrations, refereed some of the games, or just sat in the stands and watched. He was always there.

The Flight School was absolutely first class. Think about it: you're some guy who plays in a noon league back at the local health club, and now you've got Dean Smith breaking down your game for you.

Dean was paired with Georgetown's John Thompson, Arizona's Lute Olson with Kansas Roy Williams, Purdue's Gene Keady with Oklahoma State's Eddie Sutton, UNLV's Bill Bayno with Duke's Mike Krzyzewski, Georgia Tech's Bobby Cremins with Tubby Smith, former Portland Trail Blazers coach Jack Ramsay with Minnesota's Clem Haskins, Hubie Brown with Stanford's Mike Montgomery, and me with Cincinnati's Bobby Huggins.

McGuire was there too. He was the emcee for the panel discussions—talk-backs, they called them—with the coaches and campers and when Jordan did a session.

So there were eight teams, with about ten or eleven guys on a team. All the teams were named after NBA teams, which was interesting since the league wouldn't let any pro coaches attend the camp because of the lockout. I think my team was the Jazz.

The campers took it seriously, and so did I. It's like anything else—you want to win. They wanted to be treated like players. They wanted to have that experience.

I think it was fascinating. There were two coaches to a drill station, and at one point I just stepped back and thought, My God, look at these guys. They're rotating to stations, and they're going from Eddie Sutton, to Lute Olson, to Dean Smith, to Mike Krzyzewski, to Tubby Smith. It was unbelievable. There were six coaches there whose teams had won a national championship. And almost every coach there had been to the Final Four.

We did stations. We did team practices. We had games. But before the games, we had a player draft. And before the draft, we had an hour-long evaluation period to assess players for the draft. We'd go from court to court with clipboards and make notes and rank players. It must have been a harrowing experience for those players.

Here's how organized Dean Smith is: he not only had a list of players he wanted to draft, but he had an A list and a B list of "no-way" players, players there was no way he was going to pick under any circumstance. It got to be about the tenth round and my turn in the draft was coming up. I didn't have that kind of list. Dean was getting ready to leave, so I said, "Coach, what about this guy here? Is he on your no-way list, do you mind telling me?"

He looked and said, "No, he's not on list A. Let's look at list B. No, he's not on there either."

So I told Ed Janka, "Okay, we'll take the guy."

Of course, I heard it was worse the year before. They only had forty-three campers and they had the Staredown. If you've ever played pick-up basketball where they choose up sides on the court, then you know about the Staredown. That's when two guys are the captains and they pick teams from whoever is out on there.

All these campers were obviously wealthy, but there was a multi-, multi-millionaire from Indianapolis who had a mutual friend call me about four days before the Flight School started. The friend said, "This guy is coming out to the camp, and he's a friend of mine. He doesn't want to be the last guy picked. He asked me to call you. He wanted to know if you'd pick him before the final pick, just to save him that embarrassment.

"Tell him not to worry about it," I said. "He's your friend, I'll take him."

But I've been in that spot. I'm sympathetic to those guys. I know what it's like to be out there and you're fat, you're a nerd, you're no good, and all of a sudden there's five people left . . . four . . . three . . . two . . . and then you hear the captain say in a real subdued tone, "Okay, I guess I'll take Rick."

We had a makeshift draft room, but all the coaches were saying they wanted the Staredown back for next year. That's because there were too many names. They liked the idea of seeing the players.

We had the second pick of the draft. We took a guy who was real good. Jim Pierce was his name. He was thirty-five—young legs. The next pick went to the 76ers, Lute and Roy's team. They take this guy, Doug Stewart—the first guy to dunk at the camp.

Janka heard the selection and said, "Good pick. The guy is a casino host over at the Hilton."

Then there was a guy from Japan who flew over for the camp. Fabulously wealthy, but nobody wanted him on their team. He was there for the second straight year. He was terrible. God, he was bad at ball. I can't remember names, but his jersey number was number 89. I can always remember jersey numbers.

Everyone got such a kick out of this guy. He was a wonderful man, who simply didn't know how to play. It would be like me trying to go on with the New York Ballet Company, that's how out of place he looked. He was just totally out of it. But he loved basketball, and he liked Jordan.

The players enjoyed the camp, and I enjoyed them. I told them, "I really want you guys to try to win."

All the games were competitive. And it was funny, too, because you work with another head coach whose coaching stature is just as big as yours. This was a Who's Who of coaches.

We won the regular league play, but then we had a real bummer at the end and lost the championship game to the 76ers, Lute and Roy's team. In fact, Jordan gives a solid gold ring from Henry Kay jewelers of Chicago's Water Tower Place to each of the championship players. Howard Kaplan from Henry Kay's was there himself to size the players for their rings. Solid gold rings. I'm telling you, this Flight School was done extraordinarily well.

Somebody once asked me if I'd ever thought about running a camp like that. No way. Nobody would ever come to a Majerus Senior Flight School. First of all, when you think Majerus, you don't exactly think hang time. The highest I've jumped in the last twenty years was when Keith beat New Mexico in the 1997 WAC tournament. Now, if it were a Majerus Senior Food School, then maybe we'd have something.

I got paid to be a coach at Jordan's camp, but I would have done it for free. It was worth it just to hear Jordan talk. I picked up things to tell my own team. I'll tell you one thing that was really a great point. Someone asked him during the talk-back, "When you go to the foul line after you get hit, what are you thinking about right there?"

He said, "Number one, I expect to get hit. My expectation is that I'll be hit, and I'll be hit hard. Then I go to the foul line, and I try not to go to the foul line angry. I don't want those thoughts to cloud the concentration and the mechanics needed to make a foul shot." I thought that was a great point.

I'll tell you, he's good. There's a reason why he's the greatest player in the world. He's very athletic. He's very much in shape, and he's tremendously talented. But he made himself into a hell of a shooter. He does not have a shooter's stroke like Reggie Miller, Mark Price, Jeff Hornacek, Glenn Rice, and those guys have. He doesn't have the great gift Larry Bird had. It's a labored shooting stroke even to this day, to a certain extent. It's not the great, classic basketball shot that Bird had. But he made himself into a shooter.

You know that Jordan TV commercial jingle: "I want to be like

Mike"? Well, each year I show my team a video of Jordan, and I say, "Okay, you want to be like Mike? Well, here's Mike taking a charge. Here's Mike diving for a loose ball. Here's Mike running the floor. Here's Mike doing all kinds of little things that win games."

Another thing that struck me about the Flight School was the competitiveness of the coaches. We sat around and talked a few times, and you could tell how bad each guy wanted to get back to the Final Four. Krzyzewski, for example, you could just tell how bad he wants to get back there.

I want to get back there just as much as any of those guys. But I realize the limitations of my program. I'm not sure if we'll ever be able to repeat the magic of 1998.

Even though we were in the Final Four, Utah hasn't moved any closer to the Pacific Ocean or to the East Coast. So we're still remote, relative to the recruiting game, which hurts you. And we didn't get an infusion of black people into Utah just because we were in the Final Four. The weather didn't get any better; we didn't become Arizona in terms of a climate. Our facilities didn't get any better—we've got a good facility, but it's not the Delta Center.

In some ways, you think the Final Four is going to make things easier or better, but it doesn't. The same deterrents to recruiting are still here. Utah doesn't have a large black population, and the game is comprised mostly of black people. And there aren't that many players to choose from in Utah.

Now, our success has made a difference with coaches. Coaches follow basketball their whole lives. We've done so well for a decade now that they know us. Yet while we're able to get more of a look from some top recruits, there still is an apprehension about the state of Utah in the black community. We had a kid in from Louisville for a recruiting trip. He got out here, and you could just tell he didn't feel comfortable. They see the snow on the mountains, and they hear the snow is coming. And even though the snow isn't as bad here as it is in the Midwest, it's already here—they can look out their window and see it on the mountains. In Chicago, or Ann Arbor, or Minneapolis, or Bloomington, you don't see the snow until it falls from the sky. But here in Salt Lake, it's on the mountains, and some recruiter from another school will tell them the snow will be coming down the next week and an avalanche will engulf them.

It also doesn't help that there's only two or three clubs in town where you can dance. It's such a laid-back, family community. It was that way ten years ago, and it is that way now. There are more people out jogging the streets in Utah at 6:00 A.M. than there are out dancing at 11:00 P.M. When you're young, you want action. There's not a bar on our campus, which I think is kind of nice. But the downside of it is this: our kids go to the Pancake House after the game.

We're still an outpost. No twelve-, thirteen-year-old kid puts his head on a pillow at night and dreams, Oh, God, if only I could be a Runnin' Ute. But if you look at the other teams in last year's Final Four, there are kids dreaming of going to Kentucky or North Carolina. And with Stanford, there are lots of affluent parents who are dreaming that their kid one day ends up on The Farm.

That's the thing that's funny about this supposed Final Four impact. I was in Santa Monica early last fall, and I walked into one of those sporting goods stores like Foot Locker or Champs or something like that. All I could see were Carolina hats, Stanford T-shirts, and Kentucky jerseys. There was lots of pro stuff, but I didn't see any Utah crimson and white.

The guy behind the counter came over and he was all excited and said, "Hey, you're the Utah coach."

"Yeah, I am," I said. "Where's the Utah shirts?"

He looked at me increduously and said, "Man, we don't carry *that*. We don't carry that kind of stuff."

It was like he was astounded I would even suggest the possibility of a garment bearing a Utah logo. It was like I was asking where the hood and Klan cap section was, or where I could find the Knights of Columbus sweatshirt section.

Not everyone was like that. The St. Louis Cardinals invited me to come to a game and throw out the first pitch. But, unfortunately, I couldn't do it.

Says Jeff Strohm: *"Did he tell you why he couldn't go? He canceled because Karl Malone needed help with his charity benefit.*

"My brother Joe is the director of group sales and marketing for the Cardinals. They were going to have Rick throw out the first pitch, then have him do some radio-TV with Mike Shannon. Tony LaRussa was going to give him a Cardinals jersey with 'Majerus' on the back. Even Mark McGwire was pumped. He told my brother he was looking forward to meeting him.

"Maybe next year."

11

The Official
Rick Travel Guide

Pick a place on the map, any map, and chances are I've been there. Or near there. Or plan to go there. Aside from basketball, family, and friends, the other two loves of my life are travel and food.

I've been to six of the seven continents. I've been to all fifty states at least three or four times each. If there's a good restaurant in town, I've probably eaten there. I might not remember the name, but I can remember how to get there. I am a walking Fodor's.

I'd rather read my monthly *National Geographic* than *The Sporting News* any day. I might be the first Final Four coach to go sunbathing on a nude beach in Hawaii. And I can just about guarantee you that I'm the only Division I coach to be recognized in Amsterdam's famous Red Light District.

Here's what happened: A few years ago, when I was an assistant for one of our USA Basketball select teams, Randy Ayers, P. J. Carlesimo, and myself decided to see the Red Light District—as tourists, not clients. We weren't alone. There were a lot of gawkers. Whole families were there at 3:00 A.M. looking the place over.

There was this one seedy bar where you could walk by and see things that would make a V-chip short-circuit. So, as we're walking by the window, a voice rings out from inside the bar.

"Go Utes!" yells the guy.

I couldn't believe it. Just the kind of fan we're trying to attract at Utah. I wanted to bury my head. You didn't want to be there, and you didn't want anybody to see you there.

If someone asked me to pick the one spot on earth they should visit, I'd tell them to go to Africa. The areas not spoiled by man are slowly disappearing, but the animals are unique and beyond belief in their beauty.

When I was an assistant coach for Dream Team II, I went to the Tournament of Africa with Nellie. After the tournament was finished, we flew over the Great Rift Valley to Nairobi and stayed at this very famous hotel that dated back to the days of the great white hunter. Very Hemingway-esque. Nellie went golfing for a couple of days, but I didn't go. I hooked up with some other guys and they'd just tell me stories about Africa. It was fascinating.

Nellie and I later hired a guide and went on a safari. We camped on the Massai Mara, easily the best animal reserve in Kenya and almost devoid of modern civilization. The nights are so dark; there aren't any McDonald's road signs glowing in the distance. The only light is from the stars and the moon. Otherwise, it's pitch black. You could hardly see your hand in front of your face.

One day we tracked a lion, which just happened to be in heat. I'm not sure about the exact number, but our guide said that lions in heat try to mate something like sixty-five or seventy times per day. This lion was definitely on edge because at one point it faked a charge at our vehicle. Nellie and I nearly jumped out of the truck. I almost needed another bypass. The guide just laughed.

If I weren't a coach, I think I'd like to write a travel column or be a travel editor. I love reading travel stories.

Every once in a while I'll go to the Travel Club at the U and listen to a guest lecturer. If there's something on, say, Hong Kong, I'll go listen. I come late, leave early.

I think the greatest talk radio show in the country is *Extension 720* on WGN in Chicago. I can be back in Milwaukee, get done playing ball or working out, and instead of going back to a bar and seeing some friends of mine or stopping by somebody's house, I'll just listen to *Extension 720*. There was one show where the host had a crypto-zoologist on. I was fascinated by it. Crypto-zoologists discover animals that have never been discovered before. They take safaris to Africa, and one year I was all set to go with them. The crypto-zoologists were from the University of Illinois–Chicago, and I was going to be sort of a gofer on the expedition.

But I had to cancel because it was the same year I was named to Nellie's Dream Team II staff. If you ever saw the *National Geographic* with the pygmy elephant on the cover, that was the safari I was supposed to go on. I was supposed to be with those *National Geographic* people doing the story on the crypto-zoologists.

One of these Julys, I would like to take off and go on one of those expeditions. I'll probably never do it while I'm coaching, mostly because I'd feel guilty if we lost a recruit because I was in Africa. I'm guilt-ridden about that kind of stuff. Then I tell myself I'll go to Africa in August, but then I remember I've got this little camp in Wisconsin I'm committed to . . .

After Africa, I'd go to the Great Barrier Reef. The colors and smells of both of those places are so vibrant. And the remoteness of their locations keeps everything relatively pristine.

Next, I'd take you to the Going-to-the-Sun Road in Glacier National Park in Montana. For pure beauty, it's hard to find a more spectacular sight. Kauai would run a close second.

My favorite city in the world is Fresno. Just kidding. It's Paris. I love the diversity of it. You can do so many things, almost all of which the Parisians think are a complete bore. I mean, to look at Napoleon's tomb and know this little man extended his empire into all parts of the world is amazing to me.

Like any good tourist, I walked up past the first level of the Eiffel Tower. That was enough walking to dissuade me from trying to walk to the top of it. I'll stick with the sixty-two steps I walk from the court to the concourse at the Huntsman Center.

London is another wonderful city. I went there to see Al during his Mormon mission. One of the first things I did when I got to London was go see Big Ben. I wanted to compare it to the Allen-Bradley Company Clock, which is just south of downtown Milwaukee and, according to *The Guinness Book of World Records*, is the biggest four-faced clock in the world. We called it the Polish Moon because the area around that part of town is predominantly Polish. In the clock-to-clock matchup, the Polish Moon is bigger, but it isn't as ornate as Big Ben.

I'm also a big fan of Italy. I gave a clinic in Salsomaggiore one time, which is on the Italian Riviera. Frank Layden and Pat Riley gave a clinic there, too, except Riley stayed in Milan and drove the eighty miles back and forth. I guess Salsomaggiore wasn't cosmopolitan enough for him.

The Italian people were so nice. They'd take you out to dinner, then to an ancient village, then to the countryside. You'd go to these wonderful little restaurants and there was never a written menu. Whatever was made fresh that day, that's what you ate. At one restaurant they had pumpkin ravioli that was almost the specialty of the region. They also took me over to Pisa, so I could see the Leaning Tower.

I had a host during the trip. He said, "Usually the men like to go to Milan and shop for the day." Milan is one of the world's fashion capitals. But I'm not exactly a clothes horse and anyway, he said they probably didn't make sweaters in my size.

"Perhaps there is something else you would rather do than shop?" he said.

I rented a motorscooter. The town I was staying in was famous for its hot springs baths, so I rode my motorscooter down to the spa.

I also went down to the town square at night and did some people-watching. You'd go down there—here in this remote town in Italy—and people would be playing Beach Boys songs.

I've been to Venice. It wasn't very romantic, but I rode a gondola with Dick Hunsaker. I mean, as a kid you see pictures of Venice, the city of canals, and you think, I wonder what that place is like? I was lucky enough to find out.

My most miserable Italian sightseeing experience was in Rome. I had a one-day stopover, so I tried to squeeze in as many things as possible. It was a miserably hot day, and I literally ran into the Vatican and out again. At the end of the day, I saw nothing.

Says Jon Huntsman: *"Did he tell you about our trip?*

"Rick loves to go to countries, try out restaurants, see the people, so I took him on a trip once where we were going to cover fourteen countries in fourteen days. This was the Jon Huntsman Plan, not the Rick Majerus Plan.

"He brought Mike Schneider with him, and I had six or seven of my executives with me. Our first stop was Japan, where I had a ninety-minute meeting outside of Tokyo. I hired a tour bus for Rick, Mike, and some of my family members and they took a quick tour of the country. They zoomed up and back, and then we climbed aboard the plane and I told the pilot, 'Fly low over the rest of Japan on the way to Korea, because I want Rick to see the rest of Japan. See if you can get permission to fly at 10,000 feet instead of 45,000.'

"We went to South Korea, where I had a quick business meeting. Then I walked Rick around the beach at night, and he toured one of our chemical

plants in Pusan the next morning. We got back in the plane and told the pilot to fly low again.

"Then we went to China. We got into Beijing, where I was scheduled to have dinner with the minister of finance and the minister of economics. Rick was wearing his usual clothes: a jockstrap, shorts, and T-shirt. Well, here's the minister of finance and the minister of economics, and all these long, black limousines waiting to meet us, and Rick gets off the plane looking as if he'd just finished playing a basketball game. They had this huge banquet for us that night, and Rick sat there in his gym clothes. Those people could never quite figure out who he was. They didn't know if he was a sumo wrestler or what. They knew he was a Great American Somebody, but they never figured out who this goliath was.

"The next morning I arranged for somebody to take Rick out to the Great Wall of China. But I only gave him two hours to get out there, see the wall, and get back. Then we went to Tiananmen Square, where I gave him ten minutes. We were out of China by noon the next day. We flew low out of China.

"Indonesia was our fourth country. By now, Rick was getting a little whizzed off about my sightseeing methods. He was also getting a little self-conscious about his attire.

"In Indonesia there are seven individuals who have kind of built that country over the years. They're called the Magnificent Seven. My business partners involve two of those very powerful people.

"I said, 'Rick, we have a luncheon with these people. I'd like you and Mike to come over there.'

"Well, in Indonesia you don't wear suits. You wear very light, short-sleeved white shirts. It's quite informal. I'm on the top floor of this building owned by one of the Magnificent Seven, with a beautiful panorama of Jakarta, and in walks Rick wearing a beautiful dark blue suit, white shirt, and tie. People looked at him so aghast because he was overdressed. Rick sat through that luncheon, and he could hardly swallow anything because of the tie choking him.

"From there we flew over Bali, and Singapore, where my son used to be U.S. ambassador, and then hit Australia.

"We got into this little place in Melbourne—Rick, Mike, myself, and two of my sons—and Rick said, 'Jon, you are the worst guy to travel with I've ever been with. How can you go to all these countries and not see anything?'

"He had had enough. He said his style of traveling and my style of traveling were different, that he'd catch up with me in about ten days.

"We shook hands, and that was the last I ever saw of Rick on that trip."

Early in my career at Utah, I took my team to Europe and we played the Russians in an exhibition game. Shortly after the game, it was announced that the Russian people had essentially been granted their freedom, that communism, at least in the Cold War sense, was no more. We were driving to Amsterdam and with us were some Russians and their host. The host was listening to a Beach Boys song on the radio, and that's when I turned to Mike Schneider, who was on the trip with us, and said, "You know it's a global community when you're riding with a Russian, in Amsterdam, on the night his country gained its total independence, and you're listening to the Beach Boys."

A couple of the Russian coaches spoke English, so I talked to them about what had happened in their country. I mean, we take so much for granted in the United States. We're not monitored or held accountable for certain things. You're always suspect over there if you have tremendous wealth. Here, if you pay your taxes and you don't commit any crimes, you can pretty much live your life how you want. That's not how it was over there.

I have a lot of freedom and a lot of opportunities because of basketball. I remember reading about Lou Holtz's list of 107 things he wanted to accomplish in life. Things like appearing on *The Tonight Show*, skydiving, being invited to dinner at the White House. I don't have a list like that, but I know I'd like to go to New Zealand and ride a motorcycle through that country. I'd like to fly-fish in New Zealand and Chile, mostly because you're just about guaranteed to catch something. You don't have to be that good a fly-fisherman.

Of course, I would never want to go fly-fishing with Bobby Knight. He's an expert, or damn close to it. With him, you probably have to stay out until you catch a fish. I'd give it a couple of hours and call it a day. And I don't want to camp in a tent after I fish. I'd like to fish and then go back to a hotel.

There are some other destination sites on my wish list: I want to go to Mardi Gras. I'd also like to see the Amazon and the rain forests. I've been to the Kentucky Derby. That was fun.

Says ABC's Lesley Visser, longtime friend: *"This was 1994, the year Go For Gin won the Derby. Rick had never been to a Kentucky Derby, so I told him I'd take care of everything. I'd make sure he got a hotel room, tickets to the big black-tie ball at the governor's mansion, a pass for Derby Day. I'd even rent him a tuxedo.*

" 'All you have to do is get us a limo to Frankfort and back,' I told him.

"Everything was all arranged. We met in the hotel lobby at six o'clock. He looked great, except he couldn't get the bow tie around his neck. He said something was funny with the button.

"Meanwhile, I didn't see the limousine waiting for us. So I asked him about it and he said, 'No, no, don't worry, I'll get us one.'

"So he went over to the bellboy, gave him five dollars, and said, 'Can you get us a limo?'

"This is Derby Week. There aren't any limos available for miles.

" 'It doesn't look good, Coach,' the bellboy said.

"We ended up driving to the Governor's Ball in a Chevy Lumina, but I made him park the car two miles away from the mansion. I wasn't about to let anybody see me drive up in a rented Chevy Lumina."

When I go someplace I always try to find the best restaurants, the nicest walk, the best place to run.

I like good food. I really enjoy good food. But I'm not a food snob or food elitist. I don't know if I'd make a good food critic. Some critics talk in all these technical food terms, I couldn't do that. But I know what tastes good and what doesn't. Like, if you asked me what's the best pasta I've ever eaten, it was that pumpkin ravioli in a little town outside Salsomaggiore. They had a couple of different pastas, a fish of the day, a rabbit dish.

One of my favorite meals would be a double brat soaked in Budweiser on a German hard roll with fried onions and secret County Stadium sauce. That's perfection. That's a great meal.

Chicago is probably my favorite town. Great restaurants. I'm always happy to go back to Chicago because of the Italian restaurants. In Utah, we don't have an Italian restaurant that has a name ending in a vowel. That's not a good sign. In Utah, you're eating Italian at a place like Olson's, or something, and ordering baked manicotti by Chef Boyardee.

My favorite Italian place in Chicago is probably Rosebud. There are two of them: one on Taylor Street, one just off Michigan Avenue. I also like Mia Francesca, but I don't want to wait in line. Plus, I'm not good enough friends with Mike Fratello to drop his name there and get a seat. Fratello's really in with those guys.

I like going to Al's Italian Beef—not the one on Ontario, but the one on Taylor Street. And for pizza, it's Home Run Inn. For Cajun, I like Heaven on Seven.

There are places in Chicago that I love, but I only know them by menus, not names. There's a place on the South Side that serves a shrimp diablo to die for. The way they had it sauced was just terrific. All I can tell you is that you have to drive through a bad part of town to get there.

> **Says Don Donoher:** *"I drove up from Dayton one time and met him in Chicago. He says, 'Meet me at the back of Alumni Hall at DePaul.'*
>
> *"I meet him there at whatever time he said. We take his car, but he wants me to drive to the restaurant. As we're driving to the restaurant, he yells, 'Hold it! Stop the car!'*
>
> *"I thought there had been an accident. Maybe I hit somebody.*
>
> *"No, that wasn't it. Somebody was selling barbecue ribs from one of those sidewalk carts. Rick gets out of the car, buys some ribs—remember, this is on our way to dinner—and we sit outside and eat the ribs.*
>
> *"We get back in the car and he says, 'You know, those ribs weren't very good. But we had to stop because they might have been good.' "*

In Milwaukee, there's ten great Italian restaurants. I love Giovanni's. For casual, I'd go to Barbiere's Italian Inn for pizza. In fact, they still have a clipping up on the wall from when I was at Ball State.

If you want the best custard cones, you go to Mack's in Waukesha. I was doing a speech out there when somebody told me about it. It's a mom-and-pop place. The custard has a high butterfat content, higher than most custard places. They have a flavor of the day, and they turn the custard over every two hours. It's the guy's only store, so he takes a lot of pride in it.

If you're in Atlanta, you go to the Hickory Hut for ribs. If you're in Birmingham, you go to Dreamland for ribs.

Like I always say: some guys smoke, some guys drink, some guys chase women. I'm a big barbecue sauce guy. I'm like that guy in the *Odd Couple*, and I don't mean the neat guy. I go into my room and find pieces of pizza under the laundry.

San Francisco, one of my favorite places, has an Italian place near the marina that I love. There's a Chinese place in P. J. Carlesimo's building—right behind the Hyatt on Embarcadero—that is really good. Another good place is the Fog City Diner.

In Los Angeles, there's Valentino, but you've got to get dressed up. And if you want to go really, really casual, get the chopped Italian salad and an eggplant mamma mia at Alejo's on Manchester and Lincoln. I love Vito's on Oceanside.

Seattle is a great town for food. There's a place in the Magnolia

District that I love. A great view. There's a Thai place, as well as a great pizza place by Green Lake. The Metropolitan Grill in downtown Seattle is good.

In Honolulu, I go to Nick's Fish Market.

I'm not big on wearing a coat and tie, but I would wear one for Il Mulino in New York. There's another place, right next to the Embassy Suites, across the light on the south side of the street, which is great—but I couldn't tell you the name of it. And in Jersey, there are two great pasta places by the Seton Hall campus. I could drive you to them tomorrow. One of them is P.J.'s favorite, Bella Italia.

I'm great with menus and directions, bad with names. The same with players. I can't remember an opposing player's name, but I can tell you his jersey number.

My general philosophy on dining is this: Am I in the area? How am I dressed? How quickly do I want to get served?

Those are the questions I base my dining decisions on.

Says Jeff Strohm: *"I had just started working for him. We flew into North Carolina and on the way to the hotel we stopped at a convenience store.*

"As I was waiting in the car, Coach came sprinting out of the store. I thought somebody had been robbed and shot. I thought people were dying in there.

"He rushed over to me and said, 'Jeff! Jeff! You've got to come in right now. You've got to try these doughnuts. They're the best doughnuts in the world.' "

Says Donny Daniels: *"Usually after a night game at home, the manager will come in and take a pizza order for the staff. Early in Coach's first full season, the manager came in and Coach looked around the room, saw us sitting there, and said, 'Okay, get a pepperoni, a vegetarian, a sausage, and one with the works.' Something like that.*

"The pizzas came and the manager stacked the boxes near Coach. I reached over, opened a box, and pulled out a slice of pepperoni. Coach looked at me and said, 'Didn't you order any pizza?'

"That's when I learned the rule: 'Don't touch the pizza until Coach is done.' "

I love food, but I'd never own a restaurant because I know what a pain in the butt that is. I think owning boats, restaurants, major league baseball teams, luxury vacation cabins . . . all those things fall under the axiom, The owner's two happiest days are when he buys it and when he sells it.

Plus, owning a restaurant, you'd have to be there and you'd get bored with the menu. I like variety.

Owning a restaurant is a lot of work. It takes time. It would divert from your coaching. And it would really take time from your recruiting. It would become like a mistress where you had to be there a lot. I don't see it as a lucrative endeavor. The profit margins are cut so thin. Then you've got to have alcohol. Then you've got to have people you can trust. Then you've always got to worry about if you're getting short-changed.

I've been approached with restaurant propositions, but I've pretty much said no. If you can go in like Michael Jordan does, where you just put your name on it and someone else has the headaches, I guess that's okay. But I really respect my name, so if somebody comes in the restaurant and they get a bad roast beef sandwich, I wouldn't want to be held accountable for that. Even under the best of circumstances, somebody is going to come in and get a bad roast beef sandwich.

I don't want that responsibility.

I know I have to watch my weight. I exercise just about every day. I think I'm in good cardio-vascular shape, but I'm not always good about what I eat and when I eat.

I've been to the Duke University clinic with my dad. I go to the Pritikin clinic near L.A. with Nellie and Jon Huntsman.

So I fight a daily battle: food vs. moderation. I'm trying.

I show the kids practices. I have tapes and I show them. I love for the coach to come to practice. A lot of kids see the practice and their eyes light up. They get excited. A lot of guys come and say, "It's not for me." Hey, fair enough.

We've always been able to get a few good kids because a coach likes us or the kids saw us on TV. But we're never going to be the preeminent choice over the UCLAs, Kentuckys, Indianas, Dukes . . . that's not us.

When I recruit, I really make a point of never saying anything about another coach's personality. I will point out style-of-play situations. I'll say, "Look, do you want to play in the NBA? Are you better off coming to practice every day at Utah playing man-to-man defense, and playing man-to-man in every game, with NBA terminology and rules and techniques and fundamentals? Or do you want to play a zone in college?"

There's a place for zones in college, but I couldn't coach a zone as good as John Chaney does. He plays a great zone, but I think there's a liability there in pro ball. Just like there's a certain liability offensively to my system. I think I give my guys a certain freedom, but I might err on overstructure, too much emphasis on shot selection, too much discipline.

We have now had an NBA first-round draft pick in 1997 with Keith and with Doleac in 1998. I expect Andre to be a first-round pick in 1999, with the distinct possibility of Hanno joining him. I also think Britton will be a first-round pick by the time he leaves Utah.

So I think this system speaks for itself. Part of it has been the players wanting to come here. Part of it is the players buying into everything we talk about. Part of it is us and the way we coach. Part of it is our commitment to academics.

Salt Lake City is a big small town. There's a certain measure of celebrity that comes with being the basketball coach here. And with us reaching the Final Four in 1998, there was probably more attention.

I like meeting people. I appreciate the compliments they give to the team. If an autograph or a quick picture makes them feel good, then I'm almost always happy to do it. It isn't unusual for me to strike up a conversation with people, ask them if they're going to the game that night, maybe even offer them a couple of tickets. My only request: you've got to cheer for the Utes.

There's a Second City–like troupe in Salt Lake City called the Happy Valley Players. For the last twenty years or so, they've put on a show spoofing anything connected with the city and the state: politics,

BYU, Temple weddings, clothes, conservatism, hairstyles, the entire Mormon lifestyle and culture, news of the day, and me.

The annual *Saturday's Voyeur* show is always a huge hit. I saw it late last summer and I laughed so damn hard. The plot line has something to do with a gay guy at BYU coming to me for advice. He's thinking of leaving the church and he's looking for life's answers.

I loved the show, but it was tough watching the actor who played me. I knew I didn't look like Robert Redford, but I thought I was okay looking. But the guy who played me—and he sort of looked like me—wasn't the most striking man in the world. It would have been like Lute Olson turning on his TV and seeing, "The Lute Olson Story," starring Jamie Farr.

It was a comedy and a parody. Nobody was spared. I think my character was going out with Linda Tripp.

After the show, I went backstage and took pictures with the cast. Most of them were huge Ute fans.

Celebrity is a weird thing. George Karl and I were in McCall, Idaho. We were on a beach at this lakefront hotel. Hardly anybody knew George, but they all knew me. It was more of a college ball crowd. Our games are shown in Idaho, and that had something to do with it. Plus, in pro basketball, you're either a fan or you're not. If I were to go to New York with George, everybody would know him.

I've been involved with basketball my entire adult life. But sometimes I can't believe I coached teams with the knowledge and expertise that I had then. I'm such a better coach than when I coached my first game at Marquette. Now I've weathered every storm, every trap, every run and jump, every Dale Brown freak defense. You see things come out and it's the "wheel," or the old "air force shuffle." Somebody resurrected a book on an offense last year that was supposed to be really innovative. But I had seen that same offense in a book called *The Trident Offense*. Jerry Tarkanian's "amoeba defense" is based on another guy's sliding zone.

There are more than 300 Division I schools, and I've got to venture a guess that I've played 250 of them. Coaches such as Dean Smith and Bob Knight, they've seen just about everybody. Dean probably missed some of the lower-end schools, but I doubt that he missed playing any of the top 125 schools.

I'm a pack rat. I've picked up stuff from Bobby Knight. Knight really gave me the basis of my passing game.

Don Donewald gave me some good post play.

Nellie is really the best in terms of the overall package: dealing with the media, dealing with the players, evaluations, a sense of work ethic. Nellie taught me to look at what players could do and then put them in spots where they could succeed, as opposed to dwelling on what they couldn't do. Nellie also taught me the importance of respecting players, and understanding that they're human and will make mistakes—just like coaches.

Del Harris is the best *Xs* and *Os* guy in the game. He has the most organized package relative to any defensive scheme. He has a tremendous feel for the game offensively. He has a great grasp of team defense, the utilization of disrupting and defending.

From George Karl, I learned disruption, player-coach relationships, conditioning, and shooting emphasis.

The Laydens—Scott and Frank—have helped me a lot. Scott, who's the vice president of basketball operations for the Jazz, is really a great evaluator of talent. I pick his brain a lot. We look at players. He talks a lot about compatibility and character. Frank, who's the Jazz president, took my team one time when we were in Houston and actually walked them through the press offense. He talked to them for forty-five minutes.

I owe a lot to Donoher. Most of my zone offense principles are from him. The same goes for my press offense. I've also picked up a lot of things from Don Meyer at Lipscomb University.

Hank Raymonds was a very compassionate man who taught me the importance of fundamentals. And McGuire had such a great way with players. He was a terrific communicator. He recruited well and his teams played hard and played together. Al would have been an excellent pro coach.

I've learned from everybody. And I want my players to learn. I take all of my players to watch John Stockton practice. I want them to see his commitment. He respects the sanctity of the game. If he were playing in a CYO game or making $12,000 a year, he'd still play as hard.

My life has had its share of contradictions. To this day, it's still really hard for me to believe that I couldn't get into some of the games at those playgrounds in Milwaukee. I wanted to play so much that I put together my own teams. That was the only way I could guarantee myself a spot.

I began my career sitting at the end of the Marquette bench. In the next seat over was millionaire and U.S. senator-to-be Herb Kohl. And years later, here's Herb calling me about a job or here's Herb coming to the Final Four as my guest. That just seems so weird.

And here's another thing: Herb came to the game, and Orrin Hatch came. That's an interesting thing in life. Here's two guys in red, cheering for the Utes, who are as diametrically opposed politically as you can get. Herb, a liberal, blue-collar Democratic senator from Wisconsin, and Hatch, a conservative, Mormon-positioned Republican senator from Utah. And they're pulling for the Utes, and they're pulling for me. They're both friends of mine, and I marvel at that.

One of the most gratifying things to see during our Final Four appearance was how a city and state rallied around a team. At one point, the Apostles and the hierarchy of the Mormon Church and the Prophet were outside in a parade holding red-and-white pom-poms and cheering for the Utes. The *Salt Lake Tribune* published a photo of it, but the *Deseret News*, which is owned by the church, didn't.

Some people in the church were appalled and aghast by the display of partisanship. But I thought it was the height of ecumenicalism. I thought it was a good thing, and I derive great satisfaction from that picture and that scene. It crossed all the boundaries. It's a Utah thing. The significance was probably lost on others. But it's as if the Pope were waving pom-poms for Southern Methodist and the Mustangs were having a parade through the Vatican. In the Mormon church, the Prophet is the pope.

At the end of the day, what I take from being a coach has nothing to do with money, contracts, celebrity, material things. I don't wear my national championship ring from Marquette. I gave Huntsman my 300-victory game ball, as well as a chair from the Final Four. And I'll probably give my Final Four ring to Chase Peterson.

I get my satisfaction from my players, from their progress as students and people. I like to win, sure, but there's more to it than that.

One of my favorite short stories is by Mark Twain. It's called, "The Five Boons of Life." It's only a few pages long, but has always held a special meaning for me. If you can contemplate that story, read it a few times, you'll shake and shiver. It's a very powerful story.

A young man is given his choice of five gifts—fame, love, riches, pleasure, death—and told to select carefully, because only one of them is truly valuable. By life's end, he realizes he has chosen the four that matter least, that death is "that dear and sweet and kindly one."

But it is too late. He has no more chances.

I've thought about that story many times. Life is to be enjoyed and cherished and shared. I've tried to do that. I think I understand what's important. It isn't the trappings or, as Twain put it, "the lendings" of material success. Instead, it is a friend's trust. The remembrance of a father. The unconditional love of a mother. The joy of team. The purity of a game I love.

My life is on a napkin, but the napkin is filled with friends, families, and warm memories. I am truly happy in life. How lucky is that?